A gift for

_____

From

_____

Date

_____

YOU CAN
COUNT
ON GOD

-365 Devotions-

MAX LUCADO

THOMAS NELSON ·

Since 1798

January

Under His Wings

He will cover you with his feathers. He will shelter you with his wings. His faithful promises are your armor and protection.

PSALM 91:4 NLT

To read today's scripture is to read the words of a man who, in the innermost part of his being, believed in the steady hand of a good God. He was protected by God's strength, preserved by God's love. He lived beneath the shadow of God's wings.

Do you?

Stabilize your soul with the sovereignty of God. He reigns supreme over every detail of the universe. "There is no wisdom, no insight, no plan that can succeed against the LORD" (Proverbs 21:30). "[God] does as he pleases with the powers of heaven and the peoples of the earth. No one can hold back his hand or say to him: 'What have you done?'" (Daniel 4:35). He "sustains all things" (Hebrews 1:3 NRSV). He can "whistle for the fly that is in the farthest part of the rivers of Egypt" (Isaiah 7:18 NKJV). He names the stars and knows the sparrows. Great and small, from the army of a great country to the army of ants in my backyard, everything is under his control.

Anxious for Nothing

Jesus Still Rescues

*"My Father, who has given them to Me, is greater than all;
and no one is able to snatch them out of My Father's hand."*

JOHN 10:29 NKJV

With Christ's resurrection, he poleaxed the devil and turned every grave into short-term housing. Holding confetti and lining up for a Pearly Gate victory parade, heaven's angels were ready to celebrate. But the party would have to wait.

Jesus wanted to cook fish tacos for his friends. He wanted to restore the heart and the ministry of Peter. He perceived the layers of guilt and shame on the heart of his friend. As if with a cotton swab of grace, he began to wipe them away.

So Christ restored Peter with three personal commissions: "Feed My lambs" (John 21:15 NKJV). "Tend My sheep" (v. 16 NKJV). "Feed My sheep" (v. 17 NKJV).

Jesus had work for Peter to do, flocks for Peter to pastor. The apostle was discouraged but not disqualified.

And you? Have your fumbles and stumbles left you questioning your place in God's plan? If so, let this story remind you that Christ is not finished with you either. Jesus went on a search-and-rescue mission for Peter. He will do the same for you.

You Are Never Alone

3

Home in Jesus

"Abide in Me, and I in you."

JOHN 15:4 NKJV

ome, live in me!" Jesus invites. "Make my home your home." Odds are that you know what it means to be at home somewhere.

To be at home is to feel safe. The residence is a place of refuge and security.

To be at home is to be comfortable. You can pad around wearing slippers and a robe.

To be at home is to be familiar. When you enter the door, you needn't consult the blueprint to find the kitchen.

Our aim—our only aim—is to be at home in Christ. He is not a roadside park or hotel room. He is our permanent mailing address. Christ is our home. He is our place of refuge and security. We are comfortable in his presence, free to be our authentic selves. We know our way around in him. We know his heart and his ways.

We rest in him, find our nourishment in him. His roof of grace protects us from storms of guilt. His walls of providence secure us from destructive winds. His fireplace warms us during the lonely winters of life. He is our home.

Anxious for Nothing

Choose Your Inheritance

*"I will give you every place where you set
your foot, as I promised Moses."*

JOSHUA 1:3

We typically think of Joshua as taking the promised land. It's more precise to think of Joshua as taking God at his word. The great accomplishment of Joshua and the Hebrew people was this: they lived out of their inheritance. In fact, the story ends with this declaration: "Then Joshua dismissed the people, each to their own inheritance" (Joshua 24:28).

Is that to say they had no challenges? The book of Joshua makes it clear that wasn't the case. The Jordan River was wide. The Jericho walls were high. The evil inhabitants of Canaan were not giving up without a fight. Still, Joshua led the Hebrews to cross the Jordan, bring down the walls of Jericho, and defeat the thirty-one enemy kings. Every time he faced a challenge, he did so with faith, because he trusted his inheritance.

What if you did the same? Standing before you is a Jericho wall of fear. Brick upon brick of anxiety and dread. It's a stronghold that keeps you out of Canaan. Circumstances say, *Cower to your fears.* Your inheritance says otherwise: *You are a child of the King. His perfect love casts out fear. Move forward.* Choose your inheritance.

Unshakable Hope

5

A Guide for the Way

"When He, the Spirit of truth, has come,
He will guide you into all truth."

JOHN 16:13 NKJV

Guide me today, Holy Spirit. Show me where you want me to go, whom you want me to talk to, what decision you want me to make. Help me discern your voice over my own and others'. Walk closely with me and whisper truth to me. Forgive me when I listen to my own desires and ignore what you are telling me.

God, I'm so grateful you sent your Spirit to empower me. Thank you for speaking to me and working in me. Stay near to me and help me hear your voice.

Father, you are good—so good that you did not leave us alone on this earth. You left us your Spirit to guide us. Because of your Spirit, I never have to feel alone or afraid. You are with me always. Amen.

Praying the Promises

Who Is the Holy Spirit?

He anointed us, set his seal of ownership on us, and put his
Spirit in our hearts as a deposit, guaranteeing what is to come.

2 CORINTHIANS 1:21–22

Ask a believer to answer the question, "Who is God the Father?"
He has a reply. Or, "Describe God the Son." She will not hesitate.
But if you want to see believers hem, haw, and search for words, ask,
"Who is the Holy Spirit?"

The Bible makes more than a hundred references to the Holy
Spirit. Jesus said more about the Holy Spirit than he did about the
church or marriage.

The Holy Spirit is central to the life of the Christian. Everything
from Acts to Revelation is a result of the work of the Holy Spirit. The
Spirit came alongside the disciples, indwelled them, and gave the early
church the push they needed to face the challenges ahead.

After Jesus ascended into heaven, the Holy Spirit became the pri-
mary agent of the Trinity on earth. He will complete what was begun
by the Father and the Son.

Do you want his power? Direction? Strength? Then "keep in step
with the Spirit" (Galatians 5:25). He directs and leads; you must obey
and follow.

Praying the Promises

An Outline of Grace

*"I am the way and the truth and the life. No one
comes to the Father except through me."*

JOHN 14:6

Paul entered the pages of Scripture as Saul, the self-professed Pharisee of all Pharisees and the most religious man in town. But all his scruples and law keeping hadn't made him a better person. He was bloodthirsty and angry, determined to extinguish anything and everyone Christian.

His attitude began to change on the road to Damascus. That's when Jesus appeared, knocked him off his high horse, and left him sightless for three days. Paul could see only one direction: inward. And what he saw, he did not like.

We aren't told when Paul realized the meaning of grace. Was it immediately on the Damascus road? Or gradually during the three-day darkness? Or after Ananias restored his sight? We don't know. But we do know that Paul got grace. Or grace got Paul. Either way, he embraced the improbable offer that God would make us right with him through Jesus Christ. Paul's logic followed a simple outline:

Our debt is enough to sink us.

God loves us too much to leave us.

So God has found a way to save us.

Unshakable Hope

8

Cast Your Cares

Cast your cares on the LORD and he will sustain you.

PSALM 55:22

Casting is an intentional act to relocate an object. When Jesus rode into Jerusalem on Palm Sunday, the crowd removed the garments off their backs and spread them in the path of Christ. Let this "throwing" be your first response to bad news. Cast your anxiety in the direction of Christ. Do so specifically and immediately.

I did a good job of "casting my problems" in a high school algebra class. My brain scans reveal a missing region marked by the sign "Intended for Algebra." Fortunately I had a wonderful, patient teacher. He issued this invitation and stuck to it: "If you cannot solve a problem, come to me and I will help you."

I wore a trail into the floor between his desk and mine. Each time I had a question, I would approach his desk and remind him, "Remember how you promised you would help?" When he said yes, instant gratitude and relief kicked in. I still had the problem, but I had entrusted it to one who knew how to solve it.

Do the same. Take your problem to Christ and tell him, "You said you would help me. Would you?"

Anxious for Nothing

Jesus Does

Our high priest is able to understand our weaknesses.

HEBREWS 4:15 NCV

You think the moon affects the tides? It does. But Christ runs the moon. You think the United States is a superpower? The United States has only the power Christ gives and nothing more. He has authority over everything. And he has had it forever.

Yet Jesus was willing to forgo the privileges of divinity and enter humanity.

He was born just as all babies are born. His childhood was a common one. There is no evidence or suggestion that he was spared the inconveniences of adolescence. As an adult he was weary enough to sit down at a well (John 4:6) and sleepy enough to doze off in a rocking boat (Mark 4:35–38). He became hungry in the wilderness and thirsty on the cross. When the soldiers pounded the nails through his skin, a thousand nerve endings cried for relief.

The Word became flesh.

If you ever wonder if God understands you, he does. If you ever wonder if God listens, he does. If you ever wonder if the Uncreated Creator can comprehend the challenges you face, he does.

Unshakable Hope

Standing on the Promises

*All of God's promises have been fulfilled
in Christ with a resounding "Yes!"*

2 CORINTHIANS 1:20 NLT

The best book of promises is the one you and God are going to write together. Search and search Scripture until you find covenants that address your needs. Clutch them as the precious pearls they are; hide them in your heart so they can pay dividends long into the future. When the Enemy comes with his lies of doubt and fear, produce the pearl. Satan will be quickly silenced. He has no reply for truth.

They work, friend. The promises of God work. They can walk you through horrific tragedies. They can buoy you in the day-to-day difficulties. They are, indeed, the great and precious promises of God.

Build your life on the promises of God. Since his promises are unbreakable, your hope will be unshakable. The winds will still blow. The rain will still fall. But in the end you will be standing—standing on the promises of God.

Unshakable Hope

Huggers Are Happier

*He took them up in His arms, laid His
hands on them, and blessed them.*

MARK 10:16 NKJV

Someone needs to create a bumper sticker that reads "Huggers are happier." That was the conclusion of researchers at Pennsylvania State University. Students were divided into two groups: readers and huggers. The huggers were instructed to give or receive a minimum of five hugs per day over the course of four weeks. The readers were told to record the number of hours each day they spent reading in the same month. Unsurprisingly the huggers fared better on the happiness scale than the readers.[1] A similar study linked hugging with a diminished rate of sickness. The more often people hugged, the less likely they were to get sick.[2]

So greet people for your sake.

And greet people for their sake. The ungreeted individual never thinks, *They ignored me because they love me*. Just the opposite. Insecurity is often the unhappy child of silence.

So greet one another. Because huggers are happier, and they make others happy too.

How Happiness Happens

Keep in Step

Never damp the fire of the Spirit, and never despise
what is spoken in the name of the Lord.

1 THESSALONIANS 5:19–20 PHILLIPS

Awhile back I purchased a new cartridge for my printer. But when I used it, no letters appeared on the page. It was half an hour before I noticed the thin strip of tape covering the outlet of the cartridge. There was plenty of ink, but until the tape was removed, no impression could be made.

Is there anything in your life that needs to be removed? Any impediment to the impression of God's Spirit? We can grieve the Spirit with our angry words and rebellion (Isaiah 63:10; Ephesians 4:30–31) or resist the Spirit in our disobedience (Acts 7:51). We can even quench the Spirit by having no regard for God's teachings.

May I ask a few blunt questions? Are you persisting in disobedience? Are you refusing to forgive someone? Are you harboring hatred? If the answer is yes, you are quenching the Spirit within you.

Do you want his power? Direction? Strength? Then "keep in step with the Spirit" (Galatians 5:25). He is the drum major; we are the marching band. He directs and leads; we obey and follow.

Unshakable Hope

If You Knew . . .

*"I will come back and take you to be with me
that you also may be where I am."*

JOHN 14:3

I don't know the day and the hour of Christ's return. But I do know
the Bible urges us to look for specific signs:

- The preaching of the gospel to all nations (Matthew 24:14;
  Mark 13:10)
- Days of distress in which saints will suffer and the creation
  will tremble (Mark 13:7–8, 19–20)
- The coming of the Antichrist, an enemy of God who will
  deceive many (2 Thessalonians 2:1–10)
- Salvation of many Jews (Romans 11:12, 25–26)

If you knew Jesus was returning tomorrow, how would you feel
today? Anxious, afraid, unprepared? If so, you can take care of your
fears by placing your trust in Christ. If your answer includes words
like *happy*, *relieved*, and *excited*, hold tightly to your joy. Heaven is
God's answer to any suffering you may face.

If you knew Jesus was coming tomorrow, what would you do today?
Then do it! Live in such a way that you would not have to change your
plans.

Because of Bethlehem

At Your Best

"A time is coming when all who are dead and in their graves will hear his voice. Then they will come out of their graves."

JOHN 5:28–29 NCV

The road on which Denalyn and I take our walks is marked by a small country graveyard. The headstones are faded beyond recognition. No dirt has been turned for a century. Yet if these words from John 5 are true, it will someday witness a miracle. The same God who shook the tomb of Joseph of Arimathea will shake the soil of this simple cemetery. The caskets will open, and the bodies of these forgotten farmers will be called into the sky.

But in what form? These bodies are decayed, some to dust. They were wracked by disease and deformity. Some were riddled with bullets or destroyed by fire. How will these bodies be worthy of heaven?

Here is Paul's answer: "The body . . . is sown a natural body, it is raised a spiritual body" (1 Corinthians 15:42, 44). Spirits will be reunited with bodies, resulting in spiritual bodies. Just as a seed becomes a plant, this fleshly body will become a spiritual body. You are going to love yours.

Unshakable Hope

Give Joy to Get Joy

*Let each of you look out not only for his own
interests, but also for the interests of others.*

PHILIPPIANS 2:4 NKJV

The studies are clear. Doing good does the doer good. A 2010 study of more than forty-five hundred American adults revealed that of the people who volunteered an average of more than one hundred hours per year, 68 percent reported feeling physically healthier. Also, 73 percent said that volunteerism "lowered my stress levels," and 89 percent stated that service "has improved my sense of well-being."[3] We elevate our joy by giving joy to others.

What would happen if everyone took on the role of a servant? How many marriages would be blessed? If politicians set out to serve their people more than serve themselves, would their country benefit? If churches were populated by sincere servants, how many would hear the invitation of a lifetime?

Do something good for someone today. It's for your own good.

How Happiness Happens

The Family Business

When a believing person prays, great things happen.

JAMES 5:16 NCV

I have a friend who owns a successful business. He employs more than five hundred people in a dozen states. He appreciates each and every one of them. Yet he treats three of his workers with partiality. They are his sons. While he hears all requests, he especially hears theirs. They are being trained to run the family business.

So are you. When God saved you, he enlisted you. He gave not only forgiveness for your past but also authority in the present and a role in the future.

This life is on-the-job training for eternity. We are part of God's family. Ruling the universe is the family business. And when you, as God's child, seek to honor the family business, God hears your requests.

"God, grant me deeper faith so I can serve you."

"God, show me where we can live and best bring glory to your name."

"God, guide my decisions so they align with your plans for my life."

Will God do what you ask? Perhaps. Or perhaps he will do more than you imagined.

Unshakable Hope

What's in Your Basket?

Andrew, Simon Peter's brother, spoke up, "Here is a boy with five small barley loaves and two small fish, but how far will they go among so many?" . . . Jesus then took the loaves.

JOHN 6:8–9, 11

Jesus didn't have to use the boy's bread. He could have turned the nearby bushes into fruit trees. He could have caused the Galilean sea to spew out an abundance of fish. Instead, he chose to use the single basket of the small boy.

What's in your basket? All you have is a wimpy prayer? Give it. All you have is a meager skill? Use it. All you have is an apology? Offer it. It's not for you and me to tell Jesus our gift is too small. God can take a small thing and do a big thing. God used the whimper of baby Moses to move the heart of Pharaoh's daughter (Exodus 2:6). He used David's sling and stone to overthrow the mighty Goliath (1 Samuel 17:48–49). He used three nails and a crude cross to redeem humanity (Matthew 27:32–54). If God can turn a basket into a buffet, don't you think he can do something with your five loaves and two fishes of faith?

You Are Never Alone

Every Person You See

*Dear friends, since God so loved us, we
also ought to love one another.*

1 JOHN 4:11

Every person you see was created by God to bear his image and deserves to be treated with dignity and respect. This means all people deserve to be seen for who they are: image bearers of God. *Would you let this truth define the way you see other people?*

Imagine the impact this idea would have on the society that embraced it. What civility it would engender! What kindness it would foster! Racism will not flourish when people believe their neighbors bear God's image. The fire of feuds will have no fuel when people believe their adversaries are God's idea. Will a man abuse a woman? Not if he believes she bears the stamp of God. Will a boss neglect an employee? Not if she believes the employee bears a divine spark. Will society write off the indigent, the mentally ill, the inmate on death row, or the refugee? Not if we believe, truly believe, that every human being is God's idea. And he has no bad ideas.

Unshakable Hope

Let Love Succeed

*Above all, love each other deeply, because
love covers over a multitude of sins.*

1 PETER 4:8

We did a lot of shouting on our elementary school playground. All the boys in Mrs. Amburgy's first-grade class bonded together to express our male superiority. We met daily at recess and marched around the playground shouting, "Boys are better than girls!" Frankly I didn't agree, but I enjoyed the fraternity.

The girls in response paraded around the school announcing their disdain for boys: "Girls are better than boys." We were a happy campus.

Shouting feels good. But does it do any good? It seems to me there is a lot of shouting going on. On the airwaves, on bumper stickers, on social media, shouting. Is it possible to have an opinion without having a fit?

"Do not argue about opinions" (Romans 14:1 NCV). It is one thing to have an opinion; it's something else to have a fight. Let's reason together. Let's work together. And if discussion fails, let love succeed. If love covers a multitude of sins, can it not cover a multitude of opinions?

Resist the urge to shout.

How Happiness Happens

The Son of God!

*When [the disciples] had rowed about three or
four miles, they saw Jesus approaching the boat,
walking on the water; and they were frightened.*

JOHN 6:19

Let's climb into the boat with the disciples on the storm-tossed sea. Look at their rain-splattered faces. What do you see? Fear, for sure. Doubt? Absolutely. You may even hear a question shouted over the wind. "Anyone know where Jesus is?"

The answer is clear and surprising: praying. Then Jesus became the answer to his own prayer.

He turned the water into a walkway and came walking to the apostles in the storm.

The followers panicked. They called him a ghost, but Jesus still came. Peter's faith became fear, but Jesus still walked on the water. The winds howled and raged, but Jesus was not distracted from his mission. He stayed on course until his point was made: he is sovereign over all storms. The disciples, for the first time in Scripture, worshipped him.

"Truly you are the Son of God" (Matthew 14:33).

With a stilled boat as their altar and beating hearts as their liturgy, they worshipped Jesus. May you and I do the same.

Unshakable Hope

God Is on His Throne

The Lord reigns forever.

PSALM 9:7

God's answer for troubled times has always been the same: heaven has an occupied throne.

During the eighth century BC, ancient Judah enjoyed a time of relative peace, thanks to the steady leadership of Uzziah, the king. Uzziah was far from perfect, yet he kept the enemies at bay for fifty-two years.

Then Uzziah died. Isaiah the prophet, who lived during the reign of this king, was left with ample reason for worry. What would happen now that Uzziah was gone?

Or, in your case, what will happen now that your job is gone? Or your health has diminished? Or the economy has taken a nosedive? Does God have a message for his people when calamity strikes? He certainly had a word for Isaiah. The prophet wrote, "In the year that King Uzziah died, I saw the Lord sitting on a throne, high and lifted up, and the train of His robe filled the temple" (Isaiah 6:1 NKJV).

Uzziah's throne was empty, but God's was occupied. He was, and is, alive, on the throne, and worthy of our endless worship.

Anxious for Nothing

God's Idea

*This is how God showed his love among us: He sent his one
and only Son into the world that we might live through him.*

1 JOHN 4:9

Someone called you a lost cause . . . a failure . . . insignificant. Don't
listen to them. They don't know what they are talking about. A
divine spark indwells you. When you say yes to God, he blows on that
holy ember, and it begins to flame. It grows day by day within you.
Are you perfect? No. But you are being made perfect. And he has a
wild and inexplicable love for you. His love for you does not depend
on you.

You are God's idea. God's child. Created in God's image.

You were conceived by God before you were conceived by your
parents. You were loved in heaven before you were known on earth.
You aren't an accident. You aren't defined by the number of pounds
you weigh, followers you have, car you drive, or clothes you wear.

You are being made into God's image. You are a diamond, a rose,
and a jewel, purchased by the blood of Jesus Christ. In the eyes of
God, you are worth dying for. Would you let this truth find its way
into your heart?

Unshakable Hope

King of Every Situation

Trust in the LORD with all your heart; do not depend on your own understanding. Seek his will in all you do, and he will show you which path to take.

PROVERBS 3:5–6 NLT

When crowds of people came to Christ for healing, "*One by one he placed his hands on them and healed them*" (Luke 4:40 MSG, emphasis mine).

Had Jesus chosen to do so, he could have proclaimed a cloud of healing blessings to fall upon the crowd. But he is not a one-size-fits-all Savior. He placed his hands on each one, individually, personally. Perceiving unique needs, he issued unique blessings.

A precise prayer gives Christ the opportunity to remove all doubt about his love and interest. Your problem becomes his pathway. The challenge you face becomes a canvas upon which Christ can demonstrate his finest work. So offer a simple prayer and entrust the problem to Christ.

Believe that Jesus is king of each and every situation.

You Are Never Alone

Providential Hope

[God] chose us in advance, and he makes
everything work out according to his plan.

EPHESIANS 1:11 NLT

A good place to see hope in action is the story of Joseph. Abused and rejected by his brothers, Joseph suffered servitude and prison. Why did God allow Joseph's suffering? Why does God permit challenges to come our way? Wouldn't an almighty God prevent them?

Not if they serve his higher purpose. Remember the rest of Joseph's story? When Pharaoh was troubled by his dreams, the butler recalled Joseph's request to remember him. He mentioned Joseph to Pharaoh, and as fast as you can say *providence*, Joseph went from prison to palace to prime minister. Joseph successfully navigated the crisis and saved not just the Egyptians but also the family of Jacob.

Years later Joseph would tell his brothers, "You intended to harm me, but God intended it for good to accomplish what is now being done, the saving of many lives" (Genesis 50:20). Two words at the heart of this passage reveal the heart of providential hope: *but God.* "You intended to harm me, but God . . ." What was intended as harm became good. Why? Because Joseph viewed the sufferings of his life through the lens of divine providence.

Can I urge you to do the same?

Anxious for Nothing

Undeserved

"If you forgive other people when they sin against you, your heavenly Father will also forgive you."

MATTHEW 6:14

Many years ago a man came to see me regarding his wife's boss. As her supervisor, the boss had overreached his bounds, demanding extra work and offering poor compensation. The husband confronted the man. To the credit of the supervisor, he owned up to his mismanagement and made amends.

The wife was grateful. But the husband was still angry. Chalk it up to a husband's intense desire to protect, but he could not forgive the man. So he came up with an idea that included a letter. He brought it to my office along with a box of matches. He read the letter to me. It was addressed to his offender and contained an account of the offending actions.

The husband then asked me to pray and watch as he burned the letter "before my anger burns me up." We did.

You might try the same. Forgiveness is the act of applying your undeserved mercy to your undeserved hurts. You didn't deserve to be hurt, but neither did you deserve to be forgiven. Being the recipient that you are of God's great grace, does it not make sense to give grace to others?

How Happiness Happens

God Can Be Trusted

The one who calls you is faithful, and he will do it.

1 THESSALONIANS 5:24

God's promises are irrevocable because of who God is.

- He is unchanging. He sees the end from the beginning. He's never caught off guard by the unexpected. He makes no mid-course corrections. He is not victimized by moods or weather. "He never changes or casts a shifting shadow" (James 1:17 NLT).
- He is faithful. "God can be trusted to keep his promise" (Hebrews 10:23 NLT).
- He is strong. He does not overpromise or underdeliver. "God is able to do whatever he promises" (Romans 4:21 NLT).
- He cannot lie. "It is impossible for God to lie" (Hebrews 6:18 NLT). A rock cannot swim. A hippo cannot fly. A butterfly cannot eat a bowl of spaghetti. You cannot sleep on a cloud, and God cannot lie. He never exaggerates, manipulates, fibs, or flatters. This verse is clear: it is impossible! Scripture could not be more forthright. "God . . . cannot lie" (Titus 1:2 ASV). Deceit is simply not an option.

God will keep his promises to you!

Unshakable Hope

It Is Better

"Give, and it will be given to you. A good measure, pressed down, shaken together and running over, will be poured into your lap. For with the measure you use, it will be measured to you."

LUKE 6:38

It is better to forgive than to hold a grudge,

... better to build up than to tear down,
... better to include than to exclude,
... better to seek to understand than to disregard,
... better to love than to hate.

God's solution for the ills of society is a quorum of unselfish, life-giving, God-loving folks who flow through neighborhoods and businesses like cleansing agents, bringing in the good, flushing out the bad. They hail from all corners of the globe, reflect all hues of skin. Liberal, conservative, rural, metropolitan, young, old. Yet they are bound together by this amazing discovery: happiness is found by giving it away.

If anyone is happier than the gift receiver, it is the gift giver.

How Happiness Happens

Our Problems Matter to Heaven

[He] is able to do exceedingly abundantly
above all that we ask or think.

EPHESIANS 3:20 NKJV

Jesus was at a wedding when Mary, his mother, came to him with a problem. "They have no more wine" (John 2:3). Folks in first-century Palestine knew how to throw a party. Weddings lasted as long as seven days. Food and wine were expected to last just as long. So Mary was concerned when she saw the servants scraping the bottom of the wine barrel.

We are not told the reason for the shortage. But we are told how it was replenished. Mary presented the problem. Christ was reluctant. Mary deferred. Jesus reconsidered. He commanded. The servants obeyed. The sommelier sipped and said something about their squirreling away the best wine for the farewell toasts. Mary smiled at her Son. Jesus raised a glass to his mother, and we are left with this message: our diminishing supplies, no matter how insignificant, matter to heaven.

You Are Never Alone

Who Do You Believe Jesus Is?

[Jesus] said to them, "But who do you say that I am?"
Peter answered and said, "The Christ of God."

LUKE 9:20 NKJV

Flip back the flaps of your soul, and you'll see a series of beliefs that serve like poles to stabilize the tent of your life and faith. Your belief system is your answer to the fundamental questions about life: Is anyone in control of the universe? Does life have a purpose? Do I have value? Is this life all there is?

Your belief system has nothing to do with your skin color, appearance, talents, or age. Your belief system is not concerned with the exterior of the tent but the interior. It is the set of convictions (poles)—all of them unseen—upon which your faith depends. If your belief system is strong, you will stand. If it is weak, the storm will prevail.

Belief always precedes behavior. For this reason the apostle Paul in each of his epistles addressed convictions before he addressed actions. To change the way a person responds to life, change what a person believes about life. The most important thing about you is your belief system.

So . . . who do you believe Jesus is?

Anxious for Nothing

Look and Consider

"Do not worry about your life, what you will eat or what
you will drink; nor about your body, what you will put on."

MATTHEW 6:25 NKJV

After Jesus rather bluntly tells us not to worry about food and clothes, he then gives two commands: "look" and "consider." He tells us to "look at the birds of the air" (Matthew 6:26 NKJV). When we do, we notice how happy they seem to be. They aren't frowning, cranky, or grumpy. Yet "they neither sow nor reap nor gather into barns" (v. 26). They don't drive tractors or harvest wheat, yet, Jesus asks us, do they appear well cared for?

He then turns our attention to the flowers of the field. "Consider the lilies" (v. 28). By the same token, they don't do anything. Even though their life span is short, God dresses them up for red-carpet appearances. Even Solomon, the richest king in history, "was not arrayed like one of these" (v. 29).

How do we disarm anxiety? Stockpile our minds with God thoughts. Draw the logical implication: if birds and flowers fall under the category of God's care, won't he care for us as well? Saturate your heart with the goodness of God.

Anxious for Nothing

Blessed Obedience

If you pay attention to the commands of the LORD your
God that I give you this day and carefully follow them,
you will always be at the top, never at the bottom.

DEUTERONOMY 28:13

Haman had it out for the Israelites. And it just so happened that Haman had a very influential position with King Xerxes of Persia. With this access to power, Haman planned to completely exterminate the Jews on Adar 13, a date somewhere around our months of February and March.

Yet there was another storyline developing that would eventually collide with Haman's story: King Xerxes selected a new queen, Queen Esther, who was Jewish.

What situation are you facing right now that stirs in you the same kind of fear the Jews had for Adar 13? Illness? Not enough money? Then take a tip from Esther. She used her influence as queen to talk to King Xerxes. She asked him to allow her people to defend themselves on Adar 13. He agreed. Because of this, the Israelites were victorious, and Haman was executed.

Esther took a step of faith, and God blessed her obedience. He will do the same for you. No matter what situation you find yourself in today, God will ultimately win.

Praying the Promises

February

Delivering Happiness

*Do not neglect to do good and to share what you
have, for such sacrifices are pleasing to God.*

HEBREWS 13:16 ESV

Albert is a mail carrier in Waco, Texas. He makes daily deliveries to the furniture store where my daughter Sara used to work. The store was wildly successful. Being a start-up, the business had a constant level of chaos. Employees were on their feet all day. It could be a stressful place.

That's why they all loved Albert. Sara described his arrival as the high point of the day. She remembers, "He'd ask how each of us was doing. He looked us in the eyes and said, 'God bless you.'"

Albert delivers more than mail. He delivers happiness. I'd like to challenge you to do the same. Here is my idea. Set out to alter the joy level of a hundred people over the next forty days. Pray for people, serve more, practice patience, and bring out the best in people. Keep a journal in which you describe the encounter and what you did. What was the setting? What did you learn?

At the end of forty days, would your world be different?

Would you be different?

I can tell you I took my own challenge, and I certainly am.

How Happiness Happens

Bringing Out the Best

We should help others do what is right
and build them up in the Lord.

ROMANS 15:2 NLT

For decades Andrea Mosconi followed the same routine six mornings a week. The Italian maestro went to the city hall in Cremona, Italy, and entered the violin museum. There he stood before the elaborate, multilocked cases and admired some of the most valuable musical instruments on the planet.

Left untouched, untuned, and unstroked, the instruments begin to lose their vibrancy. Hence, Mr. Mosconi. His job description consisted of one sentence: play music. He reverently removed each instrument from its glass case, played it for six or seven minutes, and then returned it before moving on to the next one. By the time he finished a day's work, the museum had heard the sweetest music, and the most valuable instruments had felt the tenderest care.[1]

You, Mr. Mosconi, and I have something in common. We have a chance to bring the best out of people. What could produce more joy than that?

How Happiness Happens

God Uses the Humble

*Humility is the fear of the LORD; its wages
are riches and honor and life.*

PROVERBS 22:4

Some time ago I partnered with musician Michael W. Smith for a ministry weekend in Asheville, North Carolina. The retreat was held at The Cove, a beautiful facility owned by the Billy Graham Evangelistic Association.

Before the event, Michael and I met to go over the weekend schedule. But Michael had just met with Billy Graham and was so moved that he hardly discussed the retreat. The famous evangelist was, at the time, ninety-four years old. His thoughts turned to what might be said about him at his funeral. He told Michael that he hoped his name would not be mentioned.

"What?" Michael asked.

"I hope only that the name of the Lord Jesus be lifted up."

Billy Graham preached to hundreds of millions of people. He filled stadiums on every continent. He advised every US president from Truman to Obama. Yet he didn't want to be mentioned at his own funeral.

Those who walk in pride, God is able to humble. But those who walk in humility, God is able to use.

Unshakable Hope

You Are Heard in Heaven

"Don't be afraid, Daniel. Since the first day you began
to pray for understanding and to humble yourself
before your God, your request has been heard in
heaven. I have come in answer to your prayer."

DANIEL 10:12 NLT

The moment Daniel began praying, the answer was issued. Demonic forces blocked the pathway of the angel. The impasse lasted a full three weeks until the archangel Michael arrived on the scene with his superior authority (Daniel 10:13–14). The standoff was ended, and the prayer was answered.

Have your prayers been met with a silent sky? Have you prayed and heard nothing? Are you floundering in the land between an offered and an answered prayer?

If so, I beg you, don't give up. What the angel said to Daniel, God says to you: "Since the first day that you set your mind to gain understanding and to humble yourself before your God, your words were heard" (v. 12 NIV). You have been heard in heaven. Angelic armies have been dispatched. Reinforcements have been rallied.

Do what Daniel did. Remain before the Lord.

Anxious for Nothing

Reminding God

*Put the Lord in remembrance [of His
promises], keep not silence.*

ISAIAH 62:6 AMPC

G od invites you—yes, commands you—to remind him of his
promises. Populate your prayer with "You said . . ."

"You said you would walk me through the waters" (Isaiah 43:2,
my paraphrase).

"You said you would lead me through the valley" (Psalm 23:4, my
paraphrase).

"You said you would never leave or forsake me" (Hebrews 13:5,
my paraphrase).

Find a promise that fits your problem, and build your prayer
around it. These prayers of faith touch the heart of God and activate
the angels of heaven. Miracles are set into motion. Your answer may
not come overnight, but it will come. And you will overcome.

"Prayer is essential in this ongoing warfare. Pray hard and long.
Pray for your brothers and sisters" (Ephesians 6:18 MSG).

The path to peace is paved with prayer. Less consternation, more
supplication. Fewer anxious thoughts, more prayer-filled thoughts.
As you pray, the peace of God will guard your heart and mind
(Philippians 4:7). And, in the end, what could be better?

Anxious for Nothing

All Things New

The wolf will live with the lamb, the leopard will lie down with the goat, the calf and the lion and the yearling together; and a little child will lead them.

ISAIAH 11:6

Envision this earth as it was intended to be: completely calm. Lions won't snarl. Bears won't maim. No one, no thing, will rebel. The next age will be calm because it gladly defers to God.

"No longer will there be any curse" (Revelation 22:3). No more struggle with the earth. No more shame before God. No more tension between people. No more death. No more curse. This is God's promise. He will reclaim his creation. He is a God of restoration, not destruction. He is a God of renewal, redemption, regeneration, resurrection. God loves to redo and restore.

"I am making everything new!" he announced (Revelation 21:5). Everything new. The old will be gone. Gone with hospital waiting rooms. Gone with tear-stained divorce papers. Gone with motionless ultrasounds. Gone with loneliness, foreclosure notices, and abuse. Gone with cancer. God will lay hold of every atom, emotion, insect, animal, and galaxy. He will reclaim every diseased body and afflicted mind. *I am making all things new.*

Unshakable Hope

39

Moe or Joe?

We love because he first loved us.

1 JOHN 4:19

Contrast the situation of Moe and Joe. Moe expects everyone to serve him. The moment he awakens he thinks, *Is someone going to bring me coffee?* If the service of the convenience store clerk is slow, Moe is mad. If the employees at work need more time than Moe wants to give them, Moe lets them know.

Moe expects people to cater to his plans, meet his needs, and reward him. Consequently, Moe is seldom happy.

Joe, on the other hand, measures the success of his day with this standard: *Whom can I help today?* He serves his wife by bringing her coffee. He serves the convenience store clerk by giving him a smile. He keeps a positive attitude at work.

The world doesn't exist to take care of him. He exists to take care of others. Joe goes to bed with a smile on his face.

Which one are you? Moe? Joe? Or a little of both, Mo-Jo?

Make your happiness dependent on how others serve you, and you will always be disappointed. Find happiness in serving others, and . . . well, you can complete the sentence.

How Happiness Happens

King of the Mountain

Do not think of yourself more highly than you ought.

ROMANS 12:3

The other day I saw some children at play on a large vacant lot where someone had dumped a mound of dirt. They were playing the greatest of kid games: King of the Mountain. The rules are as simple as they are brutal: fight your way to the top, and shove off anyone who threatens to take your spot. It was a slugfest of crawling, pushing, and falling.

King of the Mountain is not just a kid's game. Versions are played in every dormitory, classroom, boardroom, and bedroom. And since mountaintop real estate is limited, people get shoved around. Mark it down: if you want to be king, someone is going to suffer. Your arrogance might prompt a broken marriage, an estranged friendship, or a divided office.

Pride comes at a high price. Don't pay it. Consider the counsel of the apostle Paul: "Do not think of yourself more highly than you ought."

In other words, it is not always good to be king.

Because of Bethlehem

Never Too Late

"Anyone who loves me will obey my teaching."

JOHN 14:23

I was once called to the bedside of a dying man, an eighty-year-old scoundrel. He spent the final decade of his life with time on his hands, money at his disposal, and women on his mind. But as his health began to fail, his conscience began to stir. When the doctor told him to get his affairs in order, he called me. He wanted to get right with God. He made a deathbed confession of faith.

I left the hospital room with a scroogy scowl. *That's too easy*, I thought. A guy like him deserves to be routed through purgatory on the way to paradise.

But God didn't tell me to screen the applicants, just to teach them. And according to God's great grace, if my scoundrel friend's confession was sincere, he is walking the same heavenly streets as Paul and Peter and King David. Each a scoundrel in his own right.

It's never too late to come to Christ for help. That knock at the door of your heart? That's Jesus. All you have to do is open the door.

Because of Bethlehem

The Perfect Plan of God

In all things God works for the good of those who love him, who have been called according to his purpose.

ROMANS 8:28

In the famous lace shops of Brussels, Belgium, certain rooms used to be dedicated to the spinning of the finest lace with the most delicate of patterns. These rooms were completely dark, save for a shaft of natural light from a solitary window. Only one spinner sat in the room. The light fell upon the pattern while the worker remained in the dark.[2]

Has God permitted a time of darkness in your world? You look but cannot see him. You see only the fabric of circumstances woven and interlaced. You might question the purpose behind this thread or that. But be assured, God has a pattern. He has a plan. He is not finished, but when he is, the lace will be beautiful.

Anxious for Nothing

A Simple Greeting

Greet one another with a kiss of love. Peace to
you all who are in Christ Jesus. Amen.

1 PETER 5:14 NKJV

British minister J. H. Jowett told the story of a convict from Darlington, England. He had just been released after three years in jail when he happened to pass the mayor on the street. Expecting nothing more than cold ostracism from the public, he didn't know how to respond when the mayor paused, tipped his hat, and said in a cheery tone, "Hallo! I'm glad to see you! How are you?"

The ex-prisoner mumbled a response and went on his way. Years later the two accidentally met in another city. The mayor didn't remember the man, but the man had never forgotten the mayor. He said, "I want to thank you for what you did for me when I came out of prison."

"What did I do?"

"You spoke a kind word to me, and it changed my life!"[3]

Simply greeting one another is not that hard. But it makes a significant difference.

What is small to you may be huge to someone else.

How Happiness Happens

Some Things You Should Know

*"Do not let your hearts be troubled. You
believe in God; believe also in me."*

JOHN 14:1

Jesus wants you to know a few things. Things like the fact that you are never alone. You are never without help, hope, or strength. You are stronger than you think because God is nearer than you might imagine. He wants you to know:

"I know everything about you" (Psalm 139:1).

"I know when you sit down and when you rise up" (Psalm 139:2).

"I've numbered the hairs on your head" (Matthew 10:29–31).

"I've adopted you into my family" (Romans 8:15).

"Before you were the size of a freckle in your mother's womb, I
    knew you" (Jeremiah 1:4–5).

"You are my idea, and I have only good ideas" (Ephesians 1:11–12).

"You won't live a day longer or less than I intend" (Psalm 139:15–16).

"I love you as my own child" (1 John 3:1).

"I will take care of you" (Matthew 6:31–33).

You Are Never Alone

Believe Him

Great is our Lord, and abundant in power;
his understanding is beyond measure.

PSALM 147:5 ESV

Imagine you are ten years old, and you stumble down the stairs and twist your ankle. You roll on the floor and scream for help.

Into the room walks your dad, the world's foremost orthopedic surgeon. He examines the injury. Your anxiety kicks in.

"Dad, I'll never walk again!"

"Yes, you will."

"No one can help me!"

"I can. Do you know what I do for a living?"

Actually you don't.

The next day he drives you to his office and shows you the diplomas on his wall. Then you're off to a ringside seat for an ankle reconstruction. You begin to see your father in a different light. If he can conduct orthopedic surgery, he can likely treat a swollen ankle.

Here is what I think: our biggest fears are sprained ankles to God. And a lot of people live with unnecessary anxiety over temporary limps.

Anxious for Nothing

Be Loved

"A new commandment I give to you, that you love one another; as I have loved you."

JOHN 13:34 NKJV

The final phrase is the essential one: "as I have loved you." Have you let God love you? Please don't hurry past the question. Have you let God's love seep into the innermost recesses of your life?

If your answer is "Uh, I don't know" or "I don't think God loves a person like me," then we just stumbled upon something.

We don't love people because people are lovable. People can be cranky, stubborn, selfish, and cruel. We love people for this reason: we have come to experience and believe the love that God has for us.

We tend to skip this step. "I'm supposed to love my neighbor? All right, by golly, I will." We clench our teeth and redouble our efforts as if there were within us a distillery of affection and another bottle of love will pour forth. It won't! The source is not within us. It is only by receiving our Father's *agape* love that we can discover an agape love for others.

We cannot love if we aren't first loved. Just as hurt people hurt people, loved people love people. So let God love you!

How Happiness Happens

Words of Affirmation

Do not let any unwholesome talk come out
of your mouths, but only what is helpful for
building others up according to their needs.

EPHESIANS 4:29

Three years into my role as senior minister of our church, a former senior minister returned, not only to live in our city but also to serve on our staff. Charles Prince was thirty years my senior, Harvard educated, and a member of the Mensa society. I was in my midthirties, a rookie, and a charter member of the Dense society. The relationship could have been awkward and intimidating, but Charles preempted any stress with a visit to my office, during which he said, "There will be no tension in our relationship. I'm going to be your biggest cheerleader."

He was! For twenty-five years, right until the day he died, I could count on a post-sermon pat on the back. "You're getting better every week!" I found that hard to believe, but I always appreciated it.

Such encouragement has a Michelangelo impact on people. The sculptor saw the figure of David within the marble and carved it out. The encourager sees your best self and calls it out, not with a chisel but with words of affirmation. Be an encourager today!

How Happiness Happens

Where Is Jesus in the Storm?

*Christ Jesus . . . is at the right hand of God
and is also interceding for us.*

ROMANS 8:34

After Jesus walked on water through a storm, he went "up on a mountainside by himself to pray" (Matthew 14:23). He didn't eat. He didn't chat. He didn't sleep. He prayed even though his robe was soaked and his hair was matted. Like the disciples down on the Sea of Galilee, he, too, was in the storm, but still he prayed.

Or should we say he was in the storm, so he prayed? Was the storm the reason for his intercession? Do his actions here describe his first course of action: to pray for his followers?

Ponder this promise: Jesus, right now, at this moment, in the midst of your storm, is interceding for you. The King of the universe is speaking on your behalf. He is advocating for a special blessing to be sent your way. You do not fight the wind and waves alone. It's not up to you to find a solution. You have the mightiest Prince and the holiest Advocate standing up for you.

Where is Jesus in your storm? He is in the presence of God, praying for you.

Unshakable Hope

A Resounding Yes

*The LORD himself goes before you and will be with
you; he will never leave you nor forsake you.*

DEUTERONOMY 31:8

Administrators of one of the largest hospitals in America cite
loneliness as a major reason for overcrowded emergency rooms.
Parkland Hospital of Dallas, Texas, made this startling discovery
as they were looking for ways to unclog the system. They identified
eighty patients who went to four emergency rooms 5,139 times in a
twelve-month period, costing the system more than $14 million.

Once they identified these repeat visitors, they commissioned
teams to meet with them and determine the reason. Their conclusion?
Loneliness. Poverty and food shortage were contributing factors, but
the number one determinant was a sense of isolation. The ER provided attention, kindness, and care. Hence, the multiple return visits.
They wanted to know that someone cares.[4]

Don't we all?

If I'm facing an onslaught of challenges, will God help? When life
grows dark and stormy, does he notice? If I'm facing the fear of death,
will he help me?

Does God care? The answer is a resounding yes!

You Are Never Alone

The Kingdom

*"Yours is the kingdom and the power
and the glory forever. Amen."*

MATTHEW 6:13 NKJV

My Father in heaven, your name truly is holy. Your works are mighty. You sit on your throne. You know all and see all. Yours is the greatness and the power and the glory. Yet your kingdom is less about boundaries and castles and more about changing hearts and minds.

God, I confess that at times I want my will to be done more than I want your will to be done. I want to rule my own kingdom more than I want to be ruled by you. I want to be in charge. I want the glory. Father, forgive me.

I know the kingdom belongs to you and you alone. You are the one seated on the throne with Jesus beside you, not me. Help me remember that you are worthy of all authority. Teach me how to be a servant in your kingdom rather than someone who wants to run the kingdom.

Thank you for being a good King. Amen.

Praying the Promises

The Promise Prescription

Friendship with God is reserved for those who reverence him. With them alone he shares the secrets of his promises.

PSALM 25:14 TLB

Just as the doctor might prescribe a medication for your body, God has given promises for your heart. He shares them as gifts from friend to friend. Make it your aim to get so acquainted with these promises that you can write yourself a prescription.

- I'm feeling fearful today. Time for me to open up a bottle of Judges 6:12: "The LORD is with you." I will lay claim to the nearness of God.
- The world feels out of control. Time for a dose of Romans 8:28: "All things work together for good" (NKJV).
- I see dark clouds on the horizon. What was it Jesus told me? Oh, now I remember: "In this world you will have trouble. But take heart! I have overcome the world" (John 16:33).

Nothing lifts the weary soul like the promises of God.

Unshakable Hope

In the Season of Struggle

"Where your treasure is, there will your heart be also."

LUKE 12:34 ESV

You've probably experienced a season of God-ordained struggle, a time when there was a chill in the corner office, a dent in the savings account, a downturn. Often these days exist for a purpose: to turn our hearts back to God. Sometimes it takes a tragedy for us to hit our knees.

This is what the Israelites of Haggai's day needed. Charged by God to rebuild the temple, they had abandoned the task, distracted by worldly things. God's big thing became their small thing.

The prophet Haggai was sent to remind them of their work and to convey a promise: "'The glory of this [present] house will be greater than the glory of the former house,' says the LORD Almighty" (Haggai 2:9).

It's not too late to start again. The glory of the latter temple will be greater than the former. Or, in your case, the glory of the latter career, the latter years, will be greater than the former. Turn your heart back to him.

In God's plan, the future is always brighter, and tomorrow always has the potential to outshine today.

Praying the Promises

The High Price of Pride

[Nebuchadnezzar] was driven away from
people and ate grass like the ox.

DANIEL 4:33

When the mighty fall, the fall is mighty. One minute King Nebuchadnezzar was on the cover of *Time* magazine; the next he was banished like a creature and munching on grass. And we are left with a lesson: God hates pride.

How do we explain God's abhorrence of the haughty heart?

Simple. God resists the proud because the proud resist God. Arrogance stiffens the knee so it will not kneel, hardens the heart so it will not admit to sin. The heart of pride never confesses, never repents, never asks for forgiveness. Indeed, the arrogant never feel the need for forgiveness. Pride is the hidden reef that shipwrecks the soul.

Pride not only prevents reconciliation with God; it prevents reconciliation with people. How many marriages have collapsed beneath the weight of foolish pride? How many apologies have gone unoffered due to the lack of humility?

Pride comes at a high price. Don't pay it. Choose instead to stand on the offer of grace. "God resists the proud, but gives grace to the humble" (1 Peter 5:5 NKJV).

Unshakable Hope

For His Highest

By the grace of God I am what I am, and His grace toward me was not in vain.

1 CORINTHIANS 15:10 NKJV

Had Biddy Chambers given up, no one would have criticized her. Her God-given assignment was to partner with her husband in teaching the Bible.

They met in 1908, and by 1910 they were married, living in London, and busy about their dream of starting a Bible college. Biddy's training was in stenography. She took careful notes of her husband's lectures and turned them into correspondence courses.

Then came the setback. Complications from appendicitis rendered Biddy a widow. All dreams of a teaching ministry would need to be abandoned, right?

No. Biddy turned her husband's notes into pamphlets, and eventually they were compiled into a book. *My Utmost for His Highest* was published in 1927.[5] It has since sold more than thirteen million copies and has been translated into more than thirty-five languages. The work of Oswald Chambers surely exceeded his fondest hopes. But it was the sincere faith of his wife that made the difference.

She gave what she had to Jesus, and with it Jesus fed, and feeds, the multitudes. Let's follow her example.

You Are Never Alone

Where God Is Praised

Having disarmed the powers and authorities,
[Jesus] made a public spectacle of [the forces of
evil], triumphing over them by the cross.

COLOSSIANS 2:15

The Greek word for "devil" is *diabolos,* and it shares a root with the verb *diaballein,* which means "to split."[6] The devil is a splitter, a divider, a wedge driver. He divided Adam and Eve from God in the garden and would like to separate you from God as well. He wants to take unbelievers to hell and make life hell for believers. Every conflict is a contest with Satan and his forces.

What are our weapons? Prayer, worship, and Scripture. When we pray, we engage the power of God against the devil. When we worship, we do what Satan himself did not do: we place God on the throne. When we pick up the sword of Scripture, we do what Jesus did in the wilderness—we proclaim truth (Matthew 4:1–11).

Satan will not linger long where God is praised and prayers are offered. Satan may be vicious, but he will not be victorious. God has already won.

Praying the Promises

A Motive Check

*To each one of us grace has been given
as Christ apportioned it.*

EPHESIANS 4:7

There is a time to speak up, but before you do, check your motives. The goal is to help, never to hurt. Look at yourself before you look down on others. Rather than put them in their place, put yourself in their place.

The truth is we all drop the ball on occasion. I could relate to the mistake of the ninety-year-old woman named Marie who decided that Christmas shopping was simply too difficult for someone her age. She chose to send checks to family and friends. On each card she wrote, "Buy your own present."

She enjoyed the flurry of holiday activities. Not until after Christmas did she get around to cleaning off her desk. Imagine her chagrin when she found under a stack of papers the checks she had forgotten to include.[7]

I could have done the same thing.

Don't we owe it to one another to bear with one another?

How Happiness Happens

The Enemy

*Our fight is not against people on earth but against the rulers
and authorities and the powers of this world's darkness,
against the spiritual powers of evil in the heavenly world.*

EPHESIANS 6:12 NCV

The Bible traces Satan's activities to a moment of rebellion that occurred sometime between the creation of the universe and the appearance of the snake in the garden.

Lucifer's heart became proud. He was not content to worship; he had to be worshipped (Isaiah 14:12–15). He was not content to bow before God's throne; he had to sit upon it.

Satan succumbed to pride, and as a result he was cast out of heaven. Jesus referred to that eviction, saying, "I saw Satan fall like lightning from heaven" (Luke 10:18).

But though he is cast out of heaven, he is not out of our lives. "Be alert and of sober mind. Your enemy the devil prowls around like a roaring lion looking for someone to devour" (1 Peter 5:8). He comes "only to steal and kill and destroy" (John 10:10). You're enjoying happiness? Satan wants to steal it. You've discovered joy? He'll try to kill it. He is the Enemy of your God-given destiny and longs to be the destroyer of your soul.

Don't dismiss him.

Unshakable Hope

Jesus Will Find You

"No one can steal [you] out of my hand."

JOHN 10:28 NCV

After Jesus healed the blind man in John 9, the was-blind man found himself kicked out of the temple with no one to defend him. "When Jesus heard what had happened, he found the man" (v. 35 NLT). Christ was not about to leave that man unprotected. You can expect him to do the same for you. Others may disown you. Your family may reject you. But Jesus? He will find you. He will guide you.

> When He [Jesus] had found him, He said to him, "Do you believe in the Son of God?"
>
> He answered and said, "Who is He, Lord, that I may believe in Him?"
>
> And Jesus said to him, "You have both seen Him and it is He who is talking with you."
>
> Then he said, "Lord, I believe!" And he worshiped Him. (John 9:35–38 NKJV)

The story begins with a blind man seen by Christ. It ends with a was-blind man worshipping Christ. Is this not the desire of Jesus for us all?

You Are Never Alone

Unprejudiced Kindness

Greet my dear friend . . .

ROMANS 16:5

In Romans 16, Paul mentally went from person to person and greeted each one with a holy greeting (vv. 3–16). He saluted twenty-six people by name and, in some cases, their families. His list included

- Epenetus, his first convert in Asia;
- Mary, a hard worker;
- Ampliatus, Urbanus, Hermes, Philologus, Julia—names common among slaves;[8]
- Aristobulus, believed to have been the brother of Agrippa I and the grandson of Herod the Great;[9] and
- Narcissus, the secretary of Emperor Claudius.[10]

Paul left no one out. His example urges us to follow suit. No selective greetings allowed. No picking and choosing. Everybody greets everybody. Pecking orders leave people pecked on and picked over. You and I may carry a canteen of water, but we don't know who is thirsty. For that reason we are called to offer it to everyone.

How Happiness Happens

Leave It with God

I know whom I have believed and am persuaded that He is able to keep what I have committed to Him until that Day.

2 TIMOTHY 1:12 NKJV

Have you ever left an appliance at the repair shop? Perhaps your toaster broke or your microwave oven stopped working. You tried to fix it but had no success. So you took it to the specialist. You explained the problem and then . . .

- offered to stay and help him fix it,
- hovered next to his workbench asking questions about the progress, or
- threw a sleeping bag on the floor of the workshop so you could watch the repairman at work.

If you did any of these things, you don't understand the relationship between client and repairman. The arrangement is uncomplicated. Leave it with him to fix it. Our protocol with God is equally simple. Leave your problem with him.

God does not need our help, counsel, or assistance. (Please repeat this phrase: "I hereby resign as ruler of the universe.") When he is ready for us to reengage, he will let us know.

Anxious for Nothing

Hold On

"A branch cannot produce fruit if it is severed from the vine, and you cannot be fruitful unless you remain in me."

JOHN 15:4 NLT

If branches had seminars, the topic would be "Secrets of Vine Grabbing." But branches don't have seminars, because to attend them they would have to release the vine—something they refuse to do. The dominant duty of the branch is to cling to the vine.

The dominant duty of the disciple is the same.

We Christians tend to miss this. We banter about pledges to "make a difference for Christ" and "lead people to the Lord." Yet these are by-products of the Christ-focused life. Our goal is not to bear fruit. Our goal is to stay attached.

Maybe this image will help. When a father leads his four-year-old son down a crowded street, he takes him by the hand and says, "Hold on to me." He doesn't say, "Let's see if you can find your way home." The good father gives the child one responsibility: "Hold on to my hand."

God does the same with us. Your goal is not to know every detail of the future. Your goal is to hold the hand of the one who does and never, ever let go.

Anxious for Nothing

March

H-O-P-E

He will open the eyes of the blind and
unplug the ears of the deaf.

ISAIAH 35:5 NLT

Helen Keller wasn't yet two when an illness left her blind, deaf, and mute. When Helen was seven years old, Annie Sullivan, a young, partially blind teacher, came to the Kellers' Alabama home to serve as Helen's teacher.

Helen was as stubborn as her teacher. Locked in a frightening, lonely world, she misinterpreted Annie's teaching attempts. The result was a battle of wills.

Finally, during a fevered exchange near the water pump, Annie placed one of Helen's hands under the spout of flowing water. Into the other hand she spelled out w-a-t-e-r.

All of a sudden Helen stopped. She placed her hand on her teacher's and repeated the letters w-a-t-e-r. Annie beamed, and Helen pulled her around the yard, spelling out the words. P-o-r-c-h. P-u-m-p. It was a victory parade.[1]

Jesus gives us a similar reason to celebrate—God breaking through to our world. He is the teacher. He sends messages: H-o-p-e. L-i-f-e. He cracks the shell of our world and invites us to peek into his. And every so often a seeking soul looks up. May you be one of them.

Because of Bethlehem

That You May Believe

This miraculous sign at Cana in Galilee was the first time
Jesus revealed his glory. And his disciples believed in him.

JOHN 2:11 NLT

John's Gospel could well have been subtitled *That You May Believe.*
Why tell about the water-to-wine miracle? So you would
believe that Jesus can restore what life has taken.

Why tell about the lame man who took up his mat or the blind
man who washed the mud from his eyes? That you might believe in a
Jesus who sees a new version of us and gives new vision to us.

Why walk on water, feed the thousands, and raise the dead? That
you would believe God still calms the storms of life, still solves the
problems of life, and still brings the dead to life.

Need grace? Jesus' work of redemption is still finished.

Need reassurance that it's all true? The tomb is still empty.

Need a second chance? The coal fire is still burning on the Galilean
shore.

All these events stand together as one voice, cheering you on, calling on you to believe that this miracle-working God cares for you,
fights for you, and will come to your aid.

You Are Never Alone

If Only

*Therefore, since we are receiving a kingdom that
cannot be shaken, let us be thankful, and so worship
God acceptably with reverence and awe.*

HEBREWS 12:28

The widest river in the world is not the Mississippi, Amazon, or Nile. It is a body of water called If Only. Throngs of people stand on its banks and cast longing eyes over the waters. They desire to cross but can't seem to find the ferry. They are convinced the If Only River separates them from the good life.

If only I were thinner, I'd have the good life.

If only I were richer, I'd have the good life.

If only the kids would come. If only the kids were gone. If only I could leave home, move home, get married, get divorced.

The If Only River.

Are you standing on its shore? Does it seem the good life is always one "if only" away?

If so, then we've traced your anxiety back to one of its sources.

"If only" is the petri dish in which anxiety thrives. Replace your "if only" with "already." Look at what you already have. Treat each anxious thought with a grateful one, and prepare yourself for a new day of joy.

Anxious for Nothing

Speak Up

Admonish one another.

ROMANS 15:14 NKJV

A dmonishment is high-octane encouragement. The word literally
means "putting in mind."[2] To admonish is to deposit truth into
a person's thoughts. It might take the form of discipline, encouragement, or affirmation. It may be commendation or correction. Above
all, admonishment is truth spoken into a difficult circumstance. It
inserts the chlorine tablet of veracity into the algae of difficulty.

Admonishment speaks up.

Yes, we hold the hand of the struggler. Yes, we bring water to the
thirsty. And yes, yes, yes, we speak words of truth into moments of
despair.

Dare we sit idly by while Satan spreads his lies? By no means!
Unsheathe God's sword, the Word of God, and brandish its glimmer-
ing blade in the face of evil. "Finally, be strong in the Lord, and in the
strength of his might. Put on the whole armor of God. . . . And take
the helmet of salvation, and the sword of the Spirit, which is the word
of God" (Ephesians 6:10–11, 17 ASV).

How Happiness Happens

Jesus Stands Up for You

"I have prayed for you, that your faith should not fail."

LUKE 22:32 NKJV

Ever had anyone stand up for you? The answer is yes. Jesus stands at this very moment, offering intercession on your behalf.

"Grant Mary the strength to face this interview!"
"Issue to Tom the wisdom necessary to be a good father!"
"Defeat the devil, who seeks to rob Allison of her sleep!"

"Where is Jesus?" Peter and crew may have asked.

"Where is Jesus?" the bedridden, the enfeebled, the impoverished, the overstressed, the isolated ask.

Where is he? He is in the presence of God, praying for us. Jesus prayed for Peter. He stood up for Stephen (Acts 7:55–59). He promises to pray and stand up for you. "Therefore he is able to save completely those who come to God through him, because he always lives to intercede for them" (Hebrews 7:25).

Jesus is the sinless and perfect high priest. When he speaks, all of heaven listens.

Unshakable Hope

A Mustard-Seed Confession

"I am the resurrection and the life. Anyone who believes in me will live, even after dying. . . . Do you believe this, Martha?"

JOHN 11:25–26 NLT

D o you believe this, Martha?"
　　Look to whom Jesus asked this question: a bereaved, heart-broken sister.

Look at where Jesus stood as he asked this question: a cemetery.

Look at when Jesus asked this question: four days too late. Lazarus, his friend, was four days dead, four days buried.

Maybe she answered with the conviction of a triumphant angel, fists pumping the air. Give her reply a dozen exclamation marks if you want, but I don't. I hear a meek "Yes, Lord . . . I have always believed you are the Messiah, the Son of God, the one who has come into the world from God" (v. 27 NLT).

Martha wasn't ready to say Jesus could raise the dead. Even so, she gave him a triple tribute: "the Messiah," "the Son of God," and "the one who has come into the world." She mustered a mustard-seed confession. Her expression of belief was enough for Jesus. Yours is too.

You Are Never Alone

Heavenly Greetings

Be kindly affectionate to one another with brotherly love.

ROMANS 12:10 NKJV

One evening my wife and I joined three other couples for dinner at one of their homes. We've been friends for decades. As we were dining, the eldest son of the host family stopped by. He's been through a tough stretch, battling depression, struggling through a divorce. We rose to greet him, not because of his recent turmoil but because he is a dear friend to all of us.

We chatted and laughed at some stories. It was nice, but memorable? No. At least not to me. Later that evening he sent this text to his mom:

> Thank you again for tonight. . . . I've never felt so much love walking into a room before. . . . It felt spiritual. . . . I just had this feeling like I was being greeted in heaven or something. . . . It's like I was instantly surrounded by all this unconditional love, and it just brought me a peace like I never felt before. I think that will stay with me forever.

We never know when a gesture of kindness will touch a heart. So why not greet *everyone* with kindness?

How Happiness Happens

Hungry for Grace

God opposes the proud but gives grace to the humble.

JAMES 4:6 NLT

Wonderful freedom is found in the forest of humility. I experienced it sometime back as I sat in a circle. There were twenty of us in all. We were an assorted lot. With one exception we had nothing in common. But that one exception was significant. We were lawbreakers. Each person in the room had received a piece of paper from a uniformed officer. So there we sat in a Defensive Driving class.

I'd dreaded the day all week. Who wants to share a Saturday with strangers reviewing the Texas Driver Handbook? But I was surprised. After a short time we felt like friends. The bonding began with the introductions and confessions.

"I'm Max. I went forty-five miles per hour in a thirty-mile-per-hour zone."

"I'm Sue. I made an illegal U-turn."

As each one spoke, the rest nodded, moaned, and dabbed tears. We felt one another's pain. Charades and shams were unnecessary. Might as well admit our failures and enjoy the day. So we did, and the humility created relief. This was God's plan all along.

God gives grace to the humble because the humble are hungry for grace.

Unshakable Hope

Christ Calms the Storm

They cried out to the LORD in their trouble, and he brought them out of their distress. He stilled the storm to a whisper; the waves of the sea were hushed.

PSALM 107:28–29

Lord, in the midst of my storms, I may doubt Jesus' presence. I may wonder if he is there and if he cares. Don't let me lose hope or lose heart. Deepen my belief in you, even during the storms. Don't allow doubt to take over. Help me release control of my circumstances and surrender them to you. Jesus is interceding on my behalf, and I am so comforted by this truth.

God, there is no storm you can't calm. There is no trial that is too big for you. No obstacle you cannot overcome. You see all and know all. You are all-powerful, even over the mightiest of storms.

Father, thank you for sending Christ to calm the storm. Without him, I would be lost. I would have no hope in the midst of trials. But because of him, I know that I have an eternal intercessor. I know that my name is spoken in your throne room. I am so grateful to be known by you. Amen.

Praying the Promises

It Is Well

"Fear not, for I am with you. . . . I will strengthen you."

ISAIAH 41:10 NKJV

In November 1873, Horatio Spafford's wife, Anna, and their children set sail for Europe. Horatio stayed home to take care of some business. On December 2, he received a telegram from his wife that began "Saved alone. What shall I do?"[3] He soon learned that the ship had collided with a British vessel and had sunk. Their four daughters drowned and Anna survived. He left for England to bring Anna back home. En route, while sailing on the ship, he wrote the lyrics to a song that would become an anthem to the providence of God.

> *When peace, like a river, attendeth my way,*
> *When sorrows like sea billows roll;*
> *Whatever my lot, Thou has taught me to say,*
> *It is well, it is well, with my soul.*[4]

May we so trust in the providence of God that we can say the same. Always.

Anxious for Nothing

Jesus Came to Serve

[The mother of James and John] said to Him, "Grant that these two sons of mine may sit, one on Your right hand and the other on the left, in Your kingdom."

MATTHEW 20:21 NKJV

Sometimes we wonder if the disciples listened when Jesus spoke. Just one page prior to Matthew 20, we read how he told them to imitate the spirit of children (Matthew 19:13–15). He told the rich young ruler to quit trusting self and start trusting God (Matthew 19:16–21). He declared, "The last will be first, and the first will be last" (Matthew 20:16).

But did any of Jesus' followers ask him to explain the meaning of humility? No. The only response came from the mother of James and John as she requested cabinet positions for her sons. Jesus quickly corrected her desire.

Whoever desires to become great among you, let him be your serv-ant. And whoever desires to be first among you, let him be your slave—just as the Son of Man did not come to be served, but to serve. (Matthew 20:26–28 NKJV)

Jesus came to serve. Shouldn't we do the same?

How Happiness Happens

Two Builders

"Everyone who hears these words of mine and puts them into
practice is like a wise man who built his house on the rock."

MATTHEW 7:24

Jesus told a story about two home builders (Matthew 7:24–27). I wonder if a modern-day version of the parable might read like this:

Two people set out to build their houses. The first went to RPF Home Supply: Regrets, Pain, and Fear. He ordered lumber that was rotted by guilt, nails that were rusty from pain, and cement that was watered down with anxiety. Since his home was constructed with RPF supplies, every day was consumed with regret, pain, and fear.

The second builder chose a different supplier. She secured her supplies from Hope Incorporated. Rather than choose regret, pain, and fear, she found ample promises of grace, protection, and security. She made the deliberate, conscious decision to build a life from the storehouse of hope.

Which of the two builders was wiser? Which of the two was happier? Which of the two is most like you?

Unshakable Hope

Give Him What You Have

Jesus then took the loaves, gave thanks, and
distributed to those who were seated as much as
they wanted. He did the same with the fish.

JOHN 6:11

I remember the day email entered the world. I went to sleep one night in a world of sticky notes. I awoke the next morning in a paperless society that the avant-garde thinkers on our church staff had been dreaming of for months.

My computer illiteracy was so severe, I thought a cursor was a person who used foul language, a modem was something you flushed, and a mouse was a rodent you trapped.

I guess you could say I was overwhelmed. You know the feeling. You know the paralyzing, deer-in-the-headlights fear that surfaces when the information is too much to learn, the change is too great to make, the grief is too deep to survive, or the crowd is too numerous to feed.

Before you count your money, bread, or fish, and before you count yourself out, turn and look at the one standing next to you! Count first on Christ. He can help you do the impossible. You simply need to give him what you have and watch him work.

You Are Never Alone

The Small Stuff

Everyone should be quick to listen, slow to
speak and slow to become angry.

JAMES 1:19

During the celebration of his thirtieth wedding anniversary, a friend of mine shared the secret of their happy marriage. "Early on, my wife suggested an arrangement. She would make all the small decisions and would come to me for all the major ones. Wouldn't you know that all these years have passed, and we haven't had one major decision."

Facetious, for sure. Yet there is wisdom in acknowledging the relatively small number of major decisions in life. Don't sweat the small stuff, and you won't sweat much at all.

During the next few days you'll be tested. A driver will forget to turn on his blinker. A passenger on the airplane will talk too loudly. A shopper will have fifteen items in the "ten items or less" checkout line. Your husband is going to blow his nose like a foghorn. Your wife is going to take her half of the garage in the middle. When they do, consider whether or not it's just small stuff.

Don't give up your joy or theirs over something that's not worth sweating.

How Happiness Happens

Rejoice in the Lord

*Humble yourselves in the sight of the
Lord, and He will lift you up.*

JAMES 4:10 NKJV

The next time you fear the future, rejoice in the Lord's sovereignty. Rejoice in what he has accomplished. Rejoice that he is able to do what you cannot do. Fill your mind with thoughts of God.

"[He is] the Creator, who is blessed forever" (Romans 1:25 NKJV).

"[He] is the same yesterday, today, and forever" (Hebrews 13:8 NKJV).

"[His] years will never end" (Psalm 102:27).

He is king, supreme ruler, absolute monarch, and overlord of all history. An arch of his eyebrow and a million angels will pivot and salute. Every throne is a footstool to his. Every crown is papier-mâché next to his. He consults no advisers. He needs no congress. He reports to no one. He is in charge.

Sovereignty gives the saint the inside track to peace. Others see the problems of the world and wring their hands. We see the problems of the world and bend our knees.

Anxious for Nothing

Already Defeated

The reason the Son of God appeared
was to destroy the devil's work.

1 JOHN 3:8

S atan appears in the garden at the beginning. He is cast into the fire in the end. He tempted David, bewildered Saul, and waged an attack on Job. He is in the Gospels, the book of Acts, the writings of Paul, Peter, John, James, and Jude. Serious students of Scripture must be serious about Satan.

Jesus was. He squared off against Satan in the wilderness (Matthew 4:1–11). He pegged Satan as the one who snatches the good news from the hearts of the hearers (Matthew 13:19; Mark 4:15). Prior to the crucifixion Jesus proclaimed, "Now shall the ruler of this world be cast out" (John 12:31 RSV). Jesus saw Satan not as a mythological image, not an invention of allegory. He saw the devil as a superhuman narcissist. When Jesus taught us to pray, he did not say, "Deliver us from nebulous negative emotions." He said, "Deliver us from the evil one" (Matthew 6:13).

We play into the devil's hand when we pretend he does not exist. The devil is a real devil.

But—and this is huge—*the devil is a defeated devil.*

Unshakable Hope

79

Two Cows

Let us consider how we may spur one another on toward
love and good deeds, . . . encouraging one another.

HEBREWS 10:24–25

Two cows were grazing in a pasture when a milk truck drove by. On the side of the truck were the words "pasteurized, homogenized, standardized, vitamin A added." Noticing this, one cow said to the other, "Makes you kind of feel inadequate, doesn't it?"

Inadequacy indwells a billion hearts.

Who is going to tell people the truth? Will you? Will you distribute encouragement to the world? Will you make some happiness happen? Will you call the forgotten kid from the back of the pack to the front? Will you remind humanity that we are made in God's image? That we are chosen, destined, and loved? That God is for us, not against us? That we are in God's hand, in God's plan? Will you go face-to-face with the tidal wave of inadequacy that sucks people out to sea?

Will you encourage someone today?

How Happiness Happens

Evidence of God

Since the creation of the world His invisible attributes are
clearly seen, being understood by the things that are made.

ROMANS 1:20 NKJV

Everything in creation gives evidence of God's existence. The intricacy of snowflakes, the roar of a thunderstorm, the precision of a honeybee, the bubbling of a cool mountain stream. These miracles and a million more give testimony to the existence of a brilliant, wise, and tireless God (Psalm 19:1–4). The facts lead to a wonderful conclusion. God is . . . and God is knowable.

He has not hidden himself, but rather the opposite: he promises success to all who search for him. We can know God; we can know his heart, his joy, his passion, his plan, and his sorrows. Of course, we will never know him entirely. God is knowable, but he is incomprehensible (Isaiah 55:8–9). Our pursuit of him must be marked by humility. We will never know everything about God.

But that isn't meant to discourage us. The mark of a saint is that he or she is *growing* in the knowledge of God. Our highest pursuit is the pursuit of our Maker. And he will make himself known to all who seek him.

Praying the Promises

Written in Stone

When the LORD finished speaking to Moses on Mount
Sinai, he gave him the two tablets of the covenant law,
the tablets of stone inscribed by the finger of God.

EXODUS 31:18

Up until the miracle on Mount Sinai, God had spoken to his creation. He had spoken through divine decrees, direct address, and
human lips. God's words had come through a variety of ways. But the
miracle on Sinai inaugurated a new era of God's written Word.

I envision a lightning-like finger chiseling word after word into
stone. Upon completion, the stone tablets were given to Moses to, in
turn, give them to people. In doing so, God gave us this promise: he
will guide us.

The written Word changed the way God related to his people.
We were not present to hear his decrees. Many of us are not privy to
personal, divine conversations. But we can have a Bible. We can read
God's decrees through his written Word. We can inspect and reflect
upon them personally and endlessly.

When you set your heart toward becoming a person of the Bible,
you can trust God's promise that he will show you the way you
should go.

Praying the Promises

Keep Walking

We walk by faith, not by sight.

2 CORINTHIANS 5:7 NKJV

Bill Irwin was not the first person ever to walk the twenty-one hundred miles of the Appalachian Trail. But Bill was the first in this respect: he was blind when he did it.

He was fifty years old when he set out on the hike. He made 2 Corinthians 5:7 his mantra: "For we walk by faith, not by sight." And that is what he did. He did not use maps, GPS, or a compass. He estimated that he fell five thousand times in the eight months.[5] He battled hypothermia, cracked his ribs, and skinned his hands and knees more times than he could count.[6]

But he made it. He made the long walk by faith and not by sight.

You are doing the same. Probably not on the trails of the Appalachians, but in the trials of life. You are walking the path between offered prayer and answered prayer. Between "Help me, Lord" and "Thank you, Lord."

Trust him—and keep walking.

You Are Never Alone

Even the Cross

Being found in appearance as a man, he humbled himself
by becoming obedient to death—even death on a cross!

PHILIPPIANS 2:8

Jesus did not view his equality with God as "something to be grasped" (Philippians 2:6 NET) or "exploited" (NRSV). He refused to throw his weight around.

When people mocked him, he didn't turn them into stones. When soldiers spat on him, he didn't boomerang their spit. Just the opposite. He became "obedient to death—even death on a cross!" (v. 8).

It cannot be said too often that it was God on that cross. *God* took the nails. *God* felt the tip of the spear. *God* exhaled a final breath.

Jesus descended the ladder of incarnation one rung at a time.

He did not grasp equality with God.

He made himself nothing.

He took on the form of a servant.

He submitted himself to death.

Even death on a cross.

Down, down, down, down. From heaven's crown to Bethlehem's cradle to Jerusalem's cross. And he did this just for you.

Because of Bethlehem

What Heaven Wants

"Believe me, Peter," returned Jesus, "this very night before the cock crows twice, you will disown me three times."

MARK 14:30 PHILLIPS

When the Romans arrested Jesus, Peter and the other followers ran like scalded dogs. Peter garnered enough courage to return to the mock trial. But not enough courage to enter the court. Instead, "he sat with the servants and warmed himself at the fire" (Mark 14:54 NKJV).

When confronted about his association with Jesus, three times Peter denied he ever knew the man. And the rooster crowed.

But on Sunday, when the female followers saw the empty grave, the angel told them:

Don't be alarmed. . . . You are looking for Jesus the Nazarene, who was crucified. He has been resurrected! He is not here! See the place where they put Him. But go, tell His disciples and Peter. (Mark 16:6–7 HCSB)

My goodness, did you see what I just saw? It's as if all of heaven had watched Peter fall. Now all of heaven wanted to help him back on his feet. It's what all of heaven wants for each of us.

You Are Never Alone

Full-Service Salvation

[He] is able to keep you from stumbling.

JUDE V. 24 NKJV

Jesus not only did a work *for* us; he does a work *within* us. "The mystery in a nutshell is just this: Christ is in you" (Colossians 1:27 MSG). He commandeers our hands and feet, requisitions our minds and tongues. "He decided from the outset to shape the lives of those who love him along the same lines as the life of his Son" (Romans 8:29 MSG).

Having paid sin's penalty, Christ defuses sin's power. God changes us day by day. We'll never be sinless, but we will sin less. And when we do sin, we have this assurance: the grace that saved us also preserves us. We may lose our tempers, our perspective, and our self-control. But we never lose our hope because God has his hold on us. He "is able to keep you from stumbling, and to present you faultless before the presence of His glory with exceeding joy" (Jude v. 24 NKJV).

The believer has been saved from the guilt of sin, is being saved from problems of sin, and, upon the return of Christ, will be saved from the punishment for sin. Complete and full-service salvation.

Because of Bethlehem

No More Separation

Jesus cried out with a loud voice, and breathed His last. Then the veil of the temple was torn in two from top to bottom.

MARK 15:37–38 NKJV

At the moment of Jesus' death, a miracle occurred: "The veil of the temple was torn in two from top to bottom." According to Henry and Richard Blackaby, "The veil separated the people from the temple's Most Holy Place. . . . According to tradition, the veil—a handbreadth in thickness—was woven of seventy-two twisted plaits, each plait consisting of twenty-four threads. The veil was apparently sixty feet long and thirty feet wide."[7]

We aren't talking about small, delicate drapes. This curtain was a wall made of fabric. The fact that it was torn from top to bottom reveals that the hands behind the deed were divine. God himself grasped the curtain and ripped it in two.

No more division. No more separation. No more sacrifices. "No condemnation for those who are in Christ Jesus" (Romans 8:1). Heaven's work of redemption was finished. Christ's death brought new life. Whatever barrier that had separated –or might ever separate—us from God is gone.

Unshakable Hope

Two Disciples

Joseph came and took the body away.
With him came Nicodemus.

JOHN 19:38–39 NLT

As the sun set on Friday, two disciples prepared the body of Jesus for burial: Joseph of Arimathea and Nicodemus. Both men were affluent. Both were city leaders. Both were stealth followers who went public with their faith in the final days.

They had nothing to gain in this act of service. As far as they knew, they would be the final people to see their Savior. They prepared a dead body for burial, not a soon-to-be-risen body for a miracle.

They doused linen strips in a hundred pounds of burial spices (John 19:39),[8] which was "enough spices for the burial of a king."[9] Then they swaddled the corpse until it was tightly secure. Upon completion of their work, the two men carried the body to the graveyard and placed it in an unused tomb. At the insistence of the religious leaders, Pilate stationed guards at the tomb. They were told to keep the disciples out. No one mentioned the need of keeping Jesus in.

You Are Never Alone

The Name Above Every Name

*God exalted him to the highest place and gave
him the name that is above every name.*

PHILIPPIANS 2:9

It was one thing for Christ to enter a womb, quite another for him to be placed in a tomb. But the tomb could not hold him.

The one who went low is now made high. The one who descended is now exalted. No angel is higher. No political office is higher. Jesus outranks every ruler and conqueror. Jesus is, right now, in the highest place. He occupies the only true throne in the universe. Every other throne is made of papier-mâché and is doomed to pass. Not the throne of Jesus. God "gave him the name that is above every name" (v. 9).

Names carry clout. When the name *Queen Elizabeth* was announced, people turned. When the letter is signed by John F. Kennedy, it is treasured and stored in a safe-deposit box. Napoleon, Caesar, Alexander the Great—all these names turned heads. But only one name will forever cause them to bow: "At the name of Jesus every knee should bow, in heaven and on earth and under the earth" (v. 10).

Because of Bethlehem

On Sunday

"But on the third day, he will rise to life again."

MARK 10:34 NCV

It had been three days since the crucifixion. Jesus had promised that on the third day he would rise (Mark 8:31; 9:31; 10:34).

Friday was day one. Saturday was day two.

Friday evening was quiet. Saturday was sad.

On Friday the devils danced. On Saturday the demons feasted.

On Friday the disciples fled. On Saturday they wept.

On Friday heaven's finest Son died and was buried. On Saturday he spoke not a word.

On Friday the angels lowered their heads. On Saturday they kept their vigil.

But on Sunday, on the third day, in the predawn hours, in the heart of Joseph's tomb, the heart of Jesus began to beat.

Oh, to have seen the moment. To have heard the sudden intake of air. To have observed the eyes of Jesus blink open and seen a smile. Don't you know a smile spread across the Victor's face! The first breath of Christ meant the final breath of death.

You Are Never Alone

When Everything Changed

He is not here; he has risen, just as he said.

MATTHEW 28:6

It was Sunday morning after the Friday execution. The sky was dark. The disciples had scattered. Jesus was dead and buried. Yesterday's news, right? Wrong.

> There was a violent earthquake, for an angel of the Lord came down from heaven and, going to the tomb, rolled back the stone and sat on it. His appearance was like lightning, and his clothes were white as snow. . . .
>
> The angel said to the women, "Do not be afraid, for I know that you are looking for Jesus, who was crucified. He is not here; he has risen, just as he said." (Matthew 28:2–6)

Had such words never been spoken, had the body of Jesus decayed into dust in the borrowed tomb, you would not be reading these pages. But the words were spoken, and the resurrection changed everything.

Unshakable Hope

Joy *Will* Come

Jesus said to her, "Mary."
She turned toward him and cried out in Aramaic,
"Rabboni!" (which means "Teacher").

JOHN 20:16

Jesus appeared to Mary Magdalene! Of all the people to whom he could have spoken, Jesus went first to her. He'd just ripped the gates of hell off their hinges. He'd just yanked the fangs out of Satan's mouth. He'd just turned BC into AD, for heaven's sake! Jesus was the undisputed King of the universe. Ten thousand angels stood in rapt attention ready to serve. And what was his first act? To whom did he go? To Mary, the weeping, heartbroken woman who once had seven demons.

Why? Why her? As far as we know, she didn't become a missionary. No epistle bears her name. No New Testament story describes her work. Why did Jesus create this moment for Mary Magdalene? Perhaps to send this message to all the heavyhearted people: "Weeping may last through the night, but joy comes with the morning" (Psalm 30:5 NLT).

Joy comes.

Joy comes because Jesus comes. And if we don't recognize his face, he will call our names.

Unshakable Hope

No Condemnation

He was pierced for our transgressions, . . .
and by his wounds we are healed.

ISAIAH 53:5

Father, you are perfect in your ways, in your love, and in your mercy. You do not fail or fall short or sin. You are holy beyond my understanding. You sent your Son, Jesus, into this world so that I would be made holy by him and, therefore, worthy of your presence. It is only by his wounds that I am healed. You promised that there is no condemnation for those who are in Christ, but in my heart, it's not always easy for me to believe it. I may try to make myself right by doing good deeds. But I never seem to be able to do enough.

God, teach me how to live free from condemnation. Teach me how to trust and believe in this promise: in Christ, I am no longer a slave to sin. Free me from guilt and shame.

Thank you for taking care of my debt. You've rid me of the chains of sin that had taken me captive. I now live free of condemnation, fear, and guilt. Amen.

Praying the Promises

But God

But God raised him from the dead.

ACTS 2:24

God's sovereignty bids us to fight the onslaught of fret with the sword that is etched with the words *but God*.

The company is downsizing, *but God* is still sovereign.

The cancer is back, *but God* still occupies the throne.

I was an anxious, troubled soul, *but God* has been giving me courage.

The ultimate proof of providence is the death of Christ on the cross. No deed was more evil. No other day was so dark. Yet God not only knew of the crucifixion; he ordained it. As Peter told the murderers, "This man was handed over to you by God's deliberate plan and foreknowledge; and you, with the help of wicked men, put him to death by nailing him to the cross. *But God* raised him from the dead" (Acts 2:23–24, emphasis mine).

Everyone thought the life of Jesus was over—*but God*. His Son was dead and buried, but God raised him from the dead. God took the crucifixion of Friday and turned it into the celebration of Sunday.

Can he not do a reversal for you?

Anxious for Nothing

April

Watch for Joy

*Mary Magdalene went to the disciples with
the news: "I have seen the Lord!"*

JOHN 20:18

Joy comes. Watch for it. Expect it as you would the morning sunrise or the evening twilight. It came to Mary Magdalene. And it will come to you, my friend.

Keep coming to Jesus. Even though the trail is dark. Even though the sun seems to sleep. Even though everyone else is silent, walk to Jesus. Mary Magdalene did this. No, she didn't comprehend the promise of Jesus. She came looking for a dead Jesus, not a living one. But at least she came. And because she came to him, he came to her.

And you? You'll be tempted to give up and walk away. But don't. Even when you don't feel like it, keep walking the trail to the empty tomb. Open your Bible. Meditate on Scripture. Sing hymns. Talk to other believers. Place yourself in a position to be found by Jesus, and listen carefully.

Heartaches leave us with tear-streaked faces and heavy hearts. Weeping comes. But so does joy. Darkness comes, but so does the morning. Sadness comes, but so does hope. Sorrow may have the night, but it cannot have our lives.

Unshakable Hope

He Believed

*Finally the other disciple, who had reached the tomb
first, also went inside. He saw and believed.*

JOHN 20:8

John had yet to see the face of Jesus, hear the voice of Jesus, or touch
the body of Jesus. All of that would come later. Yet John believed.
What evidence led to his confession?

Here is what he tells us: along with Peter, "he . . . saw the strips of
linen cloth lying there" (John 20:5 NCV). John used a Greek term for
lying that means "still in their folds."[1] "The body is missing but the
clothes appear undisturbed."[2]

John did the math: the stone rolled away, the now-tenantless tomb,
the linens in their original state. Only one explanation made sense.
Jesus had passed through the burial wrap as if it were a sunrise mist.

Perhaps John elbowed his friend who stood next to him in the
empty tomb. "He's alive, Pete! No one took him. No one could kill
him. Come on, I'll race you! First one back gets to write the gospel!"

You Are Never Alone

What Started in Bethlehem

God was pleased for all of himself to live in Christ.

COLOSSIANS 1:19 NCV

One word describes heaven: *perfect.* One word describes us: *imperfect.* God's kingdom is perfect, but his children are not, so what is he to do? Abandon us? Start over? He could. But he loves us too much to do that.

He had a greater plan. "God was pleased for all of himself to live in Christ." All the love of God was in Jesus. All the compassion and power and devotion of God were, for a time, in the earthly body of a carpenter.

No wonder the winds obeyed when Jesus spoke; he was *God speaking.*

And no wonder ten thousand angels stood in rapt attention as Jesus was nailed to the cross; he was *God dying.*

He let people crucify him! He became sin for our sake. "He made Him who knew no sin to be sin for us" (2 Corinthians 5:21 NKJV). What started in the Bethlehem cradle culminated on the Jerusalem cross.

Because of Bethlehem

You Can Believe

God has raised this Jesus to life, and we are all witnesses of it.

ACTS 2:32

I began following Christ at the age of twenty, but somewhere around the age of twenty-two or twenty-three, I began to have some doubts. I admitted to a friend, "I'm not sure I really believe." His reply was simply, "Then, Max, where is the body of the crucified Christ?"

I've come to learn that his logic was Christian Apologetics 101. The line of reasoning goes like this: If Jesus didn't step out of the tomb, if his body is still in the grave . . .

Why didn't his enemies produce it? They knew where the body was buried. One display of the corpse and the church would have died in the cradle.

Don't you know they would have if they could have? But they had nothing to say. They had no body to display. Their silence, as it turns out, was the most convincing sermon of all.

The resurrection of Christ is the cornerstone of the Christian gospel.

Accept the invitation. Enter the tomb. Examine the facts. Even more, consider the implications. Because of the resurrection, a clear-headed, reasoned-out faith is a possibility. You can believe.

You Are Never Alone

Make Someone Smile

"The master will gird himself and have them sit down to eat, and will come and serve them."

LUKE 12:37 NKJV

In one of Jesus' appearances to his followers after his resurrection, they were on the Sea of Galilee when they heard him call out from the shore. When the disciples reached the beach, they saw the most extraordinary sight. Jesus was cooking (John 21:12)! Jesus had just ripped the gates of hell off their hinges. And now he, the unrivaled Commander of the universe, wore the apron?

Even more, he has yet to remove it. He promises a feast in heaven at which he will serve.

He was content to be called a servant.

Suppose you took that role. Be the family member who offers to wash the dishes after dinner. Be the church member who supports the pastor with prayer and notes of encouragement. Be the neighbor who mows the grass of the elderly couple.

Can you imagine the joy-giving benefits of these decisions?

Of course you can! You've experienced it. You've been unScrooged enough times to know the easiest way to make yourself smile is to make someone else smile first.

How Happiness Happens

A Resurrection Promise

"Today you will be with me in paradise."

LUKE 23:43

Jesus went on a resurrection tour. He appeared to the women near the tomb, the followers in the upper room, the disciples on the road to Emmaus, and his friends on the shore of Galilee. He spoke with them. He ate with them. They touched his body; they heard his words. They were convinced this Jesus was raised from the dead.

They also believed his resurrection was the preview and promise of ours. What God did for him, he will do for us. So what will happen when you die? Scripture reveals some intriguing assurances.

Your spirit will immediately enter into the presence of God. Your body will join you later. We believe this to be true because of verses like this one: "We are confident, I say, and would prefer to be away from the body and at home with the Lord" (2 Corinthians 5:8).

Isn't this the promise Jesus gave the thief on the cross? "Today," Christ promised, "you will be with me in paradise." No delay. No pause. The thief closed his eyes on earth and awoke in paradise. The soul of the believer journeys home, while the body of the believer awaits the resurrection.

Unshakable Hope

He Became Like Us

Though he was God, he did not think of equality
with God as something to cling to.

PHILIPPIANS 2:6 NLT

Before Bethlehem, Jesus had every advantage and benefit of deity. He was boundless, timeless, and limitless. Jesus spoke and the bespangled sky happened. He calls each star by name and can fold up the skies as a bedouin would pack his tent.

Yet the one who made everything "made himself nothing" (Philippians 2:7). Christ experienced hunger and thirst. He was taught to walk, stand, wash his face, and dress himself. His muscles grew stronger; his hair grew longer. His voice cracked when he passed through puberty. He was genuinely human.

When he was "full of joy" (Luke 10:21), his joy was authentic. When he wept for Jerusalem (Luke 19:41), his tears were as real as yours or mine. When he asked, "How long must I put up with you?" (Matthew 17:17 NLT), his frustration was honest. When he cried out from the cross, "My God, my God, why have you forsaken me?" (Matthew 27:46), he needed an answer.

He took "the very nature of a servant" (Philippians 2:7). He became like us so he could serve us! He entered the world not to demand our allegiance but to display his affection.

Because of Bethlehem

Gracious Truth, Truthful Grace

*"I do not condemn you, either. Go. From
now on do not sin any longer."*

JOHN 8:11 NASB

G race and truth. Jesus offers both.

Grace told the adulterous woman, "I do not condemn you."
Truth told her, "Go and sin no more" (John 8:11 NKJV).
Grace invited a swindler named Zacchaeus to host Jesus for
lunch.
Truth prompted him to sell half of his belongings and give to the
poor (Luke 19:1–8).
Grace washed the feet of the disciples.
Truth told them, "Do as I have done for you" (John 13:15).

Jesus shared truth but graciously. Jesus offered grace but truth-
fully. Grace and truth. Acceptance seeks to offer both.

If we offer only grace, then we gloss over the truth. If we offer only
truth, then we dismiss the joy of grace.

How Happiness Happens

The Wait Is Nearly Over

"Behold, I am coming soon."

REVELATION 22:12 ESV

As a teenager I spent many a day clearing out ditches. The routine was simple. A foreman would drive a truck full of workers to the edge of civilization and show us the ditch that had been dug with a large machine. Before pipe could be placed inside it, the excess rocks and dirt needed to be removed. He would say, "Get to work. I'll come back for you." And then he would drive off.

A root canal would have been more pleasant. By midafternoon we began thinking, *Maybe the foreman's on his way.* Sunset came and went. And just when we thought we couldn't wait any longer, a set of familiar headlights would come bouncing over the horizon. No one had to tell us to climb out of the ditch and gather our tools. We were ready when he came to take us home.

Some of you have been digging a long time. The wind is a cold one, and you've searched the horizon for the coming of the King. You're wondering, *Is he really coming for us?*

Your wait is nearly over. If all of history were merely a day, the sun would have begun to set. Christ is coming soon.

Because of Bethlehem

Set Your Eyes on Heaven

*We set our eyes not on what we see but on what
we cannot see. What we see will last only a short
time, but what we cannot see will last forever.*

2 CORINTHIANS 4:18 NCV

The verb used in the phrase "set our eyes" is *skopeó*, the great-grandfather of the English word *scope*. When you press your eye against the scope of a rifle, what happens? All your gaze is focused on one item. In the same way, lift up your eyes and look, long and hard, at the promised heaven.

Let this hope for tomorrow bring strength to today. Your finest moment will be your final moment! I know, most people say otherwise. Death is to be avoided, postponed, and ignored. But they do not have what you have. You have a promise from the living God. Your death will be swallowed up in victory! Jesus Christ rose from the dead, not just to show you his power but also to reveal your path. He will lead you through the valley of death to victory.

Unshakable Hope

When Your Ship Sinks

All the days planned for me were written in
your book before I was one day old.

PSALM 139:16 NCV

God had given Paul an assignment: carry the gospel to Rome. Though a storm threatened to sink him, Paul knew he would survive. Why? He had not yet arrived in Rome to complete his assignment. He knew God wasn't finished with him yet.

You probably don't have a clear message like Paul's. But you do have the assurance that if God has work for you to do, he will keep you alive to do it. I'm not saying you will have no more problems in your future. Quite the contrary. Paul lost the ship but lived to finish the work God had given him.

It is not easy to lose your boat: your marriage, your body, your business. Because of your boat, you've stayed afloat. And now without it you think you will sink. You're correct. You will, for a while. Waves will sweep over you. Fear will suck you under. But take heart, says Paul. Take heart, says Christ: "In this world you will have trouble, but be brave! I have defeated the world" (John 16:33 NCV).

You can lose it all, only to discover that you haven't. God has been there all along.

Anxious for Nothing

God of Victory

This God—how perfect are his deeds! How dependable his words! He is like a shield for all who seek his protection. The LORD alone is God; God alone is our defense. He is the God who makes me strong, who makes my pathway safe.

PSALM 18:30–32 GNT

Almighty God, you have promised to honor obedience. Help me walk steadfastly in your Word and in your promise. Remind me of your power. Give me the courage to take steps of faith, remembering that everything will end all right.

Thank you that even if my circumstances cause me to fear, I have the final victory in Christ. I only have to do what is right and place my trust in you. You are my hope. You are my victory.

God, you will accomplish what you set out to accomplish. You are always working for the good of those who love you. I praise you for these promises. Amen.

Praying the Promises

The Society of Bent Timber

Make allowance for each other's faults, and
forgive anyone who offends you.

COLOSSIANS 3:13 NLT

One of my favorite places on earth is a grove that sits on the Guadalupe River only minutes from my house. It's a peaceful place. Bass swim among the rocks. And trees, oh, the trees. Cypresses line the river's edge. Mesquite and Texas live oaks cluster in the draw. They weather the winters and celebrate the summers.

And they are all bent. There's not a straight trunk among them. Even so, they provide the perfect place to find peace. Fishermen doze in their shade. Birds build nests on their branches.

Humanity is like that grove of trees. Though we attempt to stand tall, none of us succeed. We twist and turn and have our gnarly bark. We are a collection of bent timber. And that's okay. There is beauty in our bentness.

So enjoy the Society of the Bent Timber. Cut people some slack. Ease up. Reduce your number of peeves, and be patient with the people who pet them. The world, for all its quirky people, is a wonderful place to live. The sooner we can find the beauty, the happier we will be.

How Happiness Happens

Resurrected Hope

Let us hold unswervingly to the hope we
profess, for he who promised is faithful.

HEBREWS 10:23

In a letter, a congregant explained to me that his wife had died of cancer a few months prior. On Easter weekend the grief was pulling him under. In one of her final acts, his wife had planted some poppy seeds in their lawn. They never grew.

He decided to make a list of his "I can'ts." Things like "I can't get over Janelle's death" and "I can't ever love again." On Saturday morning he buried the list in the soil that contained the seeds.

I'll let him tell you what happened next.

Easter Sunday, I decided to go out to my burial site where I had buried my little box of "I can'ts." . . . As I approached the site, I was taken aback. There, swaying in the light breeze, was a single red poppy![3]

God resurrected hope in the heart of the widower. And he can resurrect it in yours too.

You Are Never Alone

Anxious for . . . Nothing?

Be anxious for nothing, but in everything by
prayer and supplication, with thanksgiving, let
your requests be made known to God.

PHILIPPIANS 4:6 NKJV

We have been taught that the Christian life is a life of peace, and when we don't have peace, we assume the problem lies within us. Not only do we feel anxious, but we also feel guilty about our anxiety! The result is a downward spiral of worry, guilt, worry, guilt.

It's enough to make us wonder if the apostle Paul was out of touch with reality when he wrote, "Be anxious for nothing." "Be anxious for less" would have been a sufficient challenge. Or "Be anxious only on Thursdays." Or "Be anxious only in seasons of severe affliction."

But Paul doesn't seem to offer any leeway here. Be anxious for nothing. Nada. Zilch. Zero. Is this what he meant? Not exactly. He wrote the phrase in the present active tense, which implies an ongoing state. It's the life of *perpetual anxiety* that Paul wanted to address. The *Lucado Revised Translation* reads, "Don't let anything in life leave you perpetually breathless and in angst." The presence of anxiety is unavoidable, but the prison of anxiety is optional.

Anxious for Nothing

Words That Heal Wounds

His powerful Word is sharp as a surgeon's scalpel,
cutting through everything, whether doubt or
defense, laying us open to listen and obey.

HEBREWS 4:12–13 MSG

Scripture-based admonishment is like antibacterial cream. We may not know how it heals a wound; we just know it does. Apply it and see what happens. Make it your practice to say, "I know a verse in the Bible that might help." My go-to list includes scriptures like Romans 8:31, Philippians 1:6, and Hebrews 13:5.

After church last Sunday I met a ten-year-old boy by the name of Joshua. His mother, who was standing next to him, explained that Joshua's father was no longer a part of his son's life. The boy looked at me through sad, tear-moistened eyes. I squatted down eye level with Joshua and asked, "Do you know the story of your namesake?" He nodded. "You will do what he did," I admonished. "You will bring down Jericho's walls and pray prayers of great faith." He wasn't quite sure how to respond. But his mom? She was wiping her eyes.

Strugglers don't need our opinions. They don't need our philosophies on suffering. They need someone to admonish them with truth.

How Happiness Happens

Like Rain from Heaven

"Heaven and earth will pass away, but
my words will never pass away."

MATTHEW 24:35

A s I share these words, I'm standing on a promise.

As the rain and snow come down from heaven and stay upon the ground to water the earth, and cause the grain to grow and to produce seed for the farmer and bread for the hungry, so also is my word. I send it out, and it always produces fruit. It shall accomplish all I want it to and prosper everywhere I send it. (Isaiah 55:10–11 TLB)

Note the certainty of God's promise. God's Word "always produces fruit. It shall accomplish all I want it to and prosper everywhere I send it."

Picture God's words falling like rain from heaven on you. Imagine these promises as gentle spring showers. Receive them. Allow them to land on you, to soak you. I'm trusting that God's words will prosper in your life. Will you join me in believing this promise?

Unshakable Hope

What Are You Hooked To?

Those who wait on the LORD shall renew their strength;
they shall mount up with wings like eagles, they shall
run and not be weary, they shall walk and not faint.

ISAIAH 40:31 NKJV

Everyone is anchored to something. A retirement account or a résumé. Some are tethered to a person or career position. Yet these are surface objects. Would you anchor your boat to another boat? You want something that goes deeper and holds firmer than other floating vessels. But when you anchor to the things of this world, are you not doing the same?

Ask yourself, *Is what I'm hooked to stronger than what I'll go through?*

Salty sailors would urge you to hook on to something hidden and solid. Don't trust the buoy on the water, the sailors in the other boat, or the other boat. When the storm hits, trust no one but God.

Why? Because in him, we have an anchor that is beyond the reach of the devil and under the care of Christ. Secure your anchor in God. Build your life on his promises. The winds will still blow. The rain will still fall. But in the end, you will be standing with him.

Praying the Promises

The Power of Gratitude

Give thanks in all circumstances; for this is God's will for you.

1 THESSALONIANS 5:18

The good life begins not when circumstances change but when our attitude toward them does.

As you pray, sprinkled among your phrases "Help me . . . ," "Please give me . . . ," and "Won't you show me . . ." should be two wonderful words: "Thank you."

Gratitude is a mindful awareness of the benefits of life. Studies have linked the emotion with a variety of positive effects. Grateful people tend to be more empathetic and forgiving of others. People who keep a gratitude journal are more likely to have a positive outlook on life. Grateful individuals demonstrate less envy, materialism, and self-centeredness. Gratitude improves self-esteem and enhances relationships, quality of sleep, and longevity.[4] It's no wonder, then, that God's anxiety therapy includes a large, delightful dollop of gratitude.

Make sure you've got plenty.

Anxious for Nothing

Your Prayers Will Be Answered

"Never will I leave you; never will I forsake you."

HEBREWS 13:5

Christ will not remove all the pain this side of heaven. Did someone tell you otherwise? Did someone assure you that God permits only blue skies and rainbows and sunbeams? They misspoke. Read the Bible from the table of contents to the maps in the back, and you will not find any promise of a pain-free life on this side of death.

But you will find this assurance: "Never will I leave you; never will I forsake you."

In John 4:46–54, a father begged Jesus to come home with him and heal his son. Instead, Jesus sent him on his way, promising that the boy would live. When the father reached his home, he made this wonderful discovery: the presence and power of Jesus had gone ahead of him. Christ had supernaturally gone ahead to the nobleman's residence and not only healed the son but also won the hearts of the entire household.

Was the father's prayer answered? By all means. Yours will be as well. Perhaps the answer will come this side of heaven. Or perhaps it awaits you on the other side.

You Are Never Alone

A New Song

*"In this world you will have trouble. But take
heart! I have overcome the world."*

JOHN 16:33

My friend Chris was diagnosed with mononucleosis when he was nine years old. The doctor ordered him to stay indoors for the entire summer. Chris was a rambunctious kid. A summer indoors with no Little League, fishing trips, or bike rides? Might as well trap an eagle in a birdcage.

Chris's dad, however, resolved to find something good in the quarantine. He sold guitars in his drugstore and wasn't a half-bad guitarist himself. So he gave Chris a guitar. Each morning he taught his son a new chord or technique. Turns out, Chris had a knack for playing the guitar. By the end of the summer, Chris was beginning to write some songs of his own.

Within a few decades he was regarded as the "most sung songwriter in the world."[5] Perhaps you've heard some of his music: "How Great Is Our God," "Amazing Grace (My Chains Are Gone)," "At the Cross."

I can't help but think that Jesus was praying for nine-year-old Chris Tomlin. What Satan intends for evil, Jesus will use for good.

Unshakable Hope

Worship Works Wonders

"Worship the Lord your God and serve him only."

LUKE 4:8

We all worship someone or something. Anytime we trust an object or activity to give us life and meaning, we worship it.

When we make good things the ultimate things, we set ourselves up for disappointment. If we depend on a career or relationship to give our lives meaning, what happens when retirement comes or the relationship ends? The list of impostor gods includes sex, food, money, alcohol, success, and influence. In the correct dosage and context, these can be wonderful gifts *from* God. But they are dismal substitutes *for* God.

God-centered worship rescues us from trompe l'oeil gods who never deliver on their promises. Worship does to the soul what a spring rain does to a thirsty field. It soaks down, seeps in, and stirs life. Are you stressed? Worship God, who could store the universe in his pocket and the oceans in an eyedropper. Are you ashamed? Worship Jesus, whose love never fades. Are you bereaved? Open your heart to your Shepherd. He will lead you through the valley of sorrow. Do you feel small? A few moments in front of the throne of your loving King will evaporate any sense of insignificance. Worship works wonders.

Because of Bethlehem

Contagiously Calm

Let your gentleness be evident to all.

PHILIPPIANS 4:5

The Greek word translated in today's verse as *gentleness* (*epie-ikes*) describes a temperament that is seasoned and mature.[6] It envisions an attitude that is fitting to the occasion, levelheaded and tempered. The gentle reaction is one of steadiness, evenhandedness, fairness. It "looks humanely and reasonably at the facts of a case."[7]

This gentleness is "evident to all." Family members take note. Your friends sense a difference. Coworkers benefit from it. Others may freak out or run out, but the gentle person is sober minded and clear thinking. Contagiously calm.

The contagiously calm person is the one who reminds others, "God is in control." This is the leader who sees the challenge, acknowledges it, and observes, "These are tough times, but we'll get through them."

Let your gentleness be evident to all.

Anxious for Nothing

Our Kinsman-Redeemer

They remembered that God was their Rock,
that God Most High was their Redeemer.

PSALM 78:35

*K*insman-redeemer is a phrase that takes center stage in one of the Bible's great stories of romance and redemption, the book of Ruth.

A famine had driven Naomi's family from Bethlehem to Moab, where her husband and two sons died a few years later, leaving her a widow in a foreign land. She resolved to return to her hometown of Bethlehem, and her daughter-in-law Ruth went with her.

Boaz was everything the women were not. He was a man of means and property; they were women in need. When Boaz saw Ruth gleaning grain in his field, he asked about her, spoke to her with kindness, instructed her, and protected her. Eventually, he married her, saving Ruth and Naomi from ruin. He was their kinsman-redeemer. Boaz saw Ruth; Christ sees you. Boaz was affluent. Jesus owns every square inch of the universe. Boaz told men to leave Ruth alone. Jesus commands Satan to leave you alone.

Ask your kinsman-redeemer to take you into his care. Ask him to protect you. He has promised to do so.

Praying the Promises

Humility Is Honest

"To whom will you compare me? Or who is my equal?" says the Holy One.

ISAIAH 40:25

I'm wondering if you'd join me in a prayer of repentance—repentance from arrogance. What have we done that God didn't first do? What do we have that God didn't first give us? Have any of us ever built anything that God can't destroy? Have we created any monument that the Master of the stars can't reduce to dust?

I like the joke about the arrogant man who took God's preeminence to task. He looked up into the heavens and declared, "I can do what you can do! I can create a person out of dust! I understand the systems of life and science!"

God accepted the offer. "All right," he told the buffoon. "Let's see what you can do."

The man reached down and took a handful of dirt. But before the man could go further, God interrupted him. "I thought you said you could do what I did."

"I can."

"Then," God instructed, "get your own dirt."

Humility is healthy because humility is honest.

Unshakable Hope

Encouragement

Encourage one another daily.

HEBREWS 3:13

Tim lived in poverty. As a teenager, he worked at the local movie theater. During his breaks he would hurry across the street to a fast-food restaurant and get fries and water. John Moniz, the owner, noticed and asked why he wasn't buying more food. Tim told him he couldn't afford it.

One evening Moniz took a bag of sandwiches across the street. The two struck up a conversation that led to a mentorship. Moniz shared with Tim life lessons about discipline and responsibility. More important, Moniz taught his young friend about Jesus.

Then tragedy struck. Moniz, age thirty-seven, died of a pulmonary embolism. Much to his credit Tim chose to put the lessons Moniz had taught him to good use. He wrote a new purpose statement for his life: to have a positive effect on one billion people.

And he appears to be well on his way to reaching it. Tim Scott was sworn in to the US Senate in 2013, the first African American senator from the South since Reconstruction.[8]

It all started with a sandwich and a fellow willing to offer some encouragement. Maybe we could do something similar.

How Happiness Happens

Trust the Pilot

*Blessed is the man who trusts in the LORD, and whose
hope is the LORD. For he shall be like a tree planted
by the waters, which spreads out its roots by the river,
and will not fear when heat comes; but its leaf will be
green, and will not be anxious in the year of drought.*

JEREMIAH 17:7–8 NKJV

Many years ago I spent a week visiting the interior of Brazil with a longtime missionary pilot. He flew a circuit of remote towns in a four-seat plane that threatened to come undone at the slightest gust of wind. Wilbur and Orville had a sturdier aircraft.

I could not get comfortable. I kept thinking the plane was going to crash in some Brazilian jungle and I'd be gobbled up by piranhas or swallowed by an anaconda. I kept shifting around, looking down, and gripping my seat. (As if that would help.) Finally the pilot had enough of my squirming. He looked over at me and shouted over the airplane noise, "We won't face anything that I can't handle. You might as well trust me to fly the plane."

Is God saying the same to you?

Anxiety passes as trust increases.

Anxious for Nothing

A Defeated Rat

*God's Spirit, who is in you, is greater than
the devil, who is in the world.*

1 JOHN 4:4 NCV

My friend Carter Conlon spent many of his early years on a farm. He recalls a barnyard scene that illustrates the status of Satan. A family of cats lived in the barn. The mama cat would often be spotted in the field playing with a rat until it was exhausted. She would bring the rodent to the kittens to teach them how to catch and kill it. The rat, upon seeing the kittens, would rise up on its hind feet and prepare to fight. The rodent would bare its tiny yellow teeth and flare its little claws. Its only hope was to convince the kittens it was something other than what it was: a defeated, wimpy, outnumbered rat. It had already lost. The kittens didn't even have to fight to win the victory.[9]

Jesus has already defeated the rat as well. Be alert to the devil, but don't be intimidated by him. Evil will have its day and appear to have the sway, but God will ultimately win the day.

Unshakable Hope

Count on God

Then Jesus shouted, "Lazarus, come out!"
And the dead man came out.

JOHN 11:43–44 NLT

Lazarus, come out!" The voice of God echoed off the grotto walls until the words found their way into the corner of paradise where sat a healthy, happy Lazarus in a corner café, sipping a latte with Moses.

"Lazarus!"

He heard his name and looked at Moses. The patriarch shrugged. "You have to go, friend."

Lazarus did not want to go back to earth. Of that I'm certain. But when Jesus commands, his disciples obey. So his spirit descended from the heavens, and he reentered and reanimated his body. He stood up and lumbered toward the mouth of the tomb.

"'Now unbind him,' Jesus told them, 'and let him go home'" (v. 44 PHILLIPS).

Don't miss the message of this miracle. You are never alone. Jesus meets us in the cemeteries of life. Whether we are there to say goodbye or there to be buried, we can count on the presence of God.

You Are Never Alone

God Can Use You

"My spirit rejoices in God my Savior, for he has been mindful of the humble state of his servant."

LUKE 1:47–48

It was the servant spirit of Mary that led God to select her to be the mother of Jesus. She wasn't a scholar or a sophisticated socialite. She was simple. Plain. A peasant. She blended into the crowd. She hailed from Nazareth, a dusty village in an oppressed district in Galilee. In the social strata of her day, Mary occupied the lowest step. As a Jew she answered to the Romans. As a female she was subservient to males. As a young girl she was second to older women. She was poor, so she was beneath the upper class.

Mary was extraordinarily ordinary. Yet this virtue set her apart: "I am the servant of the Lord. Let this happen to me as you say!" (Luke 1:38 NCV).

When God wanted to bring Christ into the world, he looked for a servant. No diploma required. Bank accounts were not a factor. Place of birth didn't matter. Let all unassuming people of the world be reminded: God can use you.

How Happiness Happens

May

Encouragement All Around

Encourage each other. Live in harmony and peace.
Then the God of love and peace will be with you.

2 CORINTHIANS 13:11 NLT

Our God is "the God who gives endurance and encouragement" (Romans 15:5).

So does Jesus. "We pray that our Lord Jesus Christ and God our Father will encourage you and help you always to do and say the right thing" (2 Thessalonians 2:16–17 CEV).

When Jesus introduced the Holy Spirit to us in John 14–16, he called him the *paraklétos*, the noun form of the very word for encouragement.[1]

Scripture encourages us. "The Scriptures were written to teach and encourage us by giving us hope" (Romans 15:4 CEV).

The saints in heaven encourage us. A multitude of God's children is urging us on. Like spectators in the stands, a "crowd of witnesses" applauds from the heavens, calling on us to finish strong.

The Father, the Son, the Holy Spirit, the holy Scriptures, the saints. God places a premium on encouragement.

Seems like we should do the same.

How Happiness Happens

Today

"Seek first the kingdom of God and His righteousness,
and all these things shall be added to you."

MATTHEW 6:33 NKJV

I once wrote this resolve:

Today, I will live today. Yesterday has passed. Tomorrow is not yet. I'm left with today. So, today, I will live today.

Relive yesterday? No. I will learn from it. I will seek mercy for it. I will take joy in it. But I won't live in it.

Worry about the future? To what gain? It deserves a glance, nothing more. I can't change tomorrow until tomorrow.

Today, I will live today. I will face today's challenges with today's strength. I will dance today's waltz with today's music. I will celebrate today's opportunities with today's hope. Today.

May I laugh, listen, learn, and love. And tomorrow, if it comes, may I do so again.

A new day awaits you, my friend. A new season in which you will worry less and trust more. A season with reduced fear and enhanced faith. Can you imagine a life in which you are anxious for nothing? God can. And, with his help, you will experience it.

Anxious for Nothing

Abounding Hope

May the God of hope fill you with all joy and
peace in believing, that you may abound in
hope by the power of the Holy Spirit.

ROMANS 15:13 NKJV

G od wants us to "abound in hope by the power of the Holy Spirit."
Abound. What an extraordinary verb to use with "hope."

For about half an hour last week, the sky became a waterfall. I
had to pull my car off the road. Every square inch of the highway was
drenched. Rain *abounded.* God will drench your world with hope.

I once spent a day in Yosemite forest. I could no more number the
trees than I could count the stars. Yosemite abounded in trees. God
will turn your world into a forest of hope.

Could you use some abounding hope?

It's yours for the asking. "Grab the promised hope with both hands
and never let go. It's an unbreakable spiritual lifeline, reaching past all
appearances right to the very presence of God where Jesus, running
on ahead of us, has taken up his permanent post as high priest for us"
(Hebrews 6:18–20 MSG).

Unshakable Hope

Jesus Is the Hero

Once you were like sheep who wandered away. But now you have turned to your Shepherd, the Guardian of your souls.

1 PETER 2:25 NLT

Jesus is the one who found Peter, called Peter, orchestrated the fish catch for Peter, built the fire for Peter, cooked breakfast for Peter, took the confession of Peter, and recommissioned Peter. If the distance between Christ and Peter consisted of a hundred steps, Jesus took ninety-nine and a half.

But Peter still had to take his step. He was told to meet Jesus in Galilee, so he went. He heard Jesus was on the shore, so he jumped. He was asked questions by Christ, so he answered. He obeyed. He responded. He interacted. He stayed in communion with Christ.

Three times, in a moment of fear and weakness, he denied Jesus. Failure sires denial. And denial wants to avoid the very one we need. Don't give in to the desire. Speak to Jesus, and listen as he speaks to you. Obey him.

Peter went on to preach the inaugural sermon of the church. Can anyone turn a denying Peter into a proclaiming Peter? Jesus can. He did then. He does still.

You Are Never Alone

Vessels of the Greatest Gift

*It is God who works in you to will and to act
in order to fulfill his good purpose.*

PHILIPPIANS 2:13

God offers you the same gift he gave Mary, mother of Jesus—the indwelling Christ. Christ grew in her until the miracle of gestation became the moment of delivery. Likewise, Christ will grow in you until he comes out in your speech, your actions, your decisions.

God promised, "I will give you a new heart and put a new spirit within you; I will take the heart of stone out of your flesh and give you a heart of flesh" (Ezekiel 36:26 NKJV). Who does the work? Who removes the heart of stone? God.

We do not work; we trust the finished work of Christ. Like a growing child, we learn to walk . . . with God. We learn to talk . . . with God. We nourish ourselves on his bread and trust in his Word. Temper tantrums diminish. Prayer time increases. We seek our will less and God's will more, and he changes us from the inside out. And, in time, the most wonderful thing occurs . . . we become vessels for the greatest gift of all—Jesus Christ.

Praying the Promises

The Happiness Decision

Love is patient, love is kind.

1 CORINTHIANS 13:4

Denalyn's thirty-seven years of marriage to me, the king of quirks, qualifies her for a PhD in patience.

When I drive, my mind tends to wander. When it does, the car slows to a crawl. (*"Max, pay attention."*)

I repair things at risk of ruining them. (*"Max, I told you I could call a handyman."*)

Sending me to the grocery store is like sending me to the Amazon. I may never emerge. (*"You've been gone for two hours, and you only bought potato chips?"*)

Yet Denalyn is the happiest person within a dozen zip codes. Ask her friends or ask my daughters. They will tell you she's married to an odd duck, but she has the joy level of a kid at a carnival. Here is her secret: She's learned to enjoy my idiosyncrasies. She thinks I'm entertaining. Who would've thought?

To be clear, she lets her opinions be heard. I know when I've tested her patience. Yet I never fear failing the test and am happier for it. Happiness is less an emotion and more a decision.

How Happiness Happens

Our Sustaining God

The Son is the radiance of God's glory and the
exact representation of his being, sustaining
all things by his powerful word.

HEBREWS 1:3

The Greek word that is translated *sustaining* in Hebrews 1:3 is a term commonly used in the New Testament for "carrying" or "bringing."[2] The friends *carried* the paralyzed man to Jesus. They "sustained" the man (Luke 5:18). They guaranteed the safe delivery.

To say Jesus is "sustaining all things by his powerful word" is to say he is directing creation toward a desired aim. The use of the present participle implies that Jesus is continually active in his creation. He exercises supremacy over all things.

Distant? Removed? Not God. "He is before all things, and in him all things hold together" (Colossians 1:17). Were he to step back, the creation would collapse. His resignation would spell our evaporation. "For in him we live and move and have our being" (Acts 17:28).

With his hand at the helm of creation, spring still follows winter, and winter follows autumn. There is an order to the universe. He sustains everything. Allow him to sustain you.

Anxious for Nothing

Harmony Is Always an Option

*All these [gifts] are the work of one and the same Spirit, and
he distributes them to each one, just as he determines.*

1 CORINTHIANS 12:11

The Holy Spirit knows each saint and knows the needs of each
church. He distributes gifts according to what the church will
need in a particular region and season. When gifts are active, the
church is empowered to do the work for which it was intended. For
this reason we do not begrudge the talents of another believer or the
accomplishments of another church. Does the saxophone player envy
the tuba player? Not when each musician is playing his or her unique
part and following the lead of the conductor. When church members
do the same, the result is power. And the result is unity.

Saints are never told to create unity but rather to keep the unity
the Spirit provides (Ephesians 4:3). Harmony is always an option,
because the Spirit is always present. Gone is the excuse "I just can't
work alongside so-and-so." Maybe you can't, but the Spirit within
you can.

Fellowship is not always easy, but unity is always possible.

Unshakable Hope

The Burden Lifter

"Here I am! I stand at the door and knock."

REVELATION 3:20

I have a friend who works with churches in Papua New Guinea. Many in their culture don't knock on doors. They stand at the doorframe and politely cough. When Bible translators tried to explain the idea of Jesus knocking on the door, it made no sense to the locals. The missionaries solved the problem by rendering the verse "I stand at the door and cough."

Whether Jesus is clearing his throat or tapping on the door, the point is the same. He is gentle and polite. He never forces his way in. Yet just as we reach to open the door, the baby cries or the phone rings.

Life is crowded. Heaven knows, you already have more than you can do. And because heaven knows, Jesus comes not with a list of things for you to do but with a list of things he has already done and will do. Your death? Defeated. Your sins? Forgiven. Your fears? He will give you courage. Your questions? He will guide you.

Jesus lifts burdens; he doesn't add to them.

Because of Bethlehem

A God of Grace and Love

*Because of his great love for us, God, who is rich in mercy,
made us alive with Christ even when we were dead in
transgressions—it is by grace you have been saved.*

EPHESIANS 2:4–5

Father, sometimes I convince myself that I need to earn your salvation. I feel like I should do more, be more, and achieve more. But you simply want my faith.

Help me let go of my striving and this need to perform for you and for others. I know you want more than good deeds and religious acts—you want my belief in your promises.

You are a God of grace and love. Your well runs deep, and there is no limit to your mercy and forgiveness. You seek reconciliation with all your children through faith in Jesus.

Thank you for canceling the debt I never could have paid and for crediting my faith as righteousness in Christ. Amen.

Praying the Promises

Only One Messiah

*Now that you have purified yourselves by obeying
the truth so that you have sincere love for each
other, love one another deeply, from the heart.*

1 PETER 1:22

During the Civil War when Abraham Lincoln's wife criticized people from the South, he told her, "Don't criticize them, Mary; they are just what we would be under similar circumstances."[3]

We are never ever called to redeem the world. "Savior of humanity" is not on your job description or mine. Encourage, correct, applaud, and admonish? By all means. But save the world? In no way. There is only one Messiah and one throne. He isn't you, and the throne isn't yours.

Happiness happens not by fixing people but by accepting people and entrusting them into the care of God. Jesus did this. Otherwise, how could he have endured? No one knew humankind's hypocrisy and failings more than he. Christ knew exactly what people needed, yet he gave them time and space to grow. Aren't we wise to do the same?

How Happiness Happens

God's Version of Grace

It is by grace you have been saved, through faith—
and this is not from yourselves, it is the gift of God.

EPHESIANS 2:8

Salvation, from beginning to end, is a work of our Father. God does not stand on a mountain and tell us to climb it and find him. He comes down into our dark valley and finds us. He does all the work, from beginning to end.

An elderly woman was once asked about the security of her salvation. Though she'd dedicated her life to the Lord, a cynic asked, "How can you know that after all these years God won't let you sink into hell?"

"He would lose more than I would," the woman replied. "All I would lose would be my own soul. He would lose his good name."

Grace is entirely God's. God loving. God stooping. God offering. God caring and God carrying. This is God's version of grace. Is it yours? Guilt simmers like a toxin in far too many souls. Do not let it have a place in yours. Before you turn the page, internalize this promise that is written with the crimson blood of Christ: "There is now no condemnation for those who are in Christ Jesus" (Romans 8:1).

Unshakable Hope

Specific Prayer

Jesus asked him, "What do you want me to do for you?"

LUKE 18:40–41

What Jesus said to the blind man, he says to us: "What do you want me to do for you?" One would think the answer would be obvious. When a sightless man requests Jesus' help, isn't it apparent what he needs? Yet Jesus wanted to hear the man articulate his specific requests.

He wants the same from us. Why? I can think of three reasons.

1. A specific prayer is a serious prayer.
2. Specific prayer is an opportunity for us to see God at work.
3. Specific prayer creates a lighter load.

This is no endorsement of the demanding, conditional prayer that presumes to tell God what to do and when. Nor do I suggest that the power of prayer resides in chanting the right formula or quoting some secret code. Do not think for a moment that the power of prayer resides in the way we present it. God is not manipulated or impressed by our formulas or eloquence. But he is moved by the sincere request. After all, is he not our Father? As his children we honor him when we tell him exactly what we need.

Anxious for Nothing

What You Need to Know

"Go, wash in the pool of Siloam."

JOHN 9:7 NKJV

Jesus could have restored the blind man's sight in a second. Instead, he spackled his eyes with spit-made mud and sent him to the pool of Siloam.

The blind man groped his way to the water and began to splash his eyes. As he did, he saw the water ripple on the pool's surface. He saw his fingers open and close. With another splash he could make out the forms of people who stood to either side. From one moment to the next, he could see.

The question is often asked, "What does a person need to know to become a follower of Christ?" This story provides an answer. The man knew nothing of the virgin birth or the cost of discipleship. He knew only this: a man called Jesus made clay, put it on his eyes, and told him to wash. He received sight, not because he deserved it, earned it, or found it. He received sight because he trusted and obeyed the one who was sent to "open eyes that are blind" (Isaiah 42:7).

Nothing has changed. Trust Jesus to restore you.

You Are Never Alone

Jesus Will Carry You Home

He is able to save completely those who come to God through him, because he always lives to intercede for them.

HEBREWS 7:25

During her first-ever home-run trot, softball player Sara Tucholsky tore an ACL. She lay on the ground, clutching her knee with one hand and touching first base with the other. No one knew what to do.

Mallory Holtman played first base for the opposing team. She signaled for the shortstop to help her, and the two walked toward the injured player. "We're going to pick you up and carry you around the bases."

By the time they headed home, the spectators had risen to their feet, Sara's teammates had gathered at home plate, and Sara was smiling like a homecoming queen.[4]

God offers to do the same for you and me. You cannot make it on your own. But Jesus has the strength you do not have. He is able and willing to help in your time of need.

Let him do what he came to do. Let him carry you home.

Unshakable Hope

The Quiet Servant

*The first thing Andrew did was to find his brother
Simon and tell him, "We have found the Messiah"
(that is, the Christ). And he brought him to Jesus.*

JOHN 1:41–42

Andrew was such a servant. He was the brother of Peter. He came from the same town as James and John. Yet when we discuss the inner circle of Peter, James, and John, we don't mention Andrew. His name never appears at the top of the list of leaders. He lived in the shadow of the others.

Quiet, however, does not mean complacent. Just because Andrew avoided the limelight, that doesn't mean he lacked fire. He led his brother Peter to Jesus. Peter went on to preach the first sermon. Peter led the Jerusalem church. Peter took the gospel to Gentiles. He wrote epistles that we still read. He defended the apostle Paul. Anyone who appreciates Paul's epistles owes a debt of gratitude to Peter. And anyone who has benefited from the rocklike faith of Peter owes a debt to the servant spirit of Andrew.

No doubt, the world today could use another Peter and Paul. But make no mistake, the world today needs more Andrews too. Might you be an Andrew?

How Happiness Happens

Heaven's Helpers

There stood by me this night an angel.

ACTS 27:23 NKJV

Recently after a church service, one of our members approached me in the reception line. Her eyes were full of tears and wonder as she said, "I saw your angel."

"You did?"

"Yes, he stood near you as you preached."

I find comfort in that thought. I also find many scriptures to support it. "All the angels are spirits who serve God and are sent to help those who will receive salvation" (Hebrews 1:14 NCV).

Angels still come and help us.

On the deck of a sinking ship in a raging storm, Paul received a visitor from heaven. An angel came and stood beside him. They can stand beside you. An angel protected Shadrach, Meshach, and Abednego in the fiery furnace (Daniel 3:23–26). They can protect you. An angel escorted Peter out of prison (Acts 12:5–9). They can walk you out of your bondage. "He [God] has put his angels in charge of you to watch over you wherever you go" (Psalm 91:11 NCV). Heaven has helpers to help you.

Anxious for Nothing

Words of Power

*When Jesus arrived, he learned that Lazarus had
already been dead and in the tomb for four days.*

JOHN 11:17 EXB

N ot only did Jesus not make it to the deathbed of Lazarus, but he
also didn't make it to the burial. Not only did he miss the burial,
but he was also four days late.

Martha was forthright. "Lord, if only you had been here, my brother
would not have died" (v. 21 NLT). Then she gathered herself. "But even
now I know that God will give you whatever you ask" (v. 22 NLT).

Martha was distraught, brokenhearted. And here is what Jesus
did: he looked Martha in the face and said these starchy words: "I am
the resurrection and the life. . . . Do you believe this?" (vv. 25–26 NLT).

Then Jesus did the unthinkable. He went to the tomb, wept for
his friend, and then shouted for the dead Lazarus to come out. And
Lazarus did! But don't think for a second that Lazarus was the only
miracle that day. Jesus resurrected the brother from the dead, but he
also resurrected Martha's heart from despair.

And he did both with words of power.

Speak words of power—God's words of truth—into the lives of
those around you.

How Happiness Happens

An Heir of God's Estate

In this world we are like Jesus.

1 JOHN 4:17

Suppose you are relaxing at home one evening when the doorbell rings. A well-dressed man introduces himself and says, "Might I come in and visit with you about a potential inheritance?"

Typically you wouldn't allow a stranger into your home. But did he say "inheritance"?

He produces a document from his briefcase and begins.

"We've been looking for you. Your mother inherited a large sum from her uncle. Now that inheritance is yours."

"It is?" *I can buy those new shoes at Dillard's.*

"Yes, it is quite sizable."

Maybe I should go to Nordstrom.

"You have inherited a gold mine in South Africa. It will take several years to work out all the inheritance, but in the meantime here is a down payment. Twenty million dollars."

Maybe I will buy Saks Fifth Avenue.

If this is the down payment, what is the entire inheritance going to be worth?

That, my friend, is the question. You are an heir with Christ of God's estate. He will provide what you need to face the challenges of life.

Unshakable Hope

Where's Your Focus?

Let us not become weary in doing good.

GALATIANS 6:9

Three angels once took note of a saintly man. He did so much good for so many people that the angels went to God with this request: "That man deserves a special gift. He is so unselfish. He always helps others. Let's reward him."

"Why don't you ask him what he would like?" God suggested.

The angels agreed and approached the man.

"We would like to give you a gift."

The man looked at the angels and asked, "Any gift?"

"Yes."

"Then I want to do good and not know that I did it."

From that day forward wherever the man's shadow passed, good things happened. Plants flourished. People laughed. The sick were healed. Merchants succeeded. And the man, unburdened by the knowledge of his success, smiled.

Miserable is the Christian whose focus is on self.

Blessed is the Christian whose focus is on others.

How Happiness Happens

What No One Imagined

"I am the LORD, the God of all mankind.
Is anything too hard for me?"

JEREMIAH 32:27

Once while Jesus was preaching, he realized that the multitude had nothing to eat.

"Where can we buy enough bread to feed *all these people*?" (Jesus was asking this to test Philip, because Jesus knew what he himself was going to do.) Philip responded, "Several thousand dollars' worth of bread wouldn't be enough to give even a tiny bite to *all these people!*" Then one of Jesus' other disciples, Andrew, the brother of Simon Peter, said to Jesus, "There is a boy here with five loaves of barley bread and two fish. Oh, but what are these things when there are *all these people*?" (John 6:5–9, emphasis mine)[5]

What is your version of "all these people"? Is it "all these diapers" or "all this homework," "all this dialysis," or "all these bills"? Whatever it is, you are left feeling hopeless.

Even so, notice that Jesus went right to work. The impossible challenge of feeding "all these people" became the unforgettable miracle of all these people fed. What we cannot do, Christ does!

You Are Never Alone

God Fights for You

"Do not be afraid nor dismayed because of this great multitude, for the battle is not yours, but God's."

2 CHRONICLES 20:15 NKJV

God has never promised a life with no storms. But he has promised to be there when we face them. Consider the compelling testimony of Jehoshaphat.

The Moabites formed a great and powerful confederacy with the surrounding nations and marched against Jehoshaphat (2 Chronicles 20). Jehoshaphat's response deserves a spot in the anxiety-treatment textbook. He "set himself to seek the LORD" (2 Chronicles 20:3 NKJV). He fasted (v. 3), prayed (vv. 6–12), and confessed his fears (v. 12).

God responded with this message: "The battle is not yours, but God's."

Jehoshaphat so totally believed in God that he made the remarkable decision of marching into battle with singers in front. Jehoshaphat knew the real battle was a spiritual one, so he led with worship and worshippers. By the time they reached the battlefield, the battle was over. The Hebrews never had to raise a sword (vv. 21–24).

Learn a lesson from the king. Lead with worship. And expect to see the God of ages fight for you.

Anxious for Nothing

God Isn't Finished

The LORD will work out his plans for my life—for
your faithful love, O LORD, endures forever.

PSALM 138:8 NLT

K eep in mind, we are all works in progress. You wouldn't pass judgment on the wine of a vineyard after eating only one grape or pass an opinion on the work of an artist after one brushstroke. You give the vineyard time to mature and the artist an opportunity to complete the painting.

Give God the same. He isn't finished, and some of his works— well, some of us—need extra attention. Take a cue from the apostle Paul, who told some friends: "There has never been the slightest doubt in my mind that the God who started this great work in you would keep at it and bring it to a flourishing finish on the very day Christ Jesus appears" (Philippians 1:6 MSG).

God isn't finished yet. Let the grapes mature. Give the artist some time. Applaud the progress you see. Be the cheerleader who brings out the best, not the critic who points out the rest. You'll enjoy your relationships, and so will they.

How Happiness Happens

Jesus Incarnate

He was taken up before their very eyes, and
a cloud hid him from their sight.

ACTS 1:9

In one of his broadcasts, C. S. Lewis stated, "God will invade. . . . When that happens, it's the end of the world. When the author walks on to the stage the play's over. . . . For this time it will be God without disguise. . . . It will be too late then to *choose* your side. . . . It will be the time when we discover which side we really have chosen."[6]

By the way, Jesus has not surrendered his earthly body. When Jesus ascended, he did so in a human body. Having become a man, he will never cease to be a man. God-in-the-flesh remains exactly that!

Why does this matter? There is a human being in charge of the universe. Glorified, for sure. Exalted, by all means. Utterly divine, certainly. But still, the hand that directs the affairs of humanity is the same hand that held a hammer in Nazareth. In the center of that hand is a scar, an eternal reminder of God's eternal love.

Bow before him. Humble yourself before the one who humbled himself for you.

Because of Bethlehem

When Life Gives Lemons

*God, who has called you into fellowship with
his Son, Jesus Christ our Lord, is faithful.*

1 CORINTHIANS 1:9 NCV

O ne of the toughest days of my life found me in a diner in Dalton, Georgia. I was nineteen years old, a thousand miles from home, and sleeping at the Salvation Army shelter.

On the promise of fast cash, I'd signed on to sell books door-to-door. I quickly made this discovery: no one likes a door-to-door salesman. My first day was miserable: "Hello, I'm Max . . ." Slam. "Hello, I'm Max . . ." Slam. "Hello, I'm Max . . ." Slam.

Day two wasn't any better. As I was paying my lunch bill at a diner, I spotted a display of magnets by the cash register. One was yellow, shaped like a lemon, and contained these words: "When life gives you a lemon, make lemonade."

The slogan was just enough to convince me to keep at the job. I bought the magnet and, whenever I got discouraged, I would rub my thumb over the rubber lemon and remind myself, *I can make myself miserable, or I can make myself some lemonade.*

Life comes with lemons. But we don't have to suck on them.

Anxious for Nothing

Don't Allow Hurt to Harden You

Don't repay evil for evil. Don't retaliate with insults when people insult you. Instead, pay them back with a blessing.

1 PETER 3:9 NLT

A friend's nephew recently purchased a brand-new home. He was thrilled. New marriage, new job, new life. Things were looking up until the builder found a leak. A plumber jackhammered a large hole in one of their bathrooms to reach and repair the leaking pipe. The foundation repair company proceeded to tunnel under the house and backfill the hole with a concrete substance. They filled and filled. One truckload was not enough, so they emptied a second into the hole.

When the homeowner returned from work, he couldn't get the door open. Turns out the jackhammered area of the bathroom had never been closed. The concrete had been emptied not just into the foundation but also into the residence. The furniture cemented to the floor, and the toilet looked as if it were made for someone with no legs.

Their house hardened while they weren't watching.

The same can happen to hearts. The question is not, Did you get hurt? The question is, Are you going to let the hurt harden you?

Choose forgiveness instead.

How Happiness Happens

153

A Lesson on Integrity

Not one of all the LORD's good promises to
Israel failed; every one was fulfilled.

JOSHUA 21:45

When I was twelve, I tagged along with my father as he went to buy new tires for the family car. Dad was a reliable oil field mechanic who loved his family, paid his bills, and kept his word.

He selected the tires, and we waited as they were being mounted. When it came time to pay the bill, the salesclerk requested identification. Such a practice is common today, but in the 1960s a merchant seldom asked for verification.

Dad was taken aback. "You don't believe I am who that check says I am?"

The clerk was embarrassed. "We require this of all customers."

"If you don't think I am good for my word, you can remove those tires."

We went home with the tires. And I went home with a lesson on integrity. Good people are serious about keeping their word. How much more serious would a good God be? What was said about God's faithfulness to Israel can be said about his faithfulness to us.

The question is not whether God will keep his promises but whether we will build our lives upon them.

Unshakable Hope

Cling to Christ

"I am the vine, you are the branches; the one who remains in Me, and I in him bears much fruit, for apart from Me you can do nothing."

JOHN 15:5 NASB

Jesus' allegory is simple. God is like a vine keeper. He lives and loves to coax the best out of his vines. He pampers, prunes, blesses, and cuts.

And Jesus plays the role of the vine. We nongardeners might confuse the vine and the branch. To see the vine, lower your gaze from the stringy, winding branches to the thick base below. The vine is the root and trunk of the plant. It cables nutrients from the soil to the branches. If anything good comes into our lives, he is the conduit.

And who are we? We are the branches. We bear fruit: "love, joy, peace, patience, kindness, goodness, faithfulness" (Galatians 5:22 NASB). Our gentleness is evident to all. We bask in the "peace of God" (Philippians 4:7 NASB).

And as we cling to Christ, God is honored. "My Father is glorified by this, that you bear much fruit, and so prove to be My disciples" (John 15:8 NASB).

Make it your aim to cling to Christ. Abide in him.

Anxious for Nothing

A Part of the Family

*Abraham believed God, and it was
accounted to him for righteousness.*

ROMANS 4:3 NKJV

The apostle Paul loved to talk about Abraham. In his fourteen letters he made nineteen references to the patriarch. Abraham was Paul's poster child for salvation by faith.

Abraham, remember, predated the law of Moses. Abraham was saved by God before God gave the law. So when was Abraham's faith credited to him as righteousness? It was before Abraham had done any work. This has huge ramifications. If Abraham was saved apart from lineage and law, then what does this say about Gentiles and lawbreakers like me? I am not of the bloodline of Abraham nor have I kept the law to perfection. Does God have a place for people like me? Yes!

Those who trust in Christ are included in the blessing of Abraham. We are seen as a part of the family. Gone is the fear of falling short! Gone is the anxious quest for right behavior. Gone are the nagging questions: *Have I done enough? Am I good enough?*

God's promise to Abraham was salvation by faith. God's promise to you and me is salvation by faith. Just faith. Stand on this promise.

Praying the Promises

No Arguments

"All authority in heaven and on earth has been given to me."

MATTHEW 28:18

S ome years ago I played basketball with David Robinson. Yes, the NBA All-Star, three-time Olympian, and Dream Team member. We were at a Bible retreat, and David had agreed to a game with a bunch of us fellows who hadn't dribbled a ball since middle school.

When the game began, he held back. We could tell. Even so, he played basketball at a level we could only dream about. Then, at one point—just for the fun of it, I suppose—he let loose. The same guy who had slam-dunked basketballs over Michael Jordan and Charles Barkley let it go. With three strides he roared from half court to the rim.

We gulped. David smiled.

We got the message. That's how the game is meant to be played. We may have shared the same court, but we didn't share the same power.

I'm thinking the followers of Jesus might have had a similar thought when Jesus commanded the demons to leave the possessed man, told the storm to be quiet, or instructed the dead man to rise.

No wonder no one argued when he declared, "All authority in heaven and on earth has been given to me."

Unshakable Hope

Look at God!

Not to us, LORD, not to us but to your name be the
glory, because of your love and faithfulness.

PSALM 115:1

You and I were made by God to know him and make him known. Children have a tendency to say, "Look at me!" On the tricycle: "Look at me go!" On the trampoline: "Look at me bounce!" On the swing set: "Look at me swing!" Such behavior is acceptable for children. Yet many adults spend their grown-up years saying the same. "Look at me drive this fancy car!" "Look at me make money!" "Look at me wear provocative clothes, use big words, or flex my muscles. Look at me!"

Isn't it time we grew up? We were made to live a life that says, "Look at God!" People are to look at us and see not us but the image of our Maker.

This is God's plan—to make us into his image. This is God's promise. And he will fulfill it!

Unshakable Hope

June

Be a Helper

The time has come for the wedding feast of the
Lamb, and his bride has prepared herself.

REVELATION 19:7 NLT

As I was writing a sermon about the bride of Christ, I thought, *What better way to conclude the message than to invite a bride to enter?* Unbeknownst to the audience we recruited a volunteer and dressed her in a wedding gown and veil, a veil that covered her face. At the appropriate time I signaled for the bride to begin her walk.

She did . . . straight into the back pew. Turns out the veil blocked her vision. She pinballed her way a few steps down the aisle before several people mercifully stepped out to guide her to the altar.

I intended to illustrate the beauty of the bride. In the end, however, we were given an illustration of how each of us, at one time or another, needs someone to keep us on track.

We ended up with the bride standing at the altar and a half-dozen chuckling helpers at her side. An image of what awaits us all, perhaps? When we stand before Christ, we will appreciate the influence of those who helped us.

You can do this. Do not shrink back. Be someone who helps others find their way.

How Happiness Happens

Are You Ready to Fly?

I know the Lord will continue to rescue me from every trip, trap, snare, and pitfall of evil.

2 TIMOTHY 4:18 THE VOICE

In one of Henri Nouwen's books, he tells about the lesson of trust he learned from a family of trapeze artists known as the Flying Rodleighs. One of them said:

> The secret is that the flyer does nothing and the catcher does everything. When I fly to Joe [my catcher], I have simply to stretch out my arms and hands and wait for him to catch me. . . . The worst thing the flyer can do is to try to catch the catcher. . . . If I grabbed Joe's wrists, I might break them, or he might break mine, and that would be the end for both of us. . . . The flyer must trust . . . that his catcher will be there for him.[1]

In the great trapeze act of salvation, God is the catcher, and we are the flyers. We rely solely upon God's ability to catch us. As we do, a wonderful thing happens: we fly.

Anxious for Nothing

A Good Anchor

We have this hope as an anchor for the soul, firm and secure.

HEBREWS 6:19

An anchor has one purpose—to steady the boat. To weather a blast of bad weather, you need a good anchor. You need one that can hook securely to an object that is stronger than the storm.

Why? Because you have a valuable vessel. You have a soul.

Your soul separates you from animals and unites you to God. And your soul needs an anchor. Your soul is fragile. It feels the pain of death and knows the questions of disease. Hence, your soul needs an anchor, a hooking point that is sturdier than the storm.

This anchor is not set on a boat or person or possession. No, this anchor is set in "the inner sanctuary behind the curtain, where our forerunner, Jesus, has entered on our behalf" (vv. 19–20). Our anchor, in other words, is set in the very throne room of God. Beyond the reach of the devil and under the care of Christ. Since no one can take your Christ, no one can take your hope.

Unshakable Hope

All Your Needs

"Ask, and it will be given to you."

MATTHEW 7:7 NKJV

In one of my many less-than-sane seasons of life, I competed in Half Ironman Triathlons. The event consists of a 1.2-mile swim, a 56-mile bike ride, and a 13.1-mile run.

During one of these races, I prayed the oddest prayer of my life. Four of us traveled to Florida for the race. Out of at least two hundred people, these were the three I knew.

I finished the swim, nearly dead and almost last, and began the three-hour bike trek. About a third of the way in, I reached into my shirt pocket to grab some GU. GU is a packet of easily eaten essential nutrients. Well, guess who forgot his GU? I was GU-less with a good thirty miles to go.

So I prayed, *Lord, this very well might be the only time in eternity you've heard this request . . .*

Did GU fall from heaven? Well, sort of. One of the three people I knew out of the entire field just "happened" to pedal up. When he heard of my GU-lessness, he gave me three packs.

What's my point? You can take your needs—*all your needs*—to Jesus.

You Are Never Alone

Your Happiness Quota

Be patient, bearing with one another in love.

EPHESIANS 4:2

Suppose a basket of Ping-Pong balls represents your daily quota of happiness. Each aggravation, if you allow it, can snatch a ball out of your basket.

- He left his dirty clothes on the floor. A joy ball vanishes.
- She waits until the last minute to apply her makeup. Plop! There goes another one.
- Big trucks shouldn't take up two parking places! Boing!

There go the joy balls, one by one, until the joy is gone. How can you help people smile if you have a hole in your happiness basket? You can't. For this reason the apostle Paul said, "Be patient, bearing with one another in love."

The apostle's word for *patient* is a term that combines "long" and "tempered."[2] The patient person is "long tempered." The word *tempered* literally means "taking a long time to boil."[3] In other words, not quickly overheated.

Irks come with life, but they need not diminish your life.

How Happiness Happens

When People Pray

"Our Father which art in heaven . . ."

MATTHEW 6:9 KJV

I like the story of the father who was teaching his three-year-old daughter the Lord's Prayer. She would repeat the lines after him. Finally she decided to go solo. He listened with pride as she carefully enunciated each word, right up to the end of the prayer. "Lead us not into temptation," she prayed, "but deliver us from email."

These days that seems like an appropriate request. In Philippians 4:6, we are told to "be anxious for nothing, but in everything by prayer and supplication, with thanksgiving, let your requests be made known to God" (NKJV). The terms *prayer, supplication,* and *requests* are similar but not identical. *Prayer* is a general devotion; the word includes worship and adoration. *Supplication* suggests humility. We are the supplicants in the sense that we make no demands; we simply offer humble requests. A *request* is exactly that—a specific petition. We tell God exactly what we want. We pray the particulars of our problems.

With this verse the apostle calls us to take action against anxiety. We choose prayer over despair. Peace happens when people pray.

Anxious for Nothing

Simply Stay Connected

*When you believed in Christ, he identified you
as his own by giving you the Holy Spirit.*

EPHESIANS 1:13 NLT

The Holy Spirit enters the believer upon confession of faith (Ephesians 1:13). From that point forward the Christian has access to the very power and personality of God. As the Spirit has his way in the lives of believers, a transformation occurs. They begin to think the way God thinks, love the way God loves, and see the way God sees. They minister in power and pray in power and walk in power.

This power includes the gifts of the Spirit: "love, joy, peace, forbearance, kindness, goodness, faithfulness, gentleness and self-control" (Galatians 5:22–23). These attributes appear in the life of the saint in the same way an apple appears on the branch of an apple tree. Fruit happens as a result of relationship. Sever the branch from the tree, and forget the fruit. Yet if the branch is secured to the trunk, nutrients flow, and fruit results.

So it is with the fruit of the Holy Spirit. As our relationship with God is secured and unmarred by rebellion, sin, or stubborn behavior, we can expect a harvest of fruit. It simply falls to us to stay connected.

Unshakable Hope

Mr. Happy Man

Dear friends, let us love one another, for love comes from God.

1 JOHN 4:7

It's 6:00 a.m. in Hamilton, Bermuda. Ninety-two-year-old Johnny Barnes stands on the edge of a roundabout and waves at people as they drive past. He's been here since before 4:00 a.m. He'll be here until 10:00 a.m. He's not asking for money. He's making people happy. He pulls back his right hand to retrieve a kiss and blow it in the direction of a taxi driver or commuter.

"I love you!" he shouts. "Hello, there, darlin'. I love you!"

And they love him! Bermudans call him Mr. Happy Man. They route their morning commute to see him. If he happens to miss acknowledging some commuters, they often circle the roundabout until he waves at them.

Johnny's philosophy is simple. "We human beings gotta learn how to love one another. One of the greatest joys that can come to an individual is when you're doing something and helping others."[4]

Wouldn't you love to meet a person like him? Better still, wouldn't you like to be like him?

How Happiness Happens

From Tragedy to Triumph

*The L*ord *is in his holy temple. The*
*L*ord *is on his throne in heaven.*

PSALM 11:4 NIRV

Remember Jacob's son Joseph in Egypt? Look at him in the prison. His brothers sold him out; Potiphar's wife turned him in. If ever a world caved in, Joseph's did.

Or consider Moses, watching flocks in the wilderness. His passion was to lead the slaves, not sheep.

Who could have seen any good in these dark moments? Who could have known that Joseph the prisoner was just one promotion from becoming Joseph the prime minister? Or that God was giving Moses forty years of wilderness training in the very desert through which he would lead the people?

God has made a business out of turning tragedy into triumph.

Is your day a difficult one? Then take heart. God is still on his throne. And he still makes princes out of prisoners, counselors out of captives, and Sundays out of Fridays.

He did then, for them. He does it still, for you and me.

Because of Bethlehem

Heir to Eternity

And now that you belong to Christ, you are the
true children of Abraham. You are his heirs.

GALATIANS 3:29 NLT

Lord, you are rich in mercy, love, wisdom, and grace. You never run out of these good gifts for your children, and you gave us the greatest gift of all: your Son, Jesus Christ. Through him, we get to spend eternity with you—a blessing we do not deserve and one we could have never earned.

In spite of your good and gracious gifts, my heart still longs for earthly riches. I seek wealth, success, and security, forgetting that you have already given me everything I need.

But God, you have welcomed me into your family. In Christ, I am no longer a slave to the things of this earth that will one day pass away. I am an heir of the gifts of eternity because I am yours. In you, I have an abundance of grace, wisdom, and love— the riches you provide that fulfill every empty place in my life.

Thank you for adopting me as your child. You have given me an inheritance, and I will live freely under the promise of your covering and grace. Amen.

Praying the Promises

Summon the Best

[Jesus] said to them, "But who do you say that I am?"
Simon Peter answered and said, "You are
the Christ, the Son of the living God."

MATTHEW 16:15–16 NKJV

When Jesus asked his followers, "Who do you say that I am?" I hear silence from the disciples. A throat being cleared. I see eyes lower and heads duck.

Finally Peter spoke up. He looked at the penniless rabbi from Galilee and said, "You are the Christ, the Son of the living God."

Jesus all but jumped for joy at the confession. "Blessed are you, Simon Bar-Jonah" (v. 17 NKJV). In modern-day parlance, "Way to go! You're the man! You nailed it!" He even changed the apostle's name. Simon would now be called Peter, a name that is next of kin to *petros* or Rocky. Simon, the man who expressed rock-solid faith, needed a rock-solid name. So Jesus gave it to him.

How do you suppose this made Peter feel? When his friends began calling him Rocky, when Jesus put an arm around his shoulders and said, "Love you, Rocky," do you suppose he felt encouraged? Of course he did. Jesus did to Peter what encouragers do. He summoned the best. He built Peter up.

Summon the best in those around you.

How Happiness Happens

God Still Gives Peace

The Lord disciplines the one he loves.

HEBREWS 12:6

We don't like to be rebuked, corrected, or chastened. But when we ignore God's warnings, a scolding is in order.

Did you? Are you in a storm of anxiety because you didn't listen to God? He told you that sex outside of marriage would result in chaos, but you didn't listen. He told you that the borrower is a slave to the lender, but you took on the dangerous debt. He told you to cherish your spouse and nourish your kids, but you cherished your career and nourished your vices. He cautioned you about the wrong crowd and the strong drink and the long hours. But you did not listen. And now you are in a storm of your own making.

If this describes you, receive God's rebuke. He corrects those he loves, and he loves you. So stand corrected. Confess your sin and resolve to do better. Be wiser next time. Learn from your poor choice. But don't despair. God still gives peace in the middle of a storm.

Anxious for Nothing

By His Wounds

*He personally carried our sins in his body on the
cross so that we can be dead to sin and live for
what is right. By his wounds you are healed.*

1 PETER 2:24 NLT

The God of Abraham is not a God of burdens but a God of rest. He knows we are made of flesh. He knows we cannot achieve perfection. The God of the Bible is the one who says, "Come to me, all you who are weary and burdened, and I will give you rest. Take my yoke upon you and learn from me, for I am gentle and humble in heart, and you will find rest for your souls. For my yoke is easy and my burden is light" (Matthew 11:28–30).

When you lose your temper with your child, Christ intervenes. "I paid for that." When you tell a lie and all of heaven groans, your Savior speaks up: "My death covered that sin." As you lust over someone's centerfold, gloat over someone's pain, covet someone's success, or cuss someone's mistake, Jesus stands before the tribunal of heaven and points to the blood-streaked cross. "I've already made provision. I've paid that debt. I've taken away the sins of the world."

Unshakable Hope

Trust, Wait, and Pray

You intended to harm me, but God intended it for good to accomplish what is now being done, the saving of many lives.

GENESIS 50:20

Joseph's story is one of abandonment. His brothers disliked his dreams and swagger and decided to throw him in a pit. Potiphar's wife accused Joseph of rape, and her husband took her side, tossing Joseph in prison for a crime he didn't commit.

Yet it was through suffering that Joseph came to be God's tool of rescue to the Hebrew people. Joseph would later tell his brothers, "You intended to harm me, but God intended it for good." Can he not do the same for you? Maybe you weren't thrown in jail, but you were placed in a hospital or in bankruptcy court, or, then again, maybe you were thrown in jail. And you're wondering, "Does God care?"

Scripture says yes. God uses everything to accomplish his will (Colossians 1:17).

Only in heaven will we be able to see God's purposes. Between now and our homecoming, we can only do what Joseph did. Trust. Wait. Pray. And believe.

Praying the Promises

Plunge into the Promises

*Trust in him at all times, you people; pour out
your hearts to him, for God is our refuge.*

PSALM 62:8

Secularism sucks the hope out of society. It reduces the world to a few decades between birth and hearse. Many people believe this world is as good as it gets, and let's face it. It's not that good.

But People of the Promise have an advantage. They determine to ponder, proclaim, and pray the promises of God. They are like Abraham who "didn't tiptoe around God's promise asking cautiously skeptical questions. He plunged into the promise and came up strong" (Romans 4:20 MSG).

They filter life through the promises of God. When problems surface, they can be heard telling themselves, "But God said . . ." When struggles threaten, they can be seen flipping through Scripture, saying, "I think God said something about this." When comforting others, they're prone to ask, "Do you know God's promise on this topic?"

Plunge into God's promises and you'll find unshakable hope in this shaky world.

Unshakable Hope

Listening or Reloading?

*All of you should be of one mind. Sympathize with
each other. Love each other as brothers and sisters.
Be tenderhearted, and keep a humble attitude.*

1 PETER 3:8 NLT

Raleigh Washington is an African American minister who has dedicated much of his life to racial reconciliation. He says that the most important statement in bridge building is this: "Help me understand what it's like to be you."[5] "Help me understand what it's like to be a teenager in this day and age." "Help me understand what it's like to be born into affluence." "Help me understand the challenges you face as an immigrant." "Help me understand what it's like to be a female in a gray flannel corporation."

Then sit back and listen. Really listen. Listening is a healing balm for raw emotions. (A friend admitted to me, "I often appear to be listening when actually I am reloading.")

James said it this way: "Everyone should be quick to listen, slow to speak and slow to become angry" (James 1:19).

Less reloading. More listening. That might be just what the world needs.

How Happiness Happens

Logically Speaking

*Fix your thoughts on what is true, and honorable,
and right, and pure, and lovely, and admirable. Think
about things that are excellent and worthy of praise.*

PHILIPPIANS 4:8 NLT

The transliteration of the Greek word, here rendered as *fix*, is *logizomai*. Do you see the root of an English word in the Greek one? Yes, *logic*. Paul's point is simple: anxiety is best faced with clear-headed, logical thinking. Turns out that our most valuable weapon against anxiety weighs less than three pounds and sits between our ears. Think about what you think about!

Here is how it works. You receive a call from the doctor's office. "The doctor has reviewed your tests and would like you to come into the office for a consultation."

As quickly as you can say "Uh-oh," you have a choice: anxiety or trust.

Anxiety says, "I'm in trouble. I probably have cancer. Who will raise the kids? I'm too young for this tragedy!"

There is a better way. Call on God. "Capture every thought and make it give up and obey Christ" (2 Corinthians 10:5 NCV). Slap handcuffs on the culprit and march it before the one who has all authority.

Simply refuse to let anxious thoughts have the time of day.

Anxious for Nothing

The Big News of the Bible

I will lead the blind by ways they have not known . . . I will turn the darkness into light before them.

ISAIAH 42:16

Denalyn and I moved to Brazil in 1983. We were called to plant a church, but we were naive. Brazilians were kind but less than interested in the ministry of green gringos.

Weeks. Months. One year. Two years. Slow growth in our church.

A colleague felt convicted that we weren't preaching the gospel. He urged us to meet with open Bibles and open hearts and identify the core of the good news. So we did. We read and reread Scripture. The big news of the Bible? That Jesus died for my sins and rose from the grave. Nothing more. Nothing less.

We began to focus on the gospel message, and our little church began to grow. But it all began with long bouts of fear, frustration, and failure.

Can you relate? If so, do not assume that Jesus is absent or oblivious to your struggle. Just the opposite. He is using it to reveal himself to you. He wants you to see him!

You Are Never Alone

Your Persistent Prayers

Pray for all people. Ask God to help them; intercede on their behalf, and give thanks for them.

1 TIMOTHY 2:1 NLT

Nothing activates happiness like intercessory ministry. Try it. Next time you walk through a crowded airport, lift up your heart to heaven and pray something like this: *Lord, bless that man in the gray suit. He appears to be frazzled. And give strength to the mom and the infant. Look with mercy upon those military personnel.* Before you know it, a humdrum hike becomes a significant stroll of faith.

Your Father will hear you. After all, you are his child (1 John 3:1), you are his ambassador (2 Corinthians 5:20), and you are a member of his priesthood (1 Peter 2:9).

You actually have a "seat with [Christ] in the heavens" (Ephesians 2:6 NCV). You speak on behalf of your family, neighborhood, or softball team. Be the Abraham in your cul-de-sac, the centurion in your workforce. Plead with God on their behalf.

God will not turn you away! Your persistent prayers will open God's door.

How Happiness Happens

So Many Reasons to Smile

Know that the LORD is God. It is he
who made us, and we are his.

PSALM 100:3

Just yesterday I found myself sharing a golf cart with a fellow I'd never met. We ended up on the same California course hoping to cash in on a blue sky and make a par or two. As he shared his story, I realized he had every reason to be miserable. He had battled migraines for twenty years, had lost a wife through divorce, was currently between jobs, and had moved at least once a year for the last decade.

Yet to hear him talk, you'd think he just danced Dorothy down the yellow brick road. His happiness was contagious. I had to ask him, "For a fellow with so many bad breaks in life, how is it that you smile all the time?"

He looked at me with sparkling eyes. "I get to meet people! Each human is a story. How can you not love a world when it is so full of stories!"

Let's invite the Father to kindle an equal fascination in our hearts. Think about it. If every person is a reason for joy, we have seven billion reasons to smile.

How Happiness Happens

Because He Is Jesus

*God made him who had no sin to be sin for us, so that
in him we might become the righteousness of God.*

2 CORINTHIANS 5:21

S ome have pointed to the sinlessness of Jesus as evidence that he cannot fully understand us. If he never sinned, they reason, how could he understand the full force of sin? Simple. He felt it more than we do. We give in! He never did. We surrender. He never did. He stood before the tsunami of temptation and never wavered. In that manner he understands it more than anyone who ever lived.

And then, in his grandest deed, he volunteered to feel the consequences of sin. Jesus didn't deserve to feel the shame, but he felt it. He didn't deserve the humiliation, but he experienced it. He had never sinned, yet he was treated like a sinner. He became sin. All the guilt, remorse, and embarrassment—Jesus understands it.

Does this promise matter? To the hypocrite, it does. To the person with the hangover, it does. To the cheater, slanderer, gossip, or scoundrel who comes to God with a humble spirit, it matters.

Because Jesus is human, he understands you.

Because he is divine, he can help you.

Unshakable Hope

Just Jesus

*At the name of Jesus every knee should bow, in
heaven and on earth and under the earth.*

PHILIPPIANS 2:10

Every knee will bow before Jesus. The poor. The rich. The red-carpet superstar. The street-corner panhandler.

There are people on our planet who mock the name of Jesus. They scoff at the idea of God on earth. They renounce their need for a Savior and cast aspersions on any who believe in Christ. They are self-sufficient, independent, self-made, and self-reliant. Ask them to bend a knee before Jesus, and they will laugh at you. But they will not laugh forever. A day is coming in which they will bow in his presence. Stalin will confess his name. Herod will confess his name. Even, or especially, Satan will confess his name. "All who have raged against him will come to him and be put to shame" (Isaiah 45:24).

One ruler after another will step forward. Crowns will be collected at the foot of Jesus' throne. So will Pulitzers, Nobels, and gold medals. MVP? PhD? MD? All recognitions will become instantly puny in the presence of Christ the Creator. No one will boast. Nothing will matter. No one will matter.

Just Jesus.

Because of Bethlehem

The Ultimatum

"Do to others as you would have them do to you."

LUKE 6:31

The boss had all he could take. *No more!* he resolved, and he left his staff a letter explaining why:

> I am taking a leave of absence for a month. . . . There has been a history around here of people not respecting each other and as of this moment, it's over. . . . Going forward, people are either going to treat each other with respect, dignity, and courtesy or else I will retire. . . .
> When I return . . . if nothing has changed, I will move on.

The frustrated boss even left his organization specific assignments to fulfill during his thirty-day hiatus. Among them, "Simply say 'Good morning.' It's not that hard."

When he returned, the atmosphere was different. Employees were learning the meaning of the word *considerate*. His ultimatum had its desired effect.[6]

Perhaps we need an ultimatum on society.

How Happiness Happens

Beam or Speck

*"Why do you notice the little piece of dust in your friend's eye,
but you don't notice the big piece of wood in your own eye?"*

MATTHEW 7:3 NCV

The next time you find it difficult to live with others, imagine what it is like to live with you. Or, to use the lingo of Jesus, don't obsess about the speck of dust in another person's eye while ignoring the beam in your own eye. We have eagle-eye vision when it comes to others but can be as blind as moles when we examine ourselves.

We tend to be like the fellow on the interstate. As he was driving, he received a call from his wife. She was panicked. "Honey, be careful. I just heard on the radio that some fellow is traveling down the highway on the wrong side of the road!"

The husband's reply was equally urgent. "That's not the half of it, sweetheart. It's not just one car going the wrong way. It's hundreds!"

You think the world needs more tolerance? Then be tolerant. You wish people would quit complaining? When you quit, the world is minus one whiner. If you want to change the world, begin with yourself.

How Happiness Happens

Wash Feet

"If I then, your Lord and Teacher, have washed your feet, you also ought to wash one another's feet."

JOHN 13:14 NKJV

The apostle Paul urged us to follow Jesus' lead. To give grace, not because our offenders deserve it but because we've been doused with it. "Forgiving one another, even as God in Christ forgave you" (Ephesians 4:32 NKJV).

Wearing the towel and holding the basin, Jesus said to his church, "This is how we do it."

Let others bicker and fight; we don't. Let others seek revenge; we don't. Let others keep a list of offenders; we don't. We take the towel. We fill the basin. We wash one another's feet.

Jesus could do this because he knew who he was—sent from and destined for heaven.

Do you know who you are? You are the creation of a good God, made in his image. You are destined to reign in an eternal kingdom. You are only heartbeats away from heaven.

Secure in who you are, you can do what Jesus did. Throw aside the robe of rights and expectation and make the most courageous of moves. Wash feet.

How Happiness Happens

Nothing Is Too Hard for God

Ah, Sovereign Lord, *you have made the heavens*
and the earth by your great power and outstretched
arm. Nothing is too hard for you.

JEREMIAH 32:17

The next time you feel overwhelmed, remind yourself of the one who is standing next to you. You aren't alone. You aren't without help. What bewilders you does not bewilder him. Your uphill is downhill for him. He is not stumped by your problem. When you present your needs to him, he never, ever turns to the angels and says, "Well, it finally happened. I've been handed a code I cannot crack. The demand is too great, even for me."

You may feel outnumbered, but he does not. Give him what you have, offer thanks, and watch him go to work. Your list of blessings will be so long, you'll need to buy a new hard drive for your computer so you can store it.

You Are Never Alone

Nearer Than You Think

You will call, and the LORD will answer; you will cry for help, and he will say: Here am I.

ISAIAH 58:9

I had granddaddy duty the other night with my two-and-a-half-year-old sweetheart, Rosie. Oh, the time we had. She dressed up in a wedding gown. We danced to Disney music. And to top it off, we walked to the gate in the dark.

For Rosie that ten-minute journey was a Lewis and Clark–level adventure. As we began the trek, she held up her hand and said, "Stay there, Papa Max. I go by myself."

I lingered back just far enough to let her think she was on her own. After a few steps she stopped. But I was close enough to hear her say, "Papa Max!"

I was at her side in two seconds. She looked up at me and smiled. "Come with me?" We walked the rest of the way hand in hand.

We preachers tend to overcomplicate God's love. Perhaps the best illustration is something like Rosie walking in the dark, crying out for help, and her Papa hurrying to oblige.

Your Father is nearer than you might think. And he's not about to let you walk this path without his help.

How Happiness Happens

An Open Invitation

*"The water I give will become a spring of water
gushing up inside that person, giving eternal life."*

JOHN 4:14 NCV

The Samaritan woman stopped and looked at him. The man was obviously Jewish. What was he doing here in a Samaritan city, at her well? Jews had no dealings with Samaritans at the time.

As a Samaritan, she knew the sting of racism. As a woman, she had bumped her head on the ceiling of sexism. She'd been married to five men. She knew the sound of slamming doors.

Still, he spoke to her. Jesus offered this woman not a singular drink of water but a perpetual artesian well that would quench the soul.

Some of the most incredible invitations are found in the pages of the Bible. God invited Eve to marry Adam, David to be king, Mary to birth his Son, the disciples to fish for men, and the adulterous woman to start over.

God is a God who invites. But his invitation is not just for a meal or a cup of water. It is for life. An invitation to come into his kingdom and take up residence in a tearless, graveless, painless world.

Who can come? Whoever wishes to do so.

Praying the Promises

The Peace of a Sovereign Lord

My eyes are fixed on you, Sovereign LORD; in you I take refuge.

PSALM 141:8

*S*overeignty is the term the Bible uses to describe God's perfect control and management of the universe. He preserves and governs every element. He is continually involved with all created things, directing them to act in a way that fulfills his divine purpose.

Anxiety is often the consequence of perceived chaos. If we sense we are victims of unseen, turbulent, random forces, we are troubled.

So what do we do? Control everything? Never board a plane without a parachute. Never step on a crack lest you break your mother's back. Face anxiety by taking control.

If only we could. We want certainty, but the only certainty is the lack thereof.

That's why the most stressed-out people are control freaks. Because the more they try to control the world, the more they realize they cannot. We can't take control, because control is not ours to take.

The Bible has a better idea. Rather than seeking total control, relinquish it. You can't run the world, but you can entrust it to God.

Anxious for Nothing

Already Loved

"Yes, I have loved you with an everlasting love."

JEREMIAH 31:3 NKJV

As I was about to sit down and write, my daughter Jenna stepped into my office. She is as round as a ladybug. In six weeks she will, God willing, give birth to a baby girl. Can I tell you something about that infant? I've never seen her, but I love her. She has done nothing to earn my love. But I love her. She's never brought me coffee or called me Papa. She's never sung me a song or danced me a dance. She has done nothing!

Yet I love her already. I would do anything for her, and that is not hyperbole.

Why do I love her so? Because she carries some of me. A small part for sure but a part of me nonetheless.

Why does God love you with an everlasting love? It has nothing to do with you. It has everything to do with whose you are. You are his. You carry a part of him. There is something of him in you. He made you in his image. He stamped his name on your heart. He breathed life into your lungs. And he loves you already and always.

Unshakable Hope

July

You Belong to God

*Behold what manner of love the Father has bestowed
on us, that we should be called children of God!*

1 JOHN 3:1 NKJV

When parents send their kids to summer camp, they have to sign certain documents. One of the documents asks, "Who is the responsible party?" If Johnny breaks his arm or Suzie breaks out with measles, who will be responsible? Hopefully Mom and Dad are willing to sign their names.

God signed his. When you gave your life to him, he took responsibility for you. He guarantees your safe arrival into his port. You are his sheep; he is your shepherd. Jesus said, "I am the good shepherd; I know my sheep and my sheep know me" (John 10:14).

You are a bride; he is your bridegroom. The church is being "prepared as a bride adorned for her husband" (Revelation 21:2 NKJV).

You are his child; he is your father. "You are no longer a slave but God's own child. And since you are his child, God has made you his heir" (Galatians 4:7 NLT).

You can have peace in the midst of the storm because you are not alone—because you belong to God.

Anxious for Nothing

Pet Peeves

Since God chose you to be the holy people he loves,
you must clothe yourselves with tenderhearted mercy,
kindness, humility, gentleness, and patience.

COLOSSIANS 3:12 NLT

I know a woman who has a pet peeve about facial hair. For whatever reason she does not like beards. When I grew a beard, she expressed her displeasure. More than once. On several occasions she waited in the reception line after the worship service and expressed her opinion. Each time I wondered, *Is my beard worth this frustration?*

Joy is such a precious commodity. Why squander it on a quibble?

The phrases we use regarding our pet peeves reveal the person who actually suffers. He "gets under my skin" or "gets on my nerves," or she is such a "pain in my neck." Whose skin, nerves, and neck? Ours! Who suffers? We do! Every pet peeve writes a check on our joy account.

What pets your peeve? Might I encourage you to just roll with it? Shake it off. Let it go. In other words, be patient. As we bear with one another, we preserve our joy and discover new reasons to smile.

Easy to do? No.

But essential? Absolutely. Life is too precious and brief to be spent in a huff.

How Happiness Happens

Finally Justice for All

[God] has set a day when he will judge the world.

ACTS 17:31

When you wonder if the wicked will go unpunished or injustices will go unaddressed, let this promise gratify your desire for justice. God will have the final word.

Till then follow the example of the women of a Dinka village in Sudan. Government-backed soldiers ravaged their settlement, butchering and brutalizing more than a hundred people. A remnant of survivors, wives and mothers of the murdered and missing, gathered sticks and tied them together in the form of small crosses. Before they buried the bodies and mourned their losses, they pressed the crosses into the ground. Not as memorials to their grief but as declarations of their hope. They were Jesus followers. The crossed sticks expressed their living faith in a loving God who could and will make sense of such a tragedy.[1]

Do the same with your tragedies. Place them in the shadow of the cross and be reminded: God understands injustice. He will right all wrongs and heal all wounds. He has prepared a place where life will be finally and forever . . . just.

Unshakable Hope

Seeking to Serve

Who will free me from this life that is dominated by sin and death? Thank God! The answer is in Jesus Christ our Lord.

ROMANS 7:24–25 NLT

I remember him as a large man, built like a concrete block, but I do not remember the teacher's name.

What I recall with startling detail is how he attempted to teach a handful of ten-year-old boys the meaning of Romans chapter seven, where Paul confessed the civil war that raged within his heart. When he talked about a troubled conscience and the need for forgiveness, I took note.

That night I stepped into my father's bedroom and asked him about heaven. He told me about grace. I asked Jesus to forgive me. The following Sunday I was baptized.

I've not seen that teacher since, but I've seen thousands like him. Quiet servants. The supporting cast of the kingdom of God. Those who serve because they are free. In a society that seeks to be served, we seek opportunities to serve others.

How Happiness Happens

The God of Armies

The LORD will fight for you; you need only to be still.

EXODUS 14:14

Lord, you are the God of armies, the defender of the weak. The battle truly belongs to you. You have defeated the evil one. No one can stand against you and your power and authority. You are fighting for me.

Forgive me when I try to fight my own battles. When I fear the loss of control or when I fear for my reputation, sometimes I try to take things into my own hands. If I try to fight for myself, I end up feeling exhausted and defeated by my own efforts. You have said you are fighting for me. Help me believe that truth even when I am so tempted to fight for myself.

Go before me this day as I face temptation. Go before me as I face anxiety, fear, and uncertainty. Protect me in every spiritual battle. Fight for me and help me surrender each battle to you.

God, I am so grateful that you are my Protector. Because of you, I don't have to fear the giants in my life. I know they will all fall at your feet, for you are the God of armies. Amen.

Praying the Promises

Turn the Page

"See, I am doing a new thing! Now it springs up;
do you not perceive it? I am making a way in the
wilderness and streams in the wasteland."

ISAIAH 43:19

What will God do for you? I cannot say. Those who claim they can predict the miracle are less than honest. God's help, while ever present, is ever specific. It is not ours to say what God will do. Our job is to believe he will do something. It simply falls to us to stand up, take up, and walk.

Jesus is serious about this command. When he found the just-healed man from the pool of Bethesda in the temple, he told him, "See, you have been made well. Sin no more, lest a worse thing come upon you" (John 5:14 NKJV). To indulge in inertia is to sin! Stagnant do-nothingness is deemed as a serious offense.

No more Bethesda for you. No more waking up and going to sleep in the same mess. God dismantled the neutral gear from your transmission. He is the God of forward motion, the God of tomorrow. He is ready to write a new chapter in your biography.

Turn the page.

You Are Never Alone

Expose Your Worries to Worship

*The LORD is good to those who await Him,
to the person who seeks Him.*

LAMENTATIONS 3:25 NASB

Jeremiah was the prophet to Judah during one of its darkest periods of rebellion. They called him the weeping prophet because he was one. He wept at the condition of the people and the depravity of their faith. He was anxious enough to write a book called Lamentations. But then he considered the work of God. He purposefully lifted his mind to thoughts about his King, whose "acts of mercy . . . do not end, for His compassions do not fail" (Lamentations 3:22 NASB).

Lift up your eyes. Don't get lost in your troubles. Dare to believe that good things will happen. Dare to believe that God was speaking to you when he said, "In everything God works for the good of those who love him" (Romans 8:28 NCV). The mind cannot at the same time be full of God and full of fear. Are you troubled, restless, sleepless? Then rejoice in the Lord's sovereignty. I dare you—I double-dog dare you—to expose your worries to an hour of worship. Your concerns will melt like ice on a July sidewalk.

Anxious for Nothing

A Good Big Brother

Encourage one another and build each other up.

1 THESSALONIANS 5:11

My big brother used to pick on me. For Dee no day was complete unless he had made mine miserable. But all his cruel antics were offset by one great act of grace.

Mom had given him baby-brother duty that summer day. He could go to the park if he let me tag along. He groaned but relented. He wasn't about to miss the daily baseball game. When it came time to pick teams, I took my place behind the others and braced for the worst.

But a miracle happened. When angels discuss mighty acts of divine intervention, this moment makes the list: my brother chose me. Not first, mind you. But far from last.

"Who, me?"

"Yeah, you!" my brother barked as if to downplay his largesse. I swaggered through the sad, pitiful lot of unpicked players and took my place next to my unexpected hero.

Dee didn't pick me for my skill or baseball savvy. He called my name for one reason and one reason only. He was my big brother. And on that day he decided to be a good big brother.

The New Testament has a word for such activity: encouragement.

How Happiness Happens

Need a Push?

*"I will ask the Father, and he will give you
another Helper to be with you forever."*

JOHN 14:16 NCV

Several years ago, I let my friend Pat convince me to enter a bike race. The race included a one-and-a-half-mile climb up a steep hill appropriately called the Killer Diller. It lived up to the hype.

In quick fashion the riders who belonged in the race left those of us who didn't far behind. By the time I was halfway to the top, my thighs were on fire, and I was having less-than-pleasant thoughts about my friend Patrick.

That is when I felt the push. A hand was pressing against the small of my back. It was Pat! He had already completed the race. Anticipating my utter exhaustion, he had hurried back, dismounted his bike, and scurried to give me a hand. Literally. He began pushing me up the hill!

"I told you that you would make it," he shouted. "I came to make sure you did."

The Holy Spirit promises to do the same. He will complete what was begun by the Father and the Son. The Spirit promises to give us power, unity, supervision, and holiness: P-U-S-H. Need a push?

Unshakable Hope

Say Yes to Him

God did not send his Son into the world to condemn
the world, but to save the world through him.

JOHN 3:17

*O**nly** God saves. If we could save ourselves, why would we need a
Savior? Jesus did not enter the world to help us save ourselves.
He entered the world to save us from ourselves.

As a Boy Scout, I earned a lifesaving merit badge. I never actually
saved anyone. In fact, the only people I saved were other Boy Scouts
who didn't need to be saved. During training I would rescue other
trainees. We took turns saving each other. But since we weren't really
drowning, we resisted being rescued.

"Stop kicking and let me save you," I'd say.

It's impossible to save those who are trying to save themselves.

You might save yourself from a broken heart or going broke or
running out of gas. But you aren't good enough to save yourself from
sin. You aren't strong enough to save yourself from death. You need
a Savior.

Because Jesus came, you have one.

When you say yes to him, he says yes to you.

Because of Bethlehem

Jesus Came to Bring Sight

*"I will . . . open their eyes and turn
them from darkness to light."*

ACTS 26:17–18

C hrist came to give light and sight.

Consider what Jesus is doing in the Muslim world. "More Muslims have become Christians in the last couple of decades than in the previous fourteen hundred years since Muhammad,"[2] and "about one out of every three Muslim-background believers has had a dream or vision prior to their salvation experience."[3]

For his book *The Case for Miracles*, author Lee Strobel interviewed Tom Doyle, a leading expert on contemporary dreams and visions experienced by Muslims. Doyle described a phenomenon of person after person seeing the same image: Jesus in a white robe, telling them he loves them, that he died for them, and urging them to follow him. This has been happening in Syria, Iran, and Iraq.

Jesus is in hot pursuit of the spiritually blind. He may use a vision, or the kindness of a friend, or the message of a sermon. But believe this: he came to bring sight to the blind.

You Are Never Alone

Let Christ Take It

Behold! The Lamb of God who takes away the sin of the world!

JOHN 1:29 NKJV

Denalyn and I enjoyed a nice dinner at a local restaurant the other night. About the same time we received our bill, we received a visit from a church member. He spotted us and came over to say hello. After we chatted for a moment, he reached down and took our bill and said, "I'll take this."

When he took it, guess what I did? I just let him do what he wanted to do: I let him take it away.

Someday we will all stand before God. All of us will be present. All of us will have to give an account for our lives. Every thought, every deed, every action. Were it not for the grace of Christ, I would find this to be a terrifying thought.

Yet, according to Scripture, Jesus came to "take away the sins of the world" (John 1:29 PHILLIPS). On the day when I appear before the judgment seat of God, I will point to Christ. When my list of sins is produced, I will gesture toward him and say, "He took it."

Let him take yours.

Anxious for Nothing

Shifting the Burden

Give all your worries and cares to God, for he cares about you.

1 PETER 5:7 NLT

We have the opportunity to offer heartfelt prayers for every person we see. We can pray for the attendant at the grocery store, the nurse in the doctor's office, the maintenance staff in the office building. You don't have to tell them of your intercessory prayer. Then again, I'm surprised at the welcome response from people when I say, "I'd like to pray for you. Do you have any particular needs?"

Not surprisingly, when we seek to bless others through prayer, we are blessed. The act of praying for others has a boomerang effect. It allows us to shift the burden we carry for others to the shoulders of God. He invites us to cast all our cares upon him (1 Peter 5:7 KJV). Impossible burdens are made bearable because we pray about them. Don't fret about politicians. Pray for them. Don't grow angry at the condition of the church. Pray for her. Don't let the difficulties of life suck you under. Give them to God before they get to you.

Rather than assuming you can do nothing to help others, assume the posture of prayer.

How Happiness Happens

Because of the Miracle

"Anyone who has seen me has seen the Father."

JOHN 14:9

Because of Bethlehem's miracle, you can answer these fundamental questions: Does God care if I'm sad? Look at the tear-streaked face of Jesus as he stands near Lazarus's tomb (John 11:1–36). Does God notice when I'm afraid? Note the resolve in the eyes of Jesus as he marches through the storm to rescue his friends (Matthew 14:22–33). Does God know if I am ignored or rejected? Find the answer in the compassionate eyes of Christ as he stands to defend the adulterous woman (John 8:1–11).

"[Jesus] radiates God's own glory and expresses the very character of God" (Hebrews 1:3 NLT). Jesus himself stated,

"Anyone who has seen me has seen the Father."

"Anyone who has seen me weep has seen the Father weep."

"Anyone who has seen me laugh has seen the Father laugh."

"Anyone who has seen me determined has seen the Father determined."

Would you like to see God? Take a look at Jesus.

Because of Bethlehem

JULY 15

Debt-Free

*Abraham believed God, and it was
credited to him as righteousness.*

JAMES 2:23

I have a credit card. If I were to write a check to pay the balance on the card, the debt on the card would be removed, and I would be credited a zero balance. I would have no debt. No obligation.

According to Paul, God has done the same with our spiritual debt. He presents Abraham as an example. Abraham had not a credit-card debt but a spiritual debt. He had sinned. He was a good man, I am certain, but not good enough to live debt-free. He was continually racking up debt: Every time he cursed his camel. Every time he flirted with a handmaiden. Every time he wondered where in the world God was leading him and if God knew where in the world he was headed.

But for all the bad things Abraham did, there was one good thing he chose to do. He believed. He put his faith in God. And because he believed, a wonderful, unspeakably great thing happened to his debt.

It was returned to zero!

God's promise to Abraham was salvation by faith. God's promise to you and me is salvation by faith. Just faith.

Unshakable Hope

He Cleans Up Our Mess

Jesus said to them, "Come and eat breakfast."

JOHN 21:12 NKJV

When I was six, my brother and I were playing a game of tag, running up and down the aisles of a grocery store. I crashed into a stand-alone display of honey. Bottles flew every direction—glass bottles of honey! The store manager appeared.

"Whose boy are you?" he barked.

There I sat on the floor, covered with honey. I looked at the manager. I wondered how many years in prison I was going to get. Then, from behind me, I heard the voice of my mom. "He belongs to me," she said. "We'll clean up this mess."

Jesus felt the same way about Peter: "He belongs to me. I can clean up this mess."

The cleanup would take place over breakfast on the shore of the Sea of Galilee. We might expect Jesus to go nuclear on Peter: dredge up the past, rehearse the promises Peter broke, call down every "I told you so" from heaven. A divine snarl or two seems in order.

But no. Just this: "Come and eat breakfast."

Who would've imagined this invitation?

By the way, it's the same invitation he offers you.

You Are Never Alone

207

God Doesn't Delay

"Don't you think God will surely give justice to his chosen people who cry out to him day and night? Will he keep putting them off? I tell you, he will grant justice to them quickly!"

LUKE 18:7–8 NLT

Read the story of the persistent widow in Luke's gospel (18:1–8), and you might wonder, *What is this story doing in the Bible?*

A corrupt official. A persistent gadfly. Reluctant benevolence. No compassion or concern. Is there a message in this account? Is God a reluctant judge? Are we the marginalized widow? Is prayer a matter of pestering God until he breaks down and gives us what we want?

No, this is a parable of contrast, not comparison. God is not the reluctant judge in this story. And you are not the widow. The widow in the story had nowhere to turn. But as a child of the King, you are at the front of the line. You, at any moment, can turn to God.

God doesn't delay. He never places you on hold or tells you to call again later. God loves the sound of your voice. Always. He doesn't hide when you call. He hears your prayers.

Anxious for Nothing

David's Question

The LORD has established his throne in heaven, and his kingdom rules over all.

PSALM 103:19

In the prayer journal of King David, we read this question: "When the foundations for good collapse, what can good people do?" (Psalm 11:3 NCV).

Isn't David's question ours? When all that is good falls apart, what can good people do?

When terrorists attack, when diseases rage, when families collapse, when churches divide . . . when all that is good falls apart, what can good people do? What is the godly response to the unexpected mishaps and calamities of life?

Curiously, David didn't answer his question with an answer. He answered it with a declaration. "The LORD is in his holy temple. The LORD is on his throne in heaven" (v. 4 NIRV).

His point is unmistakable: When everything shakes, God remains unshaken. He is in his holy temple. His plan will not be derailed. God is unaffected by our storms. He is undeterred by our problems. We don't have to be worried by our worries. The Lord is on his throne.

Because of Bethlehem

Pigeonholes Are for Pigeons

"The Lord does not look at the things people look at. People look at the outward appearance, but the Lord looks at the heart."

1 SAMUEL 16:7

I happened to be walking through downtown on a Saturday afternoon when I spotted a haggard-looking man sitting on the concrete steps of a building. He wore a stocking cap, dirty clothes, and a full beard. A can of his favorite beverage sat at his feet.

I set aside my discomfort and sat down beside him. I had taken him for a homeless, unemployed drifter. I was wrong.

Turns out he had just gotten off work from an all-night shift as a stagehand. We talked for a few moments about his career—several decades of setting it up and tearing it down for the best of country music. He also told me that God had blessed his life and that he felt the favor of the Lord. I'd misjudged him. I walked away a bit embarrassed.

Learn from my experience. Let every person you meet be a new person in your mind. None of this labeling or these preconceived notions. Pigeonholes work for pigeons, not for people.

How Happiness Happens

Jesus Sees You

As [Jesus] went along, he saw a man blind from birth.

JOHN 9:1

No one else saw the blind man. The followers of Jesus may have observed him. He may have entered their field of vision. But they did not see him.

The disciples saw only a theological case study. "His disciples asked him [Jesus], 'Rabbi, who sinned, this man or his parents, that he was born blind?'" (v. 2). They didn't see a human being. They saw a topic of discussion.

Jesus, by contrast, saw a man who was blind from birth, a man who'd never seen a sunrise, who couldn't distinguish purple from pink. He dwelled in a dark world. Other men his age had learned a craft; he sat on the side of the road. Others had an income; he begged for money. Others had reason to hope; he had reason to despair.

Then Jesus *saw* him.

And Jesus sees you. You and I aren't invisible. We may feel like nameless beggars in the swarms of society, but this story—and dozens of others like it—assure us that Jesus spots us on the side of the road. He takes the initiative. He makes the first move.

You Are Never Alone

211

Strength Is on the Way

So you are no longer a slave, but God's child; and since you are his child, God has made you also an heir.

GALATIANS 4:7

I recently spent the better part of an hour reciting the woes of my life to my wife. I felt overwhelmed by commitments and deadlines. I'd been sick with the flu. There was tension at the church between some coworkers. We'd received word of friends who were getting a divorce.

If you could have read my mind, you would have thought you were perusing the textbook for Pessimism 101. *My work is in vain. I'm going to move to the Amazon jungle and live in a hut.*

After several minutes Denalyn interrupted me with a question. "Is God in this anywhere?" (I hate it when she does that.)

What had happened to me? I wasn't turning to God. I'd limited my world to my own strength, wisdom, and power. No wonder I was in a tailspin. For such moments God gives this promise: "We are heirs—heirs of God and co-heirs with Christ" (Romans 8:17).

Strength is on the way. The gauge may be bouncing on Empty, but we will not run out of fuel. Our Father will not allow it.

Unshakable Hope

The Very Peace of God

"Peace I leave with you; my peace I give you. I do not give to you as the world gives. Do not let your hearts be troubled and do not be afraid."

JOHN 14:27

In this life of faith, as we do our part—rejoice in the Lord, pursue a gentle spirit, pray about everything, and cling to gratitude—God does his part. He bestows upon us the peace of God. Note, this is not a peace *from* God. Our Father gives us the very peace *of* God. He downloads the tranquility of the throne room into our world, resulting in an inexplicable calm. We should be worried, but we aren't. We should be upset, but we are comforted. The peace of God transcends all logic, scheming, and efforts to explain it.

This kind of peace is not a human achievement. It is a gift from above. Jesus promises you his vintage of peace! The peace that calmed his heart when he was falsely accused. The peace that steadied his voice when he spoke to Pilate. The peace that kept his thoughts clear and heart pure as he hung on the cross. This was his peace. This can be your peace.

Anxious for Nothing

The God Who Stoops

*All have sinned and fall short of the glory of God,
and all are justified freely by his grace through
the redemption that came by Christ Jesus.*

ROMANS 3:23–24

Before sending the Flood that would cover the earth, God promised safety for Noah and his family. All of humanity at the time was wicked, "but Noah found grace in the eyes of the LORD" (Genesis 6:8 NKJV). This is the first time we see the word *grace* in Scripture. We might expect *grace* to debut in David's psalm or Jesus' sermon or Paul's epistle. But it doesn't. Grace comes when the Flood does.

Noah found a God who would stoop down and help him. Indeed, "stoop" is the Hebrew meaning of the word *grace*. God stooped and entered Noah's world. Grace is the God who stoops, who descends, who condescends and reaches.

The Noah story is our story. The world is corrupt. The judgment is sure. But the salvation is certain. God has provided us a way of escape.

We are saved not by a boat but by Jesus Christ. He is our ark. We enter into him. We trust him. He, and he alone, keeps us safe from the evil that floods about us.

Praying the Promises

Together, We Are Poetry

*We are His workmanship, created in Christ
Jesus for good works, which God prepared
beforehand that we should walk in them.*

EPHESIANS 2:10 NKJV

We are His workmanship." The word *workmanship* comes from the Greek word *poiéma*, which could be translated "poetry."[4] We are the poetry of God! What Longfellow did with pen and paper, our Maker has done with us. We are an expression of his creative best.

Together we are God's poetry. Independently we are nothing but small pieces on God's page. You may be a verb, she may be a noun, and I'm probably a question mark. We're just letters, marks from God's hand.

What letter, then, has a right to criticize another? Dare the *p* accuse the *q* of being backward? Dare the *m* mock the *w* for being too open-minded? Who are we to tell the writer how to form us or when to use us? We need each other. By ourselves we are just letters on a page, but collectively we are poetry.

How Happiness Happens

Made for His Glory

*"Bring to me all the people who are mine, whom I
made for my glory, whom I formed and made."*

ISAIAH 43:7 NCV

Pop psychology is wrong when it tells you to look inside yourself
and find your value. The magazines are wrong when they suggest you are only as good as you are thin, muscular, pimple-free, or
perfumed. Religious leaders lie when they urge you to grade your
significance according to your church attendance, self-discipline, or
spirituality.

According to the Bible you are good simply because God made you
in his image. Period. He cherishes you because you bear a resemblance
to him. And you will only be satisfied when you engage in your role
as an image bearer of God. Such was the view of King David: "As for
me, I will see Your face in righteousness; I shall be satisfied when I
awake in Your likeness" (Psalm 17:15 NKJV).

Lay hold of this promise, and spare yourself a world of confusion
and fear. How much sadness would evaporate if every person simply
chose to believe this: *I was made for God's glory and am being made
into his image.*

Unshakable Hope

Search and Rescue

"The Son of Man came to seek and to save the lost."

LUKE 19:10

Jesus' time on earth was a search-and-rescue mission. He rescued a woman hiding in Samaria. Five husbands had dumped her like the morning garbage. The sixth wouldn't marry her. Christ went out of his way to help her (John 4:4–29).

He rescued a demoniac in the caves. Evil spirits had driven the man to mutilate himself, slashing himself with stones. One word from Christ stopped the hurting (Mark 5:1–15).

He spotted pint-size Zacchaeus in Jericho. The tax collector had swindled enough people to stockpile his retirement. Yet he would have given it all for a clean conscience and a good friend. One lunch with Jesus and he found both (Luke 19:1–10).

Jesus' ministry went on like this for three years. He changed person after person; no one quite knew how to respond to this carpenter who commanded the dead. Just when he seemed poised for a crown, he died on a cross.

All so that he could search for and rescue you.

Because of Bethlehem

The Devil's Speciality

"The thief comes with the sole intention of
stealing and killing and destroying."

JOHN 10:10 PHILLIPS

The devil is always messing with our minds. He brings only gloom and doom. By the time he was finished with Job, the man was sick and alone. By the time he had done his work in Judas, the disciple had given up on life. The devil is to hope what termites are to an oak; he'll chew you up from the inside.

Exaggerated, overstated, inflated, irrational thoughts are the devil's specialty.

No one will ever love me.

It's all over for me.

Everyone is against me.

I'll never lose weight, get out of debt, or have friends.

What lugubrious, monstrous lies! No problem is unsolvable. No life is irredeemable. No one's fate is sealed. No one is unloved or unlovable. But Satan wants us to think we are.

Satan is the master of deceit. But he is not the master of your mind. You have a power he cannot defeat. You have God on your side. He will help you as well. Guard your thoughts and trust your Father.

Anxious for Nothing

Take the Plunge

"Don't be afraid; just believe."

MARK 5:36

Perhaps you can envision a middle-aged man going goofy in the motel swimming pool. His four-year-old daughter stands on the edge and watches. It's not easy convincing a kid to jump into the pool. It was time, I believed, for Jenna to take the plunge. She wasn't so sure.

"I'll catch you!" I told Jenna. "You'll love it! Just trust me!" And finally she jumped. She took the plunge.

I caught her, as I promised.

She survived, as I promised she would.

And she loved it. All because she believed.

We preachers tend to complicate this thing of belief. We've been known to write papers about the exact moment of salvation and the evidence of repentance.

Call me simple, but I think God is a good Father. I think he knows something about life. And I think he invites us to take the step, to take the plunge, to jump—not into a pool but into a relationship with him that is vibrant, joyous, and, yes, fun! It's not always easy, mind you. But certainly it's worth the risk, and by all means it's better than life in a deck chair on the poolside.

You Are Never Alone

Yet Another Cleansing

Purify me from my sins, and I will be clean;
wash me, and I will be whiter than snow.

PSALM 51:7 NLT

Heaven must have a warehouse that contains row after row of ceramic bowls. Each bowl has a name affixed to it. One particularly well-worn basin bears the name Max. Every day, multiple times a day, Jesus sends an angel to fetch it. "Lucado needs another cleansing." The angel wings his way over to the warehouse, retrieves it, and carries it to Christ. The Master takes my container, fills it with cleansing grace, and washes away my sins. All my betrayals sink like silt to the bottom of the bowl. Jesus throws them out.

Have you considered how often Christ washes you?

Suppose I were somehow to come into possession of your sin-history video. Every contrary act. Every wayward thought. Every reckless word. Would you want me to play it on a screen? By no means. You'd beg me not to. And I would beg you not to show mine.

Don't worry. I don't have it. But Jesus does. He's seen it. And he has resolved, "My grace is enough. I can cleanse these people. I will wash away their betrayals." And he does.

How Happiness Happens

Our Father, the King

*Yours is the kingdom, O Lord, and You
are exalted as head over all.*

1 CHRONICLES 29:11 NKJV

In our society, we don't like to talk about kings and kingdoms. We find the notion of absolute rule repulsive and medieval. Yet this is the consistent teaching of Scripture. God is King. The entire creation, both humans and nature, answers to him.

And this truth is the greatest of the kingdom secrets: the King is our Father. Remember how Jesus taught us to pray? "Our Father in heaven, hallowed be Your name. Your kingdom come" (Matthew 6:9–10 NKJV).

If our Father is the King, everything changes. He listens when we call. He cares when we fall. He includes us at his table. Our King loves us, but his kingdom is not about us. It's about God.

God is creating an everlasting commonwealth, and he invites us to be a part of it. There is only one condition: the kingdom has one King. You and I are welcome to enter the throne room, but we have to surrender our crowns at the door.

Praying the Promises

In the Storms

*When evening came, his disciples went down to
the lake, where they got into a boat and set off
across the lake for Capernaum. . . . A strong wind
was blowing and the waters grew rough.*

JOHN 6:16–18

The disciples were "in the middle of the sea, tossed by the waves" (Matthew 14:24 NKJV). They were too far from the shore, too long in the struggle, and too small against the waves. And Jesus was nowhere to be seen. Have you ever encountered a dangerous, seemingly godforsaken storm?

Too far from the shore. Too far from a solution.

Too long in the struggle. Too long in the court system, the hospital.

Too small against the waves. Too small and too alone.

The storm controlled the disciples. Storms can dominate our lives as well. But then the unimaginable happened. "They saw Jesus approaching the boat, walking on the water" (John 6:19).

We want more description. Was Jesus' hair blown back? Was he ankle-deep? Was his robe wet? John gives no details, just this economical statement: "They saw Jesus . . . walking on the water."

That is all we need to know. Before Jesus stills the storms, he comes to us in the midst of our storms.

You Are Never Alone

August

Good for the Doer

We should love one another.

1 JOHN 3:11 NLT

The people in our world can be moody, fickle, and stubborn. And that just describes my wife's husband. If we are going to find the joy that comes through giving joy away, we need a plan. We need instruction. No wonder the Bible has so much to say about finding joy in the act of sharing it. The New Testament contains more than fifty "one another" statements, practical principles for making happiness happen. I've condensed them into a list of ten: (1) Encourage one another (1 Thessalonians 5:11). (2) Bear with one another (Ephesians 4:2). (3) Regard one another as more important (Philippians 2:4). (4) Greet one another (Romans 16:16). (5) Pray for one another (James 5:16). (6) Serve one another (Galatians 5:13). (7) Accept one another (Romans 15:7). (8) Admonish one another (Colossians 3:16). (9) Forgive one another (Ephesians 4:32). (10) Love one another (1 John 3:11).

Let's open the door to each of these "one another" passages and embark on a happiness project. I'm thinking you will discover what the Bible teaches and research affirms: doing good does good for the doer.

How Happiness Happens

Justice Will Be Served

God is a just judge.

PSALM 7:11 NKJV

There are many who fight a daily battle with anger. They've been robbed; evil people have pilfered days with their loved ones; disease has sapped health from their bodies. They believe that justice must be served.

I'm one of these people. My brother was robbed. Alcoholism heisted the joy out of his life. For two-thirds of his fifty-seven years, he battled the bottle. It cost him his family, finances, and friends. He was not innocent. I get that. He bought the liquor and made the choices. Yet I am convinced that Satan assigned a special goon squad to tempt him. When they found his weakness, they refused to let up. They took him to the mat and pounded the self-control out of him.

I'm ready to see Satan pay for his crimes against my brother. I am looking forward to that moment when I stand next to Dee, our bodies redeemed and souls secure. Together we will see the devil bound and chained and cast into a lake of fire. At that point we will begin to reclaim what the devil took.

Justice will prevail.

Unshakable Hope

Bold and Believing

*"You will call on me and come and pray
to me, and I will listen to you."*

JEREMIAH 29:12

*Lord, in Christ I have a Great High Priest who has given me
confidence to come before the throne to receive grace and mercy.
Thank you for always listening to me.*

*God, it is so easy for me to go an entire day without speaking
to you. I can get caught up in my own thoughts and tasks, forgetting I have a heavenly Father who is available to talk anytime,
day or night. Let today be different. As concerns and questions
come up, remind me to turn each of them over to you in prayer.
I lift up my family to you. I lift up my work to you. I lift up my
to-do list to you. Cover each worry with your peace. Prioritize
my day so it aligns with your will and not mine.*

*You have promised to answer when I call. So help me come
before your throne in boldness and in belief, knowing you will
hear me and knowing that you care for me. Amen.*

Praying the Promises

A Prescription for Anxiety

Rejoice in the Lord always. Again I will say, rejoice!

PHILIPPIANS 4:4 NKJV

If anyone had reason to be anxious, it was the apostle Paul in a Roman prison. Yet his prescription for anxiety begins with a call to rejoice.

Paul used every tool in the box on Philippians 4:4, hoping to get our attention. First, he employed a present imperative tense so his readers would hear him say, continually, habitually rejoice![1] And if the verb tense wasn't enough, he removed the expiration date. "Rejoice in the Lord *always*" (emphasis mine). And if perchance the verb tense and *always* were inadequate, he repeated the command: *"Again I will say*, rejoice!" (emphasis mine).

But how can a person obey this command? Rejoice always? Is it possible for any person to maintain an uninterrupted spirit of gladness? No. This is not Paul's challenge. We are urged to "rejoice *in the Lord*" (emphasis mine). This verse is a call not to a feeling but to a decision and a deeply rooted confidence that God exists, that he is in control, and that he is good.

Anxious for Nothing

The Second Chance

Jesus said to Simon Peter, "Simon son of John,
do you love me more than these?"

JOHN 21:15

We call Abraham our hero, but he once refused to call his wife his wife. We delight in the words of David. Yet David was known to delight in the wife of a friend. Rahab is one of a handful of females in the genealogy of Jesus. She was also a madam in the world's oldest profession. Paul killed Christians before he taught them. The Bible is full of famous failures.

We name our children after them. We sing songs about them. But let's be honest. There isn't a human in the Bible who didn't behave like one. And so do we.

Have you questioned whether God could ever use you after the things you've done? If so, you need to turn to a story in the book of John: the miracle of Peter's restoration.

As he did for Peter after the resurrection, Jesus not only forgives us but he restores us to our place of service. He washes us so we might once again be portraits of his goodness to hang in his gallery.

You Are Never Alone

Peace in the Storm

"When you pass through the waters, I will be with you."

ISAIAH 43:2

When mariners describe a tempest that no sailor can escape, they call it a perfect storm. Not perfect in the sense of ideal, but perfect in the sense of combining factors. All the elements, such as hurricane-force winds plus a cold front plus a downpour of rain, work together to create the perfect recipe for disaster.

You needn't be a fisherman to experience a perfect storm. All you need is a layoff *plus* a recession. A disease *plus* a job transfer. A relationship breakup *plus* a college rejection. We can handle one challenge . . . but two or three at a time? One wave after another, gale forces followed by thunderstorms? It's enough to make you wonder, *Will I survive?*

Jesus sends this message to you: "When you pass through the waters, I will be with you."

Nor'easters bear down on the best of us. Contrary winds. Crashing waves. They come. But Jesus still catches his children. He still extends his arms. He still sends his angels. Because you belong to him, you can have peace in the midst of the storm.

Anxious for Nothing

The Gift of Encouragement

"Now I say to you that you are Peter (which means
'rock'), and upon this rock I will build my church,
and all the powers of hell will not conquer it."

MATTHEW 16:18 NLT

Years ago I became friends with a preacher in Houston. After a wonderful meal together he asked me, "Do you do text messages?" (I'm old enough for him not to make assumptions.) I told him I did, so we swapped phone numbers. A few days later I received a text from him saying, "I am changing your name. You are no longer Max. You are Mighty Max!"

You might think I'd shrug off such a title. I'm a sixty-four-year-old minister. I operate in the formal world of pulpits and Bible study. Mighty Max? That's the stuff of elementary school playgrounds, right?

Not to me. When I see his name on my phone, I hurry to open the text. I love to be encouraged. We all do. So let's encourage one another.

Call someone "mighty." Call someone "special." Call someone "Rocky."

Call forth the Peter from within a Simon.

Give the gift that God loves to give: the gift of encouragement.

How Happiness Happens

Don't Settle

"You will receive power when the Holy Spirit comes on you."

ACTS 1:8

Many believers settle for a two-thirds God. They rely on the Father and the Son but overlook the Holy Spirit. On the eve of Jesus' death, as he prepared his followers to face the future without him, he made this great and precious promise: "You will receive power when the Holy Spirit comes on you."

Imagine all the promises Jesus could have made to the disciples but didn't. He didn't promise immediate success. He didn't promise the absence of disease or struggles. He never guaranteed a level of income or popularity. But he did promise the perpetual, empowering presence of the Holy Spirit. The Holy Spirit is central to the life of the Christian. Everything that happens from the book of Acts to the end of the book of Revelation is a result of the work of the Holy Spirit of Christ. The Spirit came alongside the disciples, indwelled them, and gave the early church the push they needed to face the challenges ahead.

Don't settle for a two-thirds God.

Unshakable Hope

The Promise

He will swallow up death forever.

ISAIAH 25:8

Several weeks ago I spent an hour in the office of a cemetery director. Another birthday had reminded me that the day of my departure is increasingly near. It seemed right to make burial preparations. As the gentleman was showing me the available selections, I had an idea. "Can I record a message for my tombstone?"

To his credit he didn't call me crazy. "Yes, it is possible."

So the granite stone will contain a button and an invitation: "Press for a word from Max." This is what you will hear:

Thanks for coming by. Sorry you missed me. I'm not here. I'm home. Finally home. At some point my King will call, and this grave will be shown for the temporary tomb it is. You might want to step to the side in case that happens while you are here. Again, I appreciate the visit. Hope you've made plans for your own departure. All the best, Max.

Yeah, it still needs some work. While the wording might change, the promise never will.

Unshakable Hope

Ask for Help

The LORD is my strength and my shield.

PSALM 28:7

In his fine book *The Dance of Hope*, William Frey remembers the day he tried to pull a stump out of the Georgia dirt. He was eleven.

> I . . . crowbarred for hours, but the root system was so deep I couldn't pull it out. . . . I was still struggling when my father . . . came over.
>
> "I think I see your problem," he said.
>
> "What's that?" I asked.
>
> "You're not using all your strength," he replied.
>
> I exploded and told him how hard I had worked. . . .
>
> "No," he said, "you're not using all your strength."
>
> When I cooled down I asked him what he meant, and he said, "You haven't asked me to help you yet."[2]

Some of your worries have deep root systems. Extracting them is hard, hard work. But you don't have to do it alone. Present the challenge to your Father and ask for help.

Anxious for Nothing

Grace *and* Truth

*"We must celebrate with a feast, for this son
of mine was dead and has now returned to
life. He was lost, but now he is found."*

LUKE 15:23–24 NLT

How does Jesus receive us? I know how he treated me. I was a
twenty-year-old troublemaker on a downhill path. Though I'd
made a commitment to Christ a decade earlier, you wouldn't have
known it by the way I lived. I'd spent five years claiming to be God's
child on Sunday mornings and buddying with the devil on Saturday
nights.

I was lost.

When I finally grew weary of sitting in pig slop, I got wind of
God's grace. I came to Jesus, and he welcomed me back.

Please note: Jesus didn't endorse my brawling and troublemaking.
My proclivity to boast, manipulate, and exaggerate? The chauvinistic
attitude? All that had to go. Jesus didn't gloss over the self-centered
Max I had manufactured. He didn't accept my sinful behavior.

But he accepted me, his wayward child. He didn't tell me to clean
up and then come back. He said, "Come back. I'll clean you up." He
was "full of grace and truth" (John 1:14).

Grace *and* truth.

How Happiness Happens

All Man and All God

You scrutinize my path and my lying down,
and are acquainted with all my ways.

PSALM 139:3 NASB

The one who hears your prayers understands your pain. He never shrugs or scoffs or dismisses physical struggle. He had a human body.

Are you troubled in spirit? He was too. (John 12:27)
Are you so anxious you could die? He was too. (Matthew 26:38)
Are you overwhelmed with grief? He was too. (John 11:35)
Have you ever prayed with loud cries and tears? He did too.
   (Hebrews 5:7)

He gets you.
So human he could touch his people. So mighty he could heal them. So human he spoke with an accent. So heavenly he spoke with authority. So human he could blend in unnoticed for thirty years. So mighty he could change history and be unforgotten for two thousand years. All man. Yet all God.

Unshakable Hope

Now We See

"One thing I do know. I was blind but now I see!"

JOHN 9:25

I thought my sight was normal. I assumed the other fifth graders saw what I saw when they looked at the blackboard: a patch of fuzzy lines. I had poor vision. But I didn't know it. I'd never known anything else.

Then my teacher called my mom. My mom called the optometrist. The next thing I knew I was handed my first pair of glasses. Talk about a game changer! The fuzzy lines became clear.

I still remember the exhilaration of sudden sight. I would sit in Mrs. Collins's fifth-grade classroom and lift and lower my glasses, moving from blurry to twenty-twenty. Suddenly I could see.

Christians talk like this. We love to sing the words to the old hymn: "Amazing grace! How sweet the sound that saved a wretch like me! I once was lost, but now am found; was blind, but now I see."[3] Blind. Blind to the purpose of life. Blind to the promise of eternal life. Blind to the provider of life. But now we see!

You Are Never Alone

When God Speaks

God said, "Let there be light"; and there was light.

GENESIS 1:3 NKJV

From the first chapter of Scripture, the Bible makes a case for the dependability of God. Nine times in Genesis 1, the text reiterates "God said." And without exception when God spoke, something wonderful happened. By divine fiat there were light, land, beaches, and creatures. God consulted no advisers. He needed no assistance. He spoke, and it happened. The reader is left with one conclusion: God's word is sure. What he says happens.

> By the word of the LORD the heavens were made, their starry host by the breath of his mouth. He gathers the waters of the sea into jars; he puts the deep into storehouses. Let all the earth fear the LORD; let all the people of the world revere him. For he spoke, and it came to be; he commanded, and it stood firm. (Psalm 33:6–9)

When God cleared his throat, the cosmos appeared. His authority was certain then. And it's just as certain now.

Unshakable Hope

Happy Are the Unentitled

*Do not exalt yourself in the king's presence, and
do not claim a place among his great men.*

PROVERBS 25:6

Jesus surely had a smile on his face when he gave the following instructions:

When someone invites you to dinner, don't take the place of honor. Somebody more important than you might have been invited by the host. Then he'll come and call out in front of everybody, "You're in the wrong place. The place of honor belongs to this man." Embarrassed, you'll have to make your way to the very last table, the only place left.

When you're invited to dinner, go and sit at the last place. Then when the host comes he may very well say, "Friend, come up to the front." That will give the dinner guests something to talk about! (Luke 14:8–10 MSG)

Happy are the unentitled! Expecting the applause of others is a fool's enterprise! Do yourself a favor and assume nothing. If you go unnoticed, you won't be surprised. If you are noticed, you can celebrate.

How Happiness Happens

The Lord Is Listening

"He will call on me, and I will answer him; I will be with
him in trouble, I will deliver him and honor him."

PSALM 91:15

Ask God for help. "Let your requests be made known to God" (Philippians 4:6 NKJV). Fear triggers either despair or prayer. Choose wisely.

God said, "Call on me in the day of trouble" (Psalm 50:15).

Jesus said, "Ask, and it will be given to you; seek, and you will find; knock, and it will be opened to you" (Matthew 7:7 NKJV). There is no uncertainty in that promise. No "might," "perhaps," or "possibly will." Jesus states unflinchingly that when you ask, he listens.

So ask! When anxiety and fear knock on the door, say, "Jesus, would you mind answering that?" Reduce your request to one statement. Imitate Jesus, who taught us to pray, "Give us this day our daily bread" (Matthew 6:11 NKJV). Engage in specific prayer. And engage in promise-based prayer. Stand on the firm foundation of God's covenant. "Let us then approach God's throne of grace with confidence" (Hebrews 4:16), knowing the Lord is listening.

Anxious for Nothing

The Old Jalopy

He holds all creation together.

COLOSSIANS 1:17 NLT

You might relate to the jalopy I once saw. The car clattered down the freeway, one door missing, hood dented, needing paint. On the loosely hanging bumper was this sticker: "Honk if anything falls off."

"For everything, absolutely everything, above and below, visible and invisible, rank after rank after rank of angels—*everything* got started in him and finds its purpose in him. He was there before any of it came into existence and holds it all together right up to this moment" (Colossians 1:16–17 MSG).

God holds it all together. And he will hold it together for you. You cannot face a crisis if you don't face God first. As the apostle Paul wrote, "Don't worry about anything; instead, pray about everything" (Philippians 4:6 TLB).

Cling to God. In the ER, say to him, "Lord, I need you now." Between the headstones of the cemetery, whisper, "Dear Jesus, lift me up." During the deposition, when others are grumbling beneath their breath, may you be overheard repeating this prayer: "God, you are good. I . . . need . . . help. Encourage me, please."

And he will.

Because of Bethlehem

When You Pray

*This is the confidence we have in approaching God: that
if we ask anything according to his will, he hears us.*

1 JOHN 5:14

Our prayers unlock the storehouses of heaven. When you pray, when you speak for the ones who need help to the one who can give it, something wonderful happens.

As thrilling evidence consider the case of the centurion and his servant. The soldier asked Jesus to heal the man. When Jesus asked if he should go to the man's house, the officer stopped him. "Only speak a word, and my servant will be healed" (Matthew 8:8 NKJV).

Jesus was so impressed with the faith of the soldier that he answered the request on the spot. He didn't inquire about the faith of the slave. He didn't ask if the man had confessed his sins or requested the Messiah's help. Jesus healed the slave because the centurion placed himself between the needy person and the one who could meet the need.

Let's do the same.

How Happiness Happens

It's Why Jesus Came

*You know that Christ came to take away sins
and that there is no sin in Christ.*

1 JOHN 3:5 NCV

The sinful nature is the stubborn, self-centered attitude that says, "My way or the highway." The sinful nature is all about self: pleasing self, promoting self, preserving self. Sin is selfish. I have a sin nature.

So do you. (Sorry, but we both know it's true.) Under the right circumstances you will do the wrong thing. You won't want to. You'll try not to, but you will. Why? You have a sin nature.

You were born with it. We all were. Our parents didn't teach us to throw temper tantrums; we were born with the skill. No one showed us how to steal a cookie from our sibling; we just knew. We never attended a class on pouting or passing the blame, but we could do both before we were out of diapers. The heart of the human problem is the problem of the human heart.

Each one of us entered the world with a sin nature.

God entered the world to take it away.

Because of Bethlehem

Face God First

*When Peter saw the wind and the waves, he became
afraid and began to sink. He shouted, "Lord, save me!"*

MATTHEW 14:30 NCV

D o not meditate on the mess. You gain nothing by setting your
eyes on the problem. You gain everything by setting your eyes
on the Lord.

This was the lesson Peter learned on the stormy Sea of Galilee.
He was a fisherman. He knew what ten-foot waves could do to small
boats. Maybe that is why he volunteered to leave the craft when he saw
Jesus walking on the water.

As long as Peter focused on the face of Christ, he did the impossible.
Yet when he shifted his gaze to the force of the storm, he sank like a
stone. If you are sinking, it is because you are looking in the wrong
direction.

Is God sovereign over your circumstances? Is he mightier than
your problem? Does he have answers to your questions? Yes, yes, and
yes! "God . . . is the blessed controller of all things, the king over all
kings and the master of all masters" (1 Timothy 6:15 PHILLIPS).

Rejoice in the Lord. This is step one. Do not hurry past it. Face
God before you face your problem.

Anxious for Nothing

The God Who Rescues

"I am your God and will take care of you until you are old
and your hair is gray. . . . I will give you help and rescue you."

ISAIAH 46:4 GNT

I recently went on a walk with two of my best companions: my little granddaughter, Rosie, and my faithful dog, Andy.

Andy loves to explore a dry riverbed near our house. And Rosie loves to follow right behind him. She thinks she can go wherever he goes. And when I offer to help her, she waves me away. So Andy led the way. Rosie scampered behind, and I tried to keep up.

Andy spotted a critter in a thicket of bushes and dashed into them. Rosie thought she could do the same. Andy ran straight through, but Rosie got stuck. The branches scratched her skin, and she began to cry.

"Papa Max! Will you help me?"

What did I do? I stepped into the thickets and extended my hands. She raised her arms and let me lift her out.

God will do the same for you. He doesn't think twice about stepping into the thorny thickets of our world and lifting us out.

You are never alone, never without help, never without hope.

You Are Never Alone

Pick What You Ponder

Be careful what you think, because your thoughts run your life.

PROVERBS 4:23 NCV

You can pick what you ponder.

You didn't choose your parents or siblings. You don't determine the weather. There are many things in life over which you have no choice. But the greatest activity of life is well within your dominion. You can choose what you think about.

You can be the air traffic controller of your mental airport. Thoughts circle above, coming and going. If one of them lands, it is because you gave it permission. If it leaves, it is because you directed it to do so.

Do you want to be happy tomorrow? Then sow seeds of happiness today. (Count blessings. Memorize Bible verses. Pray. Sing hymns. Spend time with encouraging people.) Do you want to guarantee tomorrow's misery? Then wallow in a mental mud pit of self-pity or guilt or anxiety today. (Assume the worst. Beat yourself up. Rehearse your regrets. Complain to complainers.) Thoughts have consequences.

Your challenge is not your challenge. Your challenge is the way you think about your challenge. Your problem is not your problem; it is the way you look at it.

Anxious for Nothing

He Gives Us Grace

"You do not realize now what I am doing,
but later you will understand."

JOHN 13:7

In Jesus' final meal with his followers, he rose from supper, took a pitcher of water, and emptied it into a bowl. The next sound was the tap of the bowl as Jesus placed it on the floor. Then the shuffle of leather as he untied and removed the first of the two dozen sandals. There was more splashing as Jesus placed two feet, dirty as they were, into the water. After washing them, he dried the feet with his towel. He then stood, emptied the basin of dirty water, filled it with fresh, and repeated the process on the next set of feet.

Later that night the disciples realized the enormity of this gesture. They had pledged to stay with their Master, but when the soldiers marched in, the disciples ran out.

I envision them sprinting until they plopped to the ground and let their heads fall forward. That's when they saw the feet Jesus had just washed. That's when they realized he had given them grace before they even knew they needed it.

Hasn't he done the same for us? Before we knew we needed grace, we were offered it.

How Happiness Happens

Shining Up an Old Coin

We . . . are being transformed into his image with ever-increasing glory, which comes from the Lord, who is the Spirit.

2 CORINTHIANS 3:18

The New Testament describes a progressive work of God to shape us into his image. As we fellowship with God, read his Word, obey his commands, and seek to understand and reflect his character, something wonderful emerges. Or, better stated, *Someone* wonderful emerges. God comes out of us. We say things God would say. We do things God would do. We forgive, we share, and we love. It is as if God is scrubbing the smudge off an old coin. In time an image begins to appear.

This was God's explanation through the apostle Paul: "You have taken off your old self with its practices and have put on the new self, which is being renewed in knowledge in the image of its Creator" (Colossians 3:9–10).

God's goal is simply this: to rub away anything that is not of him so the inborn image of God can be seen in us. When struggles come your way, could it be that God is shining up an old coin?

Unshakable Hope

We Have a Savior

*We have seen and testify that the Father has
sent his Son to be the Savior of the world.*

1 JOHN 4:14

Rick Warren tells about a time he was sitting in a parking lot. His three-year-old daughter was in the backseat in her car seat. As they waited for his wife to come out of the store, his daughter grew restless. Anticipating a short wait, Rick didn't want to remove her from her car seat. The little girl hung her head out the window and yelled, "Please, God! Get me out of this!"[4]

At some point in life, don't we all feel like Rick's daughter? We are stuck. Not stuck in a backseat, but stuck in a dying body, with bad habits, suffering the consequences of poor choices in a rebellious world. We need help.

So we shop till we drop, drink till we can't think, work till we can't stop. We take pills, take vacations, and take advice from therapists, bartenders, and big brothers. We buy new purses or Porsches. But we end up facing the same mess.

We need someone to save us from meaninglessness and meanness. God's promise is this: we have a Savior, and his name is Jesus.

Because of Bethlehem

Palace or Prison?

*My God will meet all your needs according to
the riches of his glory in Christ Jesus.*

PHILIPPIANS 4:19

If you were offered a palace with no Christ or a prison with Christ, which would you choose?

In ancient Rome, the emperor Nero had the palace, but no Christ. The legacy of his reign is deceit, fear, murder, and a severe abuse of power. Eventually, he died alone. Deified, but alone. Rich, but alone. Powerful, but alone. In the end, he had everything except happiness.

Paul, on the other hand, had nothing but happiness. Yet he literally had nothing. He was imprisoned during Nero's time. His tired body carried the marks of whippings, shipwrecks, and disease.

But if you were to ask Paul to choose between the palace and the prison, he would be quick to answer. *My purse may be empty, but my Father's is not.*

That's the promise. That was the discovery of Paul. That is the hope of the believer. Though your "Nero" might attempt to incarcerate you, your Lord will provide for you. He will give you everything you need. A palace with no Christ is a prison. A prison with Christ is a palace.

Praying the Promises

More Than You Can Imagine

No eye has seen, no ear has heard, and no mind has imagined what God has prepared for those who love him.

1 CORINTHIANS 2:9 NLT

You have everything you need to be everything God desires. Divine resources have been deposited in you.

Need more patience? It's yours. Need more joy? Ask for it. Running low on wisdom? God has plenty. Put in your order.

Your father is rich! "Yours, O LORD, is the greatness, the power, the glory, the victory, and the majesty. Everything in the heavens and on earth is yours, O LORD" (1 Chronicles 29:11 NLT).

You will never exhaust his resources. At no time does he wave away your prayer with "Come back tomorrow. I'm tired, weary, depleted."

God is affluent! Wealthy in love, abundant in hope, overflowing in wisdom.

Your imagination is too timid to understand God's dream for you. He stands with you on the eastern side of the Jordan River, he gestures at the expanse of Canaan, and he tells you what he told Joshua: be strong and of good courage, for this is your inheritance (Joshua 1:6).

Unshakable Hope

Let's Celebrate

Be happy with those who are happy.

ROMANS 12:15 NCV

Here is a helpful exercise that can turn your focus off yourself and on to others. During the next twenty-four hours, make it your aim to celebrate everything good that happens to someone else. Keep a list. Develop your "rejoice with those who rejoice" muscle (Romans 12:15). The instant you see something good done by or for another person, let out a whoop and a holler, silently if not publicly. Throw some confetti. Can you envision the fun you will have?

You won't begrudge the good weather enjoyed by Floridians; you'll celebrate their sun-kissed day. Your colleague's promotion will activate happiness, not resentment. The sight of studious Mary won't create a grumbling Martha. Just the opposite. You will thank God for the attention she gives to spiritual matters.

By the end of the day, I daresay, you will be whistling your way through life.

Make a big deal out of yourself, and brace yourself for a day of disappointments. Make a big deal out of others, and expect a blue-ribbon day. You will move from joy to joy as you regard other people's success as more important than your own.

How Happiness Happens

Do You Know Grace?

God, in his grace, freely makes us right in his sight. He did this through Christ Jesus when he freed us from the penalty for our sins.

ROMANS 3:24 NLT

My salvation has nothing to do with my work and everything to do with the finished work of Christ on the cross.

Do you know this grace? If not, we have stumbled upon a source of your anxiety. You thought the problem was your calendar, your marriage, your job. In reality it is this unresolved guilt.

Don't indulge it. Don't drown in the bilge of your own condemnation. There is a reason the windshield is bigger than the rearview mirror. Your future matters more than your past. God's grace is greater than your sin. What you did was not good. But your God is good. And he will forgive you. He is ready to write a new chapter in your life. Say with Paul, "Forgetting the past and looking forward to what lies ahead, I strain to reach the end of the race and receive the prize for which God is calling us" (Philippians 3:13–14 TLB).

Do you need to remember this grace?

Anxious for Nothing

Get Up and Walk

Heal me, LORD, and I will be healed.

JEREMIAH 17:14

Barbara Snyder hadn't walked in seven years because of multiple sclerosis. She was nearly blind. She was confined to a hospital bed in her home and given six months to live.

One day as she was listening to some prayers written for her, Barbara heard a man's voice behind her. "My child, get up and walk!" There was no man in the room. She told one of her friends, "God just told me to get up and walk. Run and get my family."

They came. What happened next was described by one of her physicians, Dr. Thomas Marshall: "She literally jumped out of bed and removed her oxygen. . . . Her vision was back . . . and she could move her feet and hands freely."[5]

Christ did the work. Christ performed the miracle. Christ intervened. But, even so, Barbara had to believe. She had to get up and walk.

So do you. So do I.

You Are Never Alone

A Different Way

If anyone is in Christ, he is a new creation; old things
have passed away; behold, all things have become new.

2 CORINTHIANS 5:17 NKJV

As God's love flows through you, you will see people in a different way. "From this time on we do not think of anyone as the world does" (2 Corinthians 5:16 NCV).

You have God living inside you. Maybe you have had trouble loving the homeless. God can love them through you. Perhaps your friends taught you to bully the weak or slander the rich. God will create a new attitude. He indwells you.

The woman at the grocery counter? She is not just an employee; she is fearfully and wonderfully made.

The husband at the breakfast table? He is not just a fellow who needs a shave; he is God's creation, destined for a heavenly assignment.

The neighbor down the street? He's not a person who forgets to mow his lawn. He is made in the image of God.

God will not let you live with your old hatred and prejudices. He will plant in your heart an appreciation for his multifaceted family. God loves a diverse creation.

How Happiness Happens

September

Special Agents of Happiness

You will fill me with joy in your presence.

PSALM 16:11

Jesus was accused of much, but he was never ever described as a grump or a self-centered jerk. He fished with fishermen and ate lunch with the little guy and spoke words of resounding affirmation. He went to so many parties that he was criticized for hanging out with rowdy people and questionable crowds. His purpose statement read "I came to give life with joy and abundance" (John 10:10 THE VOICE).

When the angels announced the arrival of the Messiah, they proclaimed "good news of a great joy" (Luke 2:10 RSV). Scripture has more than twenty-seven hundred passages that contain words like *joy, happiness, gladness, merriment, pleasure, celebration, cheer, laughter, delight, jubilation, feasting, blessing,* and *exultation.*[1] Our joy level matters to God.

This is not superficial happy talk. Jesus spoke candidly about sin, death, and the needs of the human heart. Yet he did so with hope. He brought joy to the people of first-century Palestine. And he wants to bring joy to the people of this generation, and he has enlisted some special agents of happiness to do the job. You and me.

How Happiness Happens

Do You Hear Them?

Since we are surrounded by such a great cloud of witnesses, . . .
let us run with perseverance the race marked out for us.

HEBREWS 12:1

My friend Dan once completed an Ironman Triathlon at Lake Placid, New York. The final mile of the race is run on the track of the high school stadium. The residents of Lake Placid packed the bleachers for the singular purpose of cheering on the finishers.

Dan had been swimming, biking, and running since eight o'clock that morning. His legs were cramping, and his feet were sore. Everything inside him wanted to quit. But then he heard the roar of the crowd. He quickened his pace and ran through the entrance.

The place erupted! People he'd never seen were calling his name. Little kids were chanting, "Dan! Dan! Dan!" Gone was the pain. Forgotten was the weariness. He was surrounded by a huge crowd of witnesses.

So are you. Listen carefully, my friend, and you will hear a multitude of God's children urging you on. Noah is among them. So is Mary the mother of Jesus. Your elementary school teacher shouts your name. They are part of the "great cloud of witnesses."

Unshakable Hope

Corn Bread and Buttermilk

You will keep in perfect peace all who trust in
you, all whose thoughts are fixed on you!

ISAIAH 26:3 NLT

I have a childhood memory that I cherish. My father loved corn bread and buttermilk. About ten o'clock each night, he would meander into the kitchen and crumble a piece of corn bread into a glass of buttermilk. He would stand at the counter in his T-shirt and boxer shorts and drink it.

He then made the rounds to the front and back doors, checking the locks. Once everything was secure, he would step into the bedroom I shared with my brother and say something like, "Everything is secure, boys. You can go to sleep now."

I have no inclination to believe that God loves corn bread and buttermilk, but I do believe he loves his children. He oversees your world. He monitors your life. He doesn't need to check the doors; indeed, he is the door. Nothing will come your way apart from his permission.

Listen carefully and you will hear him say, "Everything is secure. You can rest now."

Anxious for Nothing

Without End

If we walk in the light as He is in the light . . . the blood
of Jesus Christ His Son cleanses us from all sin.

1 JOHN 1:7 NKJV

C hrist has paid for you.

Receive this, the great miracle of mercy. Let the grace of God flow over you like a cleansing cascade, flushing out all dregs of guilt and shame. Nothing separates you from God. Your conscience may accuse you, but God accepts you. Others may dredge up your past, but God doesn't.

I took a break from writing to go to the beach with our family. Rosie, grandchild number one, had never seen the ocean. We all wondered how she would respond to the sight. When she saw the waves and heard the roar of the water, she watched and listened and then finally asked, "When does it turn off?"

It doesn't, sweetie.

We ask the same about God's grace. Surely it will dry up and stop flowing, right? Wrong. Surely we will exhaust his goodness, won't we? Never. We will at some point write one too many checks on his mercy and love, correct? Incorrect. His grace and goodness, his love and mercy are without end.

You Are Never Alone

Turn to Jesus

*[Jesus] said to Philip, "Where shall we buy
bread for these people to eat?"*

JOHN 6:5

In an event crafted to speak to the anxious heart, Jesus told his disciples to do the impossible: feed five thousand people. But the disciples could see only the impossibility. Did it occur to any of them to ask Jesus for help?

The stunning answer is no! Rather than count on Christ, they had the audacity to tell the Creator of the world that nothing could be done because there wasn't enough money.

Finally a boy offered his lunch basket to Andrew, who tentatively mentioned the offer to Jesus. You know the rest of the story. The day ended with twelve baskets of leftovers.

You aren't facing five thousand hungry bellies, but you are facing a deadline in two days, a child who is being bullied at school, a spouse intertwined in temptation. On one hand you have a problem. On the other you have a limited quantity of wisdom, energy, patience, or time. This time, instead of starting with what you have, start with Jesus. Before you lash out in fear, look up in faith. Take a moment. Turn to him for help.

Anxious for Nothing

The Rarest of Gifts

She came trembling with fear and knelt down in front of Jesus. Then she told him the whole story.

MARK 5:33 CEV

A desperate woman once came to see Jesus. She was out of doctors, money, and hope. Then Jesus came to town. He was on his way to treat the daughter of the synagogue leader. The crowd was thick, but she was desperate. Threading her arm through the crowd, she reached the hem of his garment. And when she touched the hem of him, the bleeding stopped. "'Who touched me?' Jesus asked" (Luke 8:45). The woman shrank back. But Jesus said it again. And this time she spoke up. She told him the whole story.

How long had it been since someone had listened to her story? Jesus had reason not to do so. The crowd was waiting, a girl was dying, but Jesus? He stopped and listened. The miracle restored her health. The listening restored her dignity. And what he did next, the woman never forgot. He called her "daughter" (Luke 8:48 NKJV). This is the only time in the Gospels that he called a woman by that name.

Do this for someone. Give the rarest of gifts: your full attention.

How Happiness Happens

Because God Loves You

God is love.

1 JOHN 4:8

Someone told you that God loves good people. Wrong. There are no good people.

Someone told you that God loves you if you love him first. Wrong. He loves people who have never thought of him.

Someone told you that God is ticked off, cranky, and vindictive. Wrong. We tend to be ticked off, cranky, and vindictive. But God?

> GOD is sheer mercy and grace;
>> not easily angered, he's rich in love.
> He doesn't endlessly nag and scold,
>> nor hold grudges forever.
> He doesn't treat us as our sins deserve,
>> nor pay us back in full for our wrongs. . .
> As parents feel for their children,
>> GOD feels for those who fear him. (Psalm
>> 103:8–13 MSG)

God loves you, and because he does, you can be assured joy will come.

Unshakable Hope

Resurrection Changed Everything

Death has been swallowed up in victory.

1 CORINTHIANS 15:54

For the Christian, the cemetery is less a place of loss and more a place of gain. The dead in Christ are to be mourned, for sure. But they are also to be envied. Funeral dirges are understandable, but a trumpet blast would be equally appropriate.

Believers hold on to the unshakable hope that hinges on the resurrection of Christ. The Christian hope depends entirely upon the assumption that Jesus Christ died a physical death, vacated an actual grave, and ascended into heaven where he, at this moment, reigns as head of the church.

The resurrection changed everything. And it proves this promise of God: he will reclaim his creation. He is a God of restoration, not destruction. He is a God of *renewal, redemption, regeneration, resur-rection.* God loves to *redo* and *restore.*

Your finest moment will be your final moment! Your death will be swallowed up in victory! Jesus Christ rose from the dead, not just to show you his power but to lead you through the valley of death.

Praying the Promises

Prayer Partner

The LORD is close to everyone who prays to him.

PSALM 145:18 NCV

When we pray for one another, we enter God's workshop, pick up a hammer, and help him accomplish his purposes.

My dad invited my brother and me to do something similar. The idea was born at our kitchen table. My brother was nine years old, and I was six.

As Dad worked on the plans to build a house for our family, we stood on tiptoe and peered over his shoulder. We peppered him with suggestions. Maybe a big window in the living room or a swing set in the kitchen.

"You boys want to help me?" he asked.

Does a one-legged duck swim in circles? Do fish get wet? Of course we wanted to help! And so it was that my brother and I pedaled our bikes to the construction project on Alamosa Street every day after school. Elementary school seemed so elementary. Who had time for math and spelling? I needed to load kitchen tiles and pick up stray nails. I wasn't just a kid in grade school. I was a partner with my papa.

Our heavenly Father has invited us to be his partner too.

Dare we accept the invitation?

How Happiness Happens

You Say, "Wonderful!"

The right word spoken at the right time is as
beautiful as gold apples in a silver bowl.

PROVERBS 25:11 NCV

A little boy said these words to his father: "Dad, let's play darts. I'll throw, and you say, 'Wonderful!'" Every person needs to hear a "wonderful." Here is why. A *discouragement* conspiracy is afoot. Companies spend billions of dollars to convince us that we are deficient. To sell new clothes, they pronounce that our clothes are out of fashion. To sell hair color, they must persuade us that our hair is dingy. Marketing companies deploy the brightest minds to convince us that we are chubby, smelly, ugly, and out-of-date. We are under attack!

Psychologist Dr. Barbara Fredrickson asserts that positive emotions allow us to see the bigger picture. By opening up the mind, positive emotions help us strengthen our relationships and even improve our physical health because they increase our energy. In contrast, negative emotions contract our mindsets.[2] Stated differently, "people have a way of becoming what you encourage them to be—not what you nag them to be."[3]

How Happiness Happens

The Grace You've Been Given

"Love your enemies! Do good to those who hate you."

LUKE 6:27 NLT

You've not been sprinkled with forgiveness. You've not been spattered with grace. You've been immersed in forgiveness, submerged in grace. Can you, standing as you are, shoulder-high in God's ocean of grace, not fill a cup and offer the happiness of forgiveness to others?

During the season I wrote these words, the world watched in horror as twenty-one Christians were martyred for their faith by ISIS terrorists. Two of the slain men were brothers. In an interview, a third brother was asked about the loss of his siblings. He said, "ISIS helped us strengthen our faith. I thank ISIS because they didn't cut the audio when [my brothers] screamed declaring their faith."

He was asked what his mother would do if she saw the ISIS member who killed her sons. He replied, "She said she would invite him home because he helped us enter the kingdom of heaven. These were my mother's words."[4]

Let's do likewise. Happiness happens when you offer to others the grace you've been given.

How Happiness Happens

In Need of Rescuing

Surely God is my salvation; I will trust and not be afraid. The LORD, the LORD himself, is my strength and my defense; he has become my salvation.

ISAIAH 12:2

Father, our world seems increasingly evil, and we are in need of rescuing. And like you did in the days of Noah, you have provided a vessel of escape for all of your children through Jesus. You care for your children so much that you sent your own Son to dwell among us so that we might be reconciled to you through grace.

Help me rely on your promise of grace because I have been found righteous through Jesus. When troubles come, use those troubles to increase my faith and draw me nearer to you.

Each step and breath I take is because of the grace you have given me. It is the greatest gift I will ever receive. I am in awe that when I was in trouble, you came near. Amen.

Praying the Promises

He Is Still the Great I AM

"Don't be afraid, I've redeemed you. I've called your name.
You're mine. When you're in over your head, I'll be there
with you. When you're in rough waters, you will not go
down. . . . I am God, your personal God, The Holy of
Israel, your Savior. . . . So don't be afraid: I'm with you."

ISAIAH 43:1–3, 5 MSG

The promise of Isaiah 43 is yours to cherish.

Don't try to weather the storms of life alone. Row the boat and bail the water, but above all bid Christ to enter your sinking craft. Believe that you are never alone, that our miracle-working God sees you, cares about you, and will come to your aid. For all you know, he may perform an immediate deliverance. You may reach your destination before you have a chance to wipe the rain off your face.

He is still the great I AM. When you find yourself in the midst of wind-whipped Galilean waters with no shore in sight, he will come to you. The next time you pray, *Is anyone coming to help me?* listen for the response of Jesus: the Lord, the great I AM, is with you in the storm.

You Are Never Alone

Your Inheritance

Since we are his children, we are his heirs. In fact,
together with Christ we are heirs of God's glory.

ROMANS 8:17 NLT

Sixty-year-old Timothy Henry Gray's body was found under an overpass in 2012. He was just a homeless cowboy who had died of hypothermia, except for this detail: as heir to the founder of Las Vegas, he stood to inherit millions of dollars.[5]

How does the heir to a fortune die like a pauper? Surely Timothy Gray knew his family history. Did it ever occur to him to investigate a potential inheritance?

Let's talk about your inheritance. Glistening in the jewel box of God's promises to you is a guarantee that you are an heir of God and coheir with Christ.

You aren't merely a slave, servant, or saint of God. No, you are a child of God. You have legal right to the family business and fortune of heaven. The will has been executed. The courts have been satisfied. Your spiritual account has been funded.

You don't have to sleep under the overpass anymore. It's time for you to live out of your inheritance.

Unshakable Hope

Grace Calms the Soul

God's readiness to give and forgive is now
public. Salvation's available for everyone!

TITUS 2:11 MSG

I can bear witness to the power of grace. I could take you to the city, to the church within the city, to the section of seats within the church auditorium. I might be able to find the very seat in which I was sitting when grace found me. I was a twenty-year-old college sophomore. For four years I had lived with the concrete block of guilt, not just from a first night of drunkenness but also a hundred more like it. The guilt had made a mess of my life, and I was headed toward a lifetime of misery. But then I heard a preacher do for me what I'm attempting to do for you: describe the divine grace that is greater than sin. When at the end of the message he asked if anyone would like to come forward and receive this grace, iron chains could not have held me back. Truth be told, chains had held me back. But mercy snapped the guilt chains and set me free. I know this truth firsthand: guilt frenzies the soul; grace calms it.

Anxious for Nothing

The Antidote

*With humility consider one another as
more important than yourselves.*

PHILIPPIANS 2:3 NASB

Not long ago, a Christian conference was being held in our city. One of the keynote speakers canceled at the eleventh hour. I received a call from the organizers. Could I fill the slot?

May I confess my first thought? *Me fill in for someone else? Me, your second choice? Your backup plan? Your plan B?* I declined the offer. My reaction was self-centered and nauseating.

Mark it down. When ministry becomes vain ambition, nothing good happens. Jesus does not get served. No wonder Paul was so insistent: "Do nothing from selfishness" (Philippians 2:3).

I am not God's MVP. You are not God's VIP.

We are not God's gift to humanity. He loves us and indwells us and has great plans for us. God can use each of us, but he doesn't need any of us.

What gift are you giving that he did not first give? What are you doing for God that God could not do alone?

How kind of him to use us.

How Happiness Happens

When Worship Happens

"Blessed is the king who comes in the name of the Lord!"

LUKE 19:38

The word *worship* actually evolved from the Old English word *weorthscipe.* "To worship, then, is to ascribe worth to someone or something."[6]

Worship happens anytime you turn your heart toward heaven and say, "You are worthy." When you clear your calendar for prayer, turn the radio dial to praise music, or use your morning jog to recite Bible verses or your lunch break to meditate, this is worship.

Worship happens in neighborhoods, in living rooms, in open pastures. And, yes, worship happens in churches. When the people of God make a public and plural declaration of God's goodness, worship is happening.

Perhaps you are wondering, *But what if I don't worship?* Oh, but you will. The question is not, Will you worship? The question is, Where will you direct your worship?

Give Jesus the gift the angels gave him, the gift of praise. Don the robe of grace, soar on wings of faith, and take your place in the heavenly chorus and sing, "Glory to God in the highest" (Luke 2:14 TLB).

Because of Bethlehem

The Debt You Owe

*There is now no condemnation for
those who are in Christ Jesus.*

ROMANS 8:1

The algebra of heaven reads something like this: heaven is a per-fect place for perfect people, which leaves us in a perfect mess. According to heaven's debt clock, we owe more than we could ever repay. And every day brings more sin and more debt.

This realization sends some people into a frenzy of good works. Life becomes an unending quest to do enough, be better, accomplish more. Yet deep within is the gnawing fear, *What if, having done all that, I've not done enough?*

Other people respond to the list not with activity but with unbelief. They throw up their hands and walk away exasperated. No God would demand so much. He must not exist. If he does exist, he is not worth knowing.

Two extremes. The legalist and the atheist. The worker desperate to impress God. The unbeliever convinced there is no God. Can you relate to either of the two? Are despair and disbelief the only options?

As you look up at the debt you can never pay, let this promise be declared: "There is now no condemnation for those who are in Christ Jesus."

Unshakable Hope

273

You Are Stronger Than You Think

Jesus told him, "Stand up, pick up your mat, and walk!"

JOHN 5:8 NLT

Life feels stuck when you make no progress. When you battle the same discouragement you faced a decade ago or struggle with the same fears you faced a year ago. When you wake up to the same hang-ups and habits.

If that is you, then pay attention to the promise of this miracle at the pool of Bethesda (John 5). This Bethesda of your life? Others avoid you because of it. Jesus walks toward you in the midst of it and says, "Stand up, pick up your mat, and walk!"

Stand up. Do something. Take action. Write a letter. Apply for the job. Reach out to a counselor. Get help.

Pick up your mat. Make a clean break with the past. Clean out your liquor cabinet. Drop the boyfriend. Put porn filters on your phone and computer. Talk to a debt counselor.

And *walk.* Lace up your boots and hit the trail. Set your sights on a new destination.

Believe in the Jesus who believes in you. You are stronger than you think.

You Are Never Alone

The Society of Seekers

He bent over and looked in at the strips of
linen lying there but did not go in.

JOHN 20:5

It might surprise you to know how often I have wrestled with doubts. You might defrock me if you knew how many times I have thought something like *Is this truly true?*

The hinge on the door called Gospel is a story about a dead man who stopped being dead, a buried man who unburied himself, a human heart that went stone-statue still for three days and then began pumping blood.

Be honest now. Does it not on occasion sound a bit far-fetched?

For some of you the answer is no. Your faith is sequoia strong.

Others of us, however, have to work through it. We have legitimate questions concerning Christianity. If this describes you, let me welcome you to the Society of Seekers. Let me assure you, it is permissible to have doubts.

Jesus welcomes an honest examination of the resurrection claim. He invites you to view his resurrected body.

The stone is still rolled back. The head cloth is still folded. The wrapping is still vacant. Examine the evidence. Look and see if you don't, like John, believe.

You Are Never Alone

Only Us

When God created mankind, he made
them in the likeness of God.

GENESIS 5:1

God created us to be more like him than anything else he made. He never declared, "Let us make oceans in our image" or "birds in our likeness." The heavens above reflect the glory of God, but they are not made in the image of God. Yet we are.

To be clear: No one is a god except in his or her own delusion. But everyone carries some of the communicable attributes of God. Wisdom. Love. Grace. Kindness. A longing for eternity. These are just some of the attributes that set us apart from the farm animal and suggest that we bear the fingerprints of the Divine Maker. We are made in his image and in his likeness.

We "take after" God in many ways. There is no exception to this promise. Every man and woman, born or preborn, rich or poor, urban or rural, is made in the image of God. Some suppress it. Others enhance it. But all were made in the image of God. Including you and me.

Unshakable Hope

Our Jesus, Our Joy

To me the only important thing about living is
Christ, and dying would be profit for me.

PHILIPPIANS 1:21 NCV

Paul's only aim was to know Jesus. Riches did not attract him. Applause did not matter to him. The grave did not intimidate him. All he wanted was more of Christ. As a result, he was content. In Jesus, Paul found all the satisfaction his heart desired.

You and I can learn the same. Christ-based contentment turns us into strong people. Since no one can take our Christ, no one can take our joy.

Can death take our joy? No, Jesus is greater than death.

Can failure take our joy? No, Jesus is greater than our sin.

Can betrayal take our joy? No, Jesus will never leave us.

Can sickness take our joy? No, God has promised, whether on this side of the grave or the other, to heal us.

Can disappointment take our joy? No, because even though our plans may not work out, we know God's plan will.

Death, failure, betrayal, sickness, disappointment—they cannot take our joy, because they cannot take our Jesus.

Anxious for Nothing

Your Prayers Matter

The eyes of the LORD are on the righteous,
and His ears are open to their cry.

PSALM 34:15 NKJV

If you have taken on the name of Christ, you have clout with the most powerful being in the universe. When you speak, God listens.

Want proof? Consider the story of Elijah. He lived under the rule of the evilest of the monarchs, King Ahab (1 Kings 21:25–26). This was a dark time in the history of Israel. The leaders were corrupt. The people worshipped Baal, a pagan god. But amid the darkness, Elijah appeared. And with a prayer, he proved who the one true God was.

Elijah told the 450 prophets of Baal, "You ask your god to send fire; I'll ask my God to send fire. The God who answers by fire is the true God" (1 Kings 18:24, my paraphrase).

Though the prophets prayed all afternoon, nothing happened. Finally, Elijah asked for his turn. He prayed, and God answered immediately.

God delighted in hearing Elijah's prayer. God delights in hearing yours too. Why? Your prayers matter to God because you matter to God.

Praying the Promises

Catched by Jesus

You are the True God—my shelter, my protector.

PSALM 43:2 THE VOICE

The Drew family was making the short drive from their house to their neighborhood pool when two-year-old Noah opened his door and fell out. Leigh Anna, the mom, felt a bump, as if she had driven over a speed bump, and braked to a quick stop. Her husband, Ben, jumped out of the car and found Noah on the pavement. "He's alive!" Ben shouted and placed him on the seat. Noah's legs were covered in blood, and he was shaking violently.

At the ER, incredibly, the tests showed no broken bones. A five-thousand-pound vehicle had run over his legs, yet little Noah had nothing but cuts and bruises to show for it.

Later that night Leigh Anna dropped to her knees and thanked Jesus for sparing her son. She then stretched out on the bed next to him. As she was lying beside him in the dark, he said, "Mama, Jesus catched me."

She said, "He did?"

Noah replied, "I told Jesus thank you, and he said you're very welcome."[7]

Have you allowed the Savior to catch you?

Anxious for Nothing

Let Love Happen

Christ's love is greater than anyone can ever know,
but I pray that you will be able to know that love.
Then you can be filled with the fullness of God.

EPHESIANS 3:19 NCV

Discover the purest source of happiness, the love of God. A love that is "too wonderful to be measured" (Ephesians 3:19 CEV).

Does God love us because of our goodness? Because of our kindness? Because of our great devotion? No, he loves us because of his goodness, kindness, and great devotion.

The reason God loves you is that he has chosen to love you.

You are loved when you don't feel lovely. You are loved by God even when you are loved by no one else. Others may abandon you, divorce you, and ignore you. God will love you. These are his words: "I'll call nobodies and make them somebodies; I'll call the unloved and make them beloved" (Romans 9:25 MSG).

Let this love happen in your life. Let this love give birth to the greatest joy: "I am beloved by heaven."

We must start here. Settle yourself into the hammock of God's affection. And as you do, to the degree you do, you will give that love to others.

How Happiness Happens

When God Sends Signs

*These are written that you may believe that
Jesus is the Messiah, the Son of God, and that by
believing you may have life in his name.*

JOHN 20:31

People see signs of God every day. Sunsets that steal the breath. Newborns that bring tears. Migrating geese that stir a smile. But do all who see the signs draw near to God? No. Many are content simply to see the signs. They do not realize that the riches of God are intended to turn us toward him. "Perhaps you do not understand that God is kind to you so you will change your hearts and lives" (Romans 2:4 NCV).

The ultimate aim of all God's messages, both miraculous and written, is to shed the light of heaven on Jesus.

When God sends signs, be faithful. Let them lead you to Scripture.

As Scripture directs, be humble. Let it lead you to worship.

And as you worship the Son, be grateful. He will lead you home.

Because of Bethlehem

A Much-Needed Message

*Jesus went around doing good and healing all who
were oppressed by the devil, for God was with him.*

ACTS 10:38 NLT

Each and every one of Jesus' miracles was an act of kindness. Someone benefited. All these events stand together as one voice, calling on you to lift your eyes and open your heart to the possibility—indeed, the reality—that the greatest force in the universe is one who means you well and brings you hope.

John recorded the miracles of Jesus not to impress us but to urge us to believe not only in the divinity of Christ but also in the tender presence of Christ. This montage of miracles proclaims, God's got this! Think it's up to you and you ain't much? Hogwash. God can carry you.

Jesus touched wounds. He spoke words of hope. Lives were improved. Blessings were bestowed. There was more to his miracles than the miracle itself. There was a message of tenderness: "I am here. I care."

You're stronger than you think because God is nearer than you know.

You Are Never Alone

Upon This Rock

Jesus replied, "Blessed are you, Simon son of Jonah, for this was not revealed to you by flesh and blood, but by my Father in heaven."

MATTHEW 16:17

In Matthew 16, Jesus asked his followers a critical question: "Who do you say that I am?" Peter gave his answer: "You are the Christ, the Son of the living God" (Matthew 16:15–16 NKJV).

Every good Hebrew knew the Christ was coming. Someone greater than Abraham, mightier than Moses, a prophet higher than Elijah. The Christ, by definition, means the "ultimate one." He wasn't the final word; he was the only Word.

Jesus, in Peter's confession, was this Christ.

"On this rock I will build My church," was Jesus' reply (Matthew 16:18 NKJV). What is the rock he was referring to? What Peter had just confessed—the belief that Jesus was the Messiah.

Rulers will come and go. But the church of Jesus Christ, built on the person of Jesus, will prevail.

Because in the midst of all this world's chaos, there is Jesus Christ and his question: "Who do you say that I am?" And there is Jesus Christ and his vow: "I will build My church."

Praying the Promises

The USS *Forgiveness*

Be kind to each other, tenderhearted, forgiving one another, just as God through Christ has forgiven you.

EPHESIANS 4:32 NLT

Some people abandon the path of forgiveness because they perceive it to be impossibly steep. So let's be realistic about the act. Forgiveness does not pardon, excuse, or ignore the offense. Forgiveness is not necessarily reconciliation. A reestablished relationship with the transgressor is not essential or always even possible.

Forgiveness is simply the act of changing your attitude toward the offender; it's moving from a desire to harm toward an openness to be at peace. A step in the direction of forgiveness is also a decisive step toward happiness.

It's no wonder then that the flotilla of "one another" scriptures includes one named the USS *Forgiveness*. "Be kind to each other, tenderhearted, forgiving one another, just as God through Christ has forgiven you."

It was not enough for the apostle Paul to say, "Forgive one another as your conscience dictates." Or "to the degree that you feel comfortable." No, Paul did what he loved to do: he used Jesus as our standard. Forgive others as Christ forgave you.

How Happiness Happens

Trust God's Promises

*You are faithful to your promises, O my
God. I will sing praises to you.*

PSALM 71:22 NLT

The heroes in the Bible came from all walks of life: rulers, servants, teachers, doctors. They were male, female, single, and married. Yet one common denominator united them: they built their lives on the promises of God. Because of God's promises, Abraham left a good home for one he'd never seen. Because of God's promises, Joshua led two million people into enemy territory. Because of God's promises, David conked a giant, Peter rose from the ashes of regret, and Paul found a grace worth dying for.

One writer went so far as to call such saints "heirs of the promise" (Hebrews 6:17 NASB). It is as if the promise was the family fortune, and they were smart enough to attend the reading of the will.

Hebrews 11 offers up a list of these "heirs." Jacob trusted God's promises. Joseph trusted God's promises. Moses trusted God's promises. Their stories were different, but the theme was the same: God's promises were polestars in their pilgrimages of faith. They had plenty of promises from which to pick. And so do we.

Unshakable Hope

October

God Muddied His Feet

*Let us, then, feel very sure that we can come
before God's throne where there is grace.*

HEBREWS 4:16 NCV

O n a trip to Israel my family and I stopped to see the traditional spot of Jesus' baptism. It's a charming place. The water invites. So I accepted the invitation and waded in to be baptized.

I declared my belief in Christ and sank so low in the water I could touch the river bottom. When I did, I felt a stick and pulled it out. A baptism memento! Some people get certificates or Bibles; I like my stick. I keep it on my office credenza so I can show it to fear-filled people.

When they chronicle their anxieties about the economy or their kids, I hand them the stick. I tell them how God muddied his feet in our world of diapers, death, digestion, and disease. How he came to earth for this very purpose—to become one of us. "Why, he might have touched this very stick," I like to say.

As they smile, I ask, "Since he came this far to reach us, can't we take our fears to him?"

Unshakable Hope

Sovereign of All

You alone are the LORD; You have made heaven, the heaven of heavens, with all their host, the earth and everything on it, the seas and all that is in them, and You preserve them all.

NEHEMIAH 9:6 NKJV

God, I believe you are sovereign over my life. You made the heavens and the earth and all that is in them. You are Alpha and Omega, the beginning and end. You are outside of time. You know everything that will happen, and you have planned it according to your purpose and will.

It is not always easy for me to trust in your sovereignty. I sometimes wonder if you care about me and what's happening in my life. Forgive me, Father, for times when I doubt your ways and your goodness. Restore my faith in you when it is weak.

Guide me during the difficult times. Give me hope as I pray and wait. Remind me of your power and authority so that I will trust your ways, even when I can't see where the path before me is going.

I am so grateful that you are in control. Amen.

Praying the Promises

The Ice Cream Truck

Therefore, whenever we have the opportunity, we should do good to everyone—especially to those in the family of faith.

GALATIANS 6:10 NLT

I have a challenge for you. Start this day by asking, *Whom can I help today? Which person can I encourage? Who needs a little sunshine?*

Maybe the new employee who occupies the cubicle down the hall. Or the neighbor whose Chihuahua wanders into your yard. Or your teacher. The one who sucks lemons for breakfast and devours students for lunch. Look for ways to lift her spirits, brighten her day, compliment her, understand her, thank her. Will the world be different because you tried?

You bet it will.

You will become the equivalent of an ice cream truck in your world. An ice cream truck used to visit my childhood neighborhood. When I heard the clanking music of the truck, I knew what to do. I wasn't alone. Kids came from everywhere. They pedaled their bikes or just ran like crazy. The ice cream truck was in the neighborhood.

Be that ice cream truck. Be the person that people are glad to see. And see if you aren't the one smiling the most.

How Happiness Happens

A New Chapter

The peace of God, which surpasses all understanding, will guard your hearts and minds through Christ Jesus.

PHILIPPIANS 4:7 NKJV

C ould you use some calm? If so, you aren't alone. The Bible is Kindle's most highlighted book. And Philippians 4:6–7 is the most highlighted passage.[1] Apparently we all could use a word of comfort.

God is ready to give it.

With God as your helper, you will sleep better tonight and smile more tomorrow. You'll learn how to view bad news through the lens of sovereignty, discern the lies of Satan, and tell yourself the truth. You will discover a life that is characterized by calm.

It will require some work on your part. Anxiety cannot be waved away with a simple pep talk. In fact, for some of you, God's healing will include the help of therapy and/or medication. Ask God to lead you to the treatment you need.

This much is sure: God made you for more than a life of mind-splitting worry. He has a new chapter for your life. And he is ready to write it.

Anxious for Nothing

Whatever He Tells You

"Dear woman, that's not our problem," Jesus
replied. "My time has not yet come."

JOHN 2:4 NLT

Early in his ministry, Jesus went to a wedding. His to-do list that day did not contain the entry "Turn water into wine." Angels were not lining up to watch miracle #1 because, as far as the Angelic Committee on Initial Miracles was concerned, the moment of the maiden miracle was scheduled for a later date.

Hence, Mary's petition was met with Jesus' hesitation.

You've heard the same. In your personal version of verse 3, you explained your shortage: no more wine, time, vigor, or vision. And then came verse 4. Silence. Quiet as a library at midnight. When no answer comes, how does your verse 5 read?

Mary's verse 5 reads like this: "Do whatever he tells you" (John 2:5 NLT).

Translation? "Jesus is in charge. I'm not." "He runs the world. I don't." "I trust Jesus. Whatever he tells you to do, do it."

Something in the explicit faith of Mary caused Jesus to change his agenda.

So make your request, and trust him to do not what you want but what is best.

You Are Never Alone

A Holy List

"The Helper, the Holy Spirit, whom the Father will send in My name, He will teach you all things, and bring to your remembrance all things that I said to you."

JOHN 14:26 NKJV

I used to know a fellow who supervised an apartment complex. When I asked him to describe his job, he said, "I keep the place running." The Holy Spirit does the same and more for the church. Want to see his to-do list?

- Comfort the believers (Acts 9:31).
- Reveal the things that are still to come (John 16:13).
- Offer prayers of intercession (Romans 8:26).
- Attest to the presence of God with signs and miracles (Hebrews 2:4; 1 Corinthians 2:4; Romans 15:18–19).
- Create a godlike atmosphere of truth (John 14:16–17), wisdom (Deuteronomy 34:9; Isaiah 11:2), and freedom (2 Corinthians 3:17).

The list of the Spirit's activities is varied, wonderful, and incomplete without this word: *holy.*

Unshakable Hope

Love One Another

I am writing to remind you, dear friends,
that we should love one another.

2 JOHN 1:5 NLT

I find at least eleven appearances of the "love one another" admonition in the Bible. The Greek word used for *love* (*agape*) in these passages denotes an unselfish affection.[2] Agape love writes the check when the balance is low, forgives the mistake when the offense is high, offers patience when stress is abundant, and extends kindness when kindness is rare. "For God so loved [*agapaó*] the world that he gave his one and only Son" (John 3:16). The agape tree is rooted in the soil of devotion. But don't think for a moment that its fruit is sour. A sweet happiness awaits those who are willing to care for the orchard.

Do you find such love difficult to muster? Scarce? If so, you may be missing a step. Love for others begins not by giving love but by receiving the love of Christ.

Do you need to start there today?

How Happiness Happens

Contingent Contentment

I have learned the secret of being content . . .
whether in abundance or in need.

PHILIPPIANS 4:12 HCSB

D oes your happiness depend on what you drive? Wear? Deposit? Spray on? If so, you have entered the rat race called materialism.

The cycle is predictable. You assume, *If I get a car, I'll be happy.* The car wears out, so you look for joy elsewhere. *If I get married . . . If we can have a baby . . . If I get the new job . . . If I can retire . . .* In each case joy comes, then diminishes. By the time you reach old age, life has repeatedly let you down. Contingent contentment turns us into wounded, worried people.

Paul advances a healthier strategy. He learned to be content with what he had. Which is remarkable since he had a jail cell instead of a house, chains instead of jewelry, a guard instead of a wife. How could he be content?

Simple. He focused on a different list. He had Christ, and Christ was enough. What he had in Christ was far greater than what he didn't have in life. Here's a suggestion: challenge yourself to say the same.

Anxious for Nothing

What Can You Do Today?

"Would you like to get well?"

JOHN 5:6 NLT

Jesus was drawn to the hurting, and one particular day he was drawn to the pool of Bethesda. His eyes landed upon a man who "had been sick for thirty-eight years. When Jesus saw him and knew he had been ill for a long time, he asked him, 'Would you like to get well?'" (John 5:5–6 NLT).

Why would Jesus pose such a question? Our only clue is the phrase "When Jesus saw him and knew he had been ill for a long time." And the response of the man convinces me: "'I can't, sir,' the sick man said, 'for I have no one to put me into the pool when the water bubbles up'" (v. 7 NLT).

Really? *No one* will help you? Thirty-eight years and absolutely no progress? In that context Christ's question takes on a firm tone: *Do you want to get well?* Or do you like being sick?

That's the question Christ asked then. That's the question Christ asks all of us.

Answer by asking the Lord a question of your own: What can I do today that will take me in the direction of a better tomorrow?

You Are Never Alone

The Prayer of Faith

Look to the LORD and his strength; seek his face always.

1 CHRONICLES 16:11

Dennis McDonald was our church's hospital chaplain for many years. On occasions I accompanied him when he visited the sick. I was always struck by the transformation that came over him. We might be walking down a hospital hallway, chatting about the weather, but when we entered the room, he went to work. He walked directly to the side of the hospital bed and leaned over until he was only inches from the face of the infirm. And he would say something like "I am Dennis, and I am here to pray for you and encourage you. God is greater than your sickness. God can heal your body. God will get you through this."

Dennis would then anoint the sick person with oil and pray, "Lord, this is your servant, whom you love and whom we love. Let your healing happen in this room. Satan, you must leave. You're a liar, and your words have no merit. This child is bought by God. We pray in Jesus' name, amen."

The prayer of faith invites God to be God, to be sovereign over a tumultuous time. Be bold in your prayers.

How Happiness Happens

God Keeps His Promises

What he says he will do, he does.

NUMBERS 23:19 NCV

One student of Scripture spent a year and a half attempting to tally the number of promises God has made to humanity. He came up with 7,487 promises![3] God's promises are pine trees in the Rocky Mountains of Scripture: abundant, unbending, and perennial. Some of the promises are positive, the assurance of blessings. Some are negative, the guarantee of consequences. But all are binding, for not only is God a promise maker; God is a promise keeper.

As God was preparing the Israelites to face a new land, he made a promise to them.

> Then the LORD said: "I am making a covenant with you. Before all your people I will do wonders never before done in any nation in all the world." (Exodus 34:10)

God did not emphasize the Israelites' strength. He emphasized his. He did not underscore their ability. He highlighted his. He equipped them for the journey by headlining his capacity to make and keep his promises.

He is the same God today. And he still keeps his promises.

Unshakable Hope

God's Playbook

Jesus performed many other signs in the presence of his disciples, which are not recorded in this book.

JOHN 20:30

Picture the aged apostle John as he shares the stories of Jesus. He's an old man. But his eyes are full of hope. He pastors a collection of Christ followers in Ephesus. He loves to tell—and they love to hear—about the day Jesus invited him to lay down the fishing net and follow him.

And John, likely knowing his days are coming to an end, takes on one final task. He seeks to tell stories Matthew, Luke, and Mark didn't and to add details to stories they told.

Before John is done, he'll lead us through two cemeteries and near one cross and invite us to eavesdrop on a breakfast chat that changed the life of an apostle. John's chosen miracles run the gamut from a wedding oversight to a violent execution, from empty bellies to empty dreams, from abandoned hopes to buried friends. And we will be careful, oh so careful, to see the signs not as entries in a history book but as samples from God's playbook.

It's the playbook for a game he's already won. For you.

You Are Never Alone

The Great Poet of Grace

All these things that I once thought very worthwhile—
now I've thrown them all away so that I can
put my trust and hope in Christ alone.

PHILIPPIANS 3:7 TLB

No one had more reason to feel the burden of guilt than Paul did. He had orchestrated the deaths of Christians. He was an ancient version of a terrorist, taking believers into custody and then spilling their blood (Acts 8:1–3 TLB).

In addition, he was a legalist to the core. Before he knew Christ, Paul had spent a lifetime trying to save himself. His salvation depended on his perfection, on his performance (Philippians 3:4–6).

Paul had blood on his hands and religious diplomas on his wall.

But then came the Damascus road moment. Jesus appeared. Once Paul saw Jesus, he couldn't see anymore. He couldn't see merit in his merits or worth in his good works anymore. He couldn't see reasons to boast about anything he had done anymore. And he couldn't see any option except to spend the rest of his life talking less about himself and more about Jesus.

He became the great poet of grace. Care to pen a few lines of your own?

Anxious for Nothing

Never Unloved

Give thanks to the God of heaven. His love continues forever.

PSALM 136:26 NCV

I read a story about a priest who was walking the shores of a lake with his uncle. They watched the sun rise, and for a full twenty minutes the two men scarcely spoke. As they resumed their walk, the priest noticed his uncle was smiling.

"Uncle Seamus," he said, "you look very happy."

"I am."

"How come?"

"The Father of Jesus is very fond of me."[4]

He's fond of you, too, dear friend.

Do you find this hard to believe? You think I'm talking to someone else? Someone who is holier, better, nicer? Someone who didn't screw up his marriage or mess up her career? Someone who didn't get hooked on pills or porn or popularity?

I'm not. I'm talking directly to you. I'm saying the greatest news in the world is not that God made the world but that God loves the world. He loves you, and his love for you will not fade if you lose your way.

You have never lived one unloved day.

Unshakable Hope

Longer, Daddy, Longer

*Look for the best in each other, and always
do your best to bring it out.*

1 THESSALONIANS 5:15 MSG

John Trent recalls a story about a young father whose daughter was going through the "terrible twos." The father decided to take the child out for breakfast and tell her how much they valued and loved her. Over pancakes he told her, "Jenny, I want you to know how much I love you, and how special you are to Mom and me. We couldn't be more proud of you."

When he finished, his daughter said, "Longer, Daddy . . . longer." The father continued to affirm and encourage her. Once again when he attempted to stop, she pleaded for him to keep going. "This father never did get much to eat that morning, but his daughter got the emotional nourishment she needed so much."[5]

Do you know someone who needs unbridled encouragement? Of course you do. Everyone needs a cheerleader. So be one.

How Happiness Happens

Facing Goliath

The LORD your God, who goes before you, He will fight for you, according to all He did for you in Egypt before your eyes.

DEUTERONOMY 1:30 NKJV

The behemoth Goliath grunted one final boast. Scrawny David loaded a single stone. Goliath raised his sword. The shepherd swung his sling. The battle was over before it began. Goliath went down. And when he did, the Philistine army ran. The Israelites, suddenly infused with courage, overtook their enemies, and a new day began for Israel.

All because David knew this: the battle was the Lord's.

Who is your Goliath? What giant seeks to liposuction the life out of your life? Does he come in the form of a disease? Is he wearing the garb of debt? Or defeat? One put-down after another?

"Our God will fight for us" (Nehemiah 4:20 NKJV).

Lay claim to this great and powerful promise. It's not just you and Goliath. You aren't alone in your struggles. The next time you hear the bully of the valley snort and strut, you remind yourself and him, "This battle belongs to the Lord."

Praying the Promises

Jesus Comes in the Storm

"It is I; don't be afraid."

JOHN 6:20

By the time Nika Maples was admitted into the ICU, doctors were beginning to fear for her survival. Lupus had ravaged her body, slurred her speech, and blurred her sight. On one particularly difficult night, she couldn't sleep at all. Nika began to pray: *God, I need you. I can't go to sleep tonight . . . Will you please send someone to hold my hand?*

Minutes passed slowly, and then someone walked into the room.

"His steps made no noise. . . . [He] took my right hand, holding it warmly. I tried to open my eyes, but could not."

Nika drifted off to sleep. When she awoke, he was still holding her hand. Nika tried again to open her eyes to see her new friend. This time she succeeded. No one was there. At that moment the pressure on her hand was gone.

She is convinced Christ was with her.[6]

He did for her what he did for the disciples. He came for her in the storm.

He will come for you too.

Unshakable Hope

What Do We Do with a Levi?

*Accept one another, then, just as Christ accepted
you, in order to bring praise to God.*

ROMANS 15:7

One of the most difficult relationship questions is "What do we
do with a Levi?"

Your Levi is the person with whom you fundamentally disagree.
You adhere to different codes of behavior, dress, and faith.

You drive a hybrid; he chugs around in a gas-guzzling truck.

You vote red, and she likes donkeys.

You love your husband, and she lives with her wife.

Your Levi is your "opposite you." "Opposite yous" can drain
your joy tank. There is a tension, an awkwardness. Anger can flare.
Inability to manage the relationship can lead to isolation, prejudice,
and bigotry.

How does God want us to respond to the Levis of the world? I
wonder if the best answer might be found in this short admonition:
"Accept one another, then, just as Christ accepted you, in order to
bring praise to God."

Accept one another. Because isn't that what Jesus does for us?

How Happiness Happens

A Sacred Moment

Jesus said, "It is finished." With that, he bowed his head and gave up his spirit.

JOHN 19:30

With a single proclamation Jesus fed more than a crowd, stilled more than a storm, and gave sight to more than one man. His announcement on Calvary was sufficient to save all who believe in him from eternal death.

The announcement? *Tetelestai.* "It is finished." This is a holy word, a sacred moment.

The artist steps back from the canvas and lowers his brush.

It is finished.

The poet reads his sonnet one final time and then places his pen on the desk.

It is finished.

The farmer gazes out over the just-harvested field, removes his hat, and wipes his brow.

It is finished.

Jesus opens his swollen eyes and looks toward the heavens. His burning lungs issue enough air for him to announce, "It is finished."

On Calvary Jesus didn't heal a servant with a proclamation; he healed all generations with an affirmation.

You Are Never Alone

If You're Seeking Joy

*My children, we should love people not only with words
and talk, but by our actions and true caring.*

1 JOHN 3:18 NCV

Patty was the picture of unselfishness. It's impossible to imagine how many kids she hugged, diapers she changed, children she taught, and hearts she encouraged.

Three months earlier a brain condition had left her unable to speak, partially paralyzed, and living in a rehabilitation center. Her spirits sank so low she did not want to eat and had trouble sleeping. One evening her daughter had an idea. She placed her mother in a wheelchair and rolled her from room to room, looking for people who needed encouragement. It didn't take long.

Though unable to speak, Patty could touch and pray. So she did both. She patted other patients and then placed her hand on their hearts and bowed her head. For the better part of the evening, she touched and prayed her way through the rehab center. That night her appetite returned, and she slept peacefully.

The words of Jesus are spot-on: "It is more blessed to give than to receive" (Acts 20:35 NKJV). Because when you do, it has a boomerang effect.

How Happiness Happens

Because God Is Near

The LORD is with me; I will not be afraid.
What can mere mortals do to me?

PSALM 118:6

D o not assume God is merely watching from a distance. Avoid the quicksand that bears the marker "God has left you!" Do not indulge this lie. If you do, your problem will be amplified by a sense of loneliness. It's one thing to face a challenge, but to face it all alone? Isolation creates a downward cycle of fret. Choose instead to be the person who clutches the presence of God with both hands.

Because the Lord is near, we can be anxious for nothing. This is Paul's point in Philippians 4. Remember, he was writing a letter. He did not use chapter and verse numbers. This system was created by scholars in the thirteenth and sixteenth centuries. The structure helps us, but it can also hinder us. The apostle intended the words of verses 5 and 6 to be read in one fell swoop. "The Lord is near; [consequently,] do not be anxious about anything."

We can calmly take our concerns to God because he is as near as our next breath!

Anxious for Nothing

God Gets Us

Christ was revealed in a human body and vindicated by the Spirit. He was seen by angels and announced to the nations. He was believed in throughout the world and taken to heaven in glory.

1 TIMOTHY 3:16 NLT

Our God gets us. Theology textbooks discuss this promise under the heading "Incarnation." The stunning idea is simply this: God, for a time, became one of us.

God became flesh in the form of Jesus Christ. He was miraculously conceived, yet naturally delivered. He was born, yet born of a virgin.

Had Jesus simply descended to earth in the form of a mighty being, we would respect him but never would draw near to him. After all, how could God understand what it means to be human?

Had Jesus been biologically conceived with two earthly parents, we would draw near to him, but would we want to worship him? After all, he would be no different than you and me.

But if Jesus was both—God and man at the same time—then we have the best of both worlds. Neither his humanity nor deity compromised. He was fully human. He was fully divine. Because of the first, we draw near. Because of the latter, we worship.

Unshakable Hope

Greeting Jesus

"The King will reply, 'Truly I tell you, whatever
you did for one of the least of these brothers
and sisters of mine, you did for me.'"

MATTHEW 25:40

Were Jesus to enter a room, every eye would turn and every person would stand. We'd wait in line for the chance to hold his hands and touch his feet. No one would miss the opportunity to welcome our Savior.

According to Jesus we have that opportunity every day. The nervous teenager in the back of the class? When you greet him, you greet Jesus. The single parent who works down the hall? As you make her feel welcome, you make Jesus feel the same. The elderly woman at the grocery store? As you open the door for her, you open the door for Christ.

By the way, the greatest greeting in history has yet to be given. And you can be certain that salutation won't be heard over a phone or through an email. The greatest of greetings will be issued by Jesus to you in person. "You did well. You are a good and loyal servant. Because you were loyal with small things, I will let you care for much greater things. Come and share my joy with me" (Matthew 25:23 NCV).

Greet one another for your sake.

How Happiness Happens

Who's in Your Boat?

*Then they were glad to take him into the boat. At once the
boat came to land at the place where they wanted to go.*

JOHN 6:21 NCV

We'd rather be spared the storms of life. Or if a storm comes, let it be mild and our deliverance quick. Let the application rejection lead to acceptance at a better college. Let the job dismissal come with a severance package and an offer of a better position. Let the marital strife turn quickly into romance.

Sometimes it does.

But when it doesn't, when we are thorax-deep in turbulence, Jesus wants us to know his name and hear him say, "I AM coming." Such was the experience of the storm-tossed disciples battling the wind and waves. The moment they invited Christ into their boat was the moment they reached their destination. "So they gladly took him aboard, and at once the boat reached the shore they were making for" (John 6:21 PHILLIPS).

Follow the example of the disciples. Welcome Jesus into the midst of your turbulent times.

Don't let the storm turn you inward. Let it turn you upward.

You Are Never Alone

Things Above

Set your mind on things above, not on things on the earth.

COLOSSIANS 3:2 NKJV

S et your mind on things above . . ." How might you do this?
A friend recently described to me her daily ninety-minute commute.

"Ninety minutes!" I commiserated.

"Don't feel sorry for me." She smiled. "I use the trip to think about God." She went on to describe how she fills the hour and a half with worship and sermons. She listens to entire books of the Bible. She recites prayers. By the time she reaches her place of employment, she is ready for the day. "I turn my commute into my chapel."

Is there a block of time you can claim for God? Perhaps you could turn off the network news and open your Bible. Set the alarm fifteen minutes earlier. Or rather than watch the TV as you fall asleep, listen to an audio version of a Christian book. "If you abide in my word, you are truly my disciples, and you will know the truth, and the truth will set you free" (John 8:31–32 ESV). Free from fear. Free from dread. And, yes, free from anxiety.

Set your mind on things above and be set free.

Anxious for Nothing

The Final Score

The God who brings peace will soon defeat
Satan and give you power over him.

ROMANS 16:20 NCV

Being a pastor, I'm often unable to watch the Sunday football games, so I record them. Yet on many Sundays a well-wishing parishioner will learn the outcome of the game and feel the burden to share it with me.

I remember one contest in particular. My beloved Dallas Cowboys were playing a must-win game. I made it as far as the parking lot when an enthusiastic fan shouted out to me, "Max, the Cowboys won!!!"

Grrr.

Even though I knew the outcome, I still wanted to watch the game. As I did, I made a delightful discovery. I could watch stress-free! The Cowboys fumbled the ball, but I didn't panic. I knew the winner. We needed a touchdown in the final minute. No problem. The victory was certain.

So is yours. Between now and the final whistle, you will have reason to be anxious. You are going to fumble the ball. The devil will seem to gain the upper hand. All that is good will appear to lose. But you do not need to worry. You and I know the final score.

Unshakable Hope

The Measure of Success

But the Lord said to her, "My dear Martha, you are worried and upset over all these details! There is only one thing worth being concerned about. Mary has discovered it, and it will not be taken away from her."

LUKE 10:41–42 NLT

It's a slippery slope, this thing of self-promotion. What begins as a desire to serve Christ metastasizes into an act of impressing people. When that happens, gifted Marthas become miserable mumblers. It's easy to see why. If your happiness depends on the applause and approval of others, you'll yo-yo up and down, based on the fickle opinion of people. If noticed, you'll strut. If unnoticed, you'll grumble.

Our generation's fascination with social media has taken addiction to adulation to a whole new level. We measure success in "likes," "retweets," "thumbs-up," and "friends." Self-images rise and fall upon the whim of clicks and Facebook entries. Social media is social comparison on steroids! Does it make sense to hinge your joy on the unpredictable reactions and reviews of people you may not even know? Absolutely not!

Hinge your joy on the one who came to bring joy.

How Happiness Happens

Not Fair

Lord, how long will You look on? Rescue me from their destructions, my precious life from the lions.

PSALM 35:17 NKJV

*I*t's not fair. When did you learn those words? What deed exposed you to the imbalanced scales of life? Did a car wreck leave you fatherless? Did friends forget you, a teacher ignore you, an adult abuse you?

How long will injustice flourish? God's answer is direct: not long.

"Judgment Day" is an unpopular term. We disdain judgment, but we value justice, yet the second is impossible without the first. One can't have justice without judgment. For that reason "we must all appear before the judgment seat of Christ" (2 Corinthians 5:10 NKJV).

From his throne Jesus will forever balance the scales of fairness. He will do so through three declarations: (1) He will publicly pardon his people (Romans 3:23–26). (2) He will applaud the service of his servants (1 Corinthians 4:5). (3) He will honor the wishes of the wicked (Romans 1:24, 26). Justice will prevail.

Remember, God will right all wrongs and heal all wounds. He has prepared a place where life will be finally and forever . . . just.

Praying the Promises

Begin with God

Be careful. Be calm and don't worry.

ISAIAH 7:4 NCV

A person would be hard-pressed to find a more practical, powerful, and inspirational passage on the topic of anxiety than Philippians 4:4–8. Take a peek at this passage, and you'll discover it has the feel of a "decision tree." A decision tree is a tool that uses a treelike graph to show decisions and their possible consequences. Paul's counsel has a similar sequential format.

You already know about the anxie-tree. (See what I did there?) We've spent more than our share of time dangling from its wimpy branches, whipped about by the winds of change and turmoil. On one occasion God sent the prophet Isaiah to soothe the concerns of an anxious king. He and his people were so frightened that "they shook with fear like trees of the forest blown by the wind" (Isaiah 7:2 NCV). Sounds as if they were sitting in a grove of anxie-trees.

The anxie-tree is not the only tree in the orchard. There is a better option: the tranquili-tree. (Aren't I clever?) It is sturdy, shady, and has ample room for you. Here is how you use it.

Begin with God.

Anxious for Nothing

In God's Image

God spoke: "Let us make human beings in our
image, make them reflecting our nature."

GENESIS 1:26 MSG

Some time ago I videotaped a message for our church. We recruited a film crew and drove to the Alamo. We selected a park bench in front of the shrine of Texas liberty, set up the equipment, and got busy.

Four workers managed lights and cameras. I sat on the bench, trying to remember my thoughts. We must have looked official. Passersby began to pause; some started to stare. *Who is that guy?*

One woman's curiosity erupted into a question that she shouted at me from behind the crew. "Are you somebody important?"

Every soul on earth has asked the same question. Not about a redhead on a park bench, mind you, but about themselves.

Am I somebody important?

It's easy to feel anything but important when the corporation sees you as a number, the boyfriend treats you like cattle, your ex takes your energy, or old age takes your dignity. Somebody important? Hardly.

When you struggle with that question, remember this promise of God: you were created by God, in God's image, for God's glory. God made you to reflect the image of God.

Unshakable Hope

Let Us Worship Together

"For where two or three are gathered together in My name, I am there in the midst of them."

MATTHEW 18:20 NKJV

Every generation has its share of "Jesus, yes; church, no" Christians. For a variety of reasons they turn away from church attendance. They do so at a great loss. Something happens in corporate worship that does not happen in private worship. When you see my face in the sanctuary and I hear your voice in the chorus, we are mutually edified. Granted, congregational worship is imperfect. We often sing off-key. Our attention tends to wander. The preacher stumbles over his words, and the organist misses her cue. Even so, let us worship. The sincerity of our worship matters more than the quality. "Let's see how inventive we can be in encouraging love and helping out, not avoiding worshiping together as some do but spurring each other on, especially as we see the big Day approaching" (Hebrews 10:24–25 MSG).

The presence of Christ deserves an abundant chorus. Let us worship together.

Because of Bethlehem

November

With Us Still

The Lord himself will give you a sign: The virgin will conceive and give birth to a son, and will call him Immanuel.

ISAIAH 7:14

You are not alone. You may feel alone. You may think you are alone. But there is never a moment in which you face life without help. God is near.

God repeatedly pledges his proverbial presence to his people.

To Abram, God said, "Do not be afraid. . . . I am your shield, your exceedingly great reward" (Genesis 15:1 NKJV).

To Hagar, the angel announced, "Do not be afraid; God has heard" (Genesis 21:17).

After Moses' death God told Joshua, "Do not be afraid; do not be discouraged, for the LORD your God will be with you wherever you go" (Joshua 1:9).

God was with David, in spite of his adultery. With Jacob, in spite of his conniving. With Elijah, in spite of his lack of faith.

Then, in the ultimate declaration of communion, God called himself Immanuel, which means "God with us." He became flesh. He became sin. He defeated the grave. And he is with us still.

Anxious for Nothing

Don't Skimp

I didn't skimp or trim in any way. Every
truth and encouragement that could have
made a difference to you, you got.

ACTS 20:20 MSG

In the mid-1930s a YMCA instructor pitched an idea for a class to his supervisor. It was based on some principles he had learned while working as a salesman in Warrensburg, Missouri. The directors couldn't afford to pay him the regular two-dollar-a-night fee, so he agreed to teach it on a commission basis.

Within a couple of years the course was so popular the instructor was earning thirty dollars a night instead of two. A publishing executive heard the messages and encouraged the instructor to compile them in a book. Dale Carnegie did. His book *How to Win Friends and Influence People* stayed on the *New York Times* bestseller list for a decade. What is the message of the book? Arguably it can be reduced to one phrase: "Encourage one another."

Here is an idea. Call a friend or relative and begin the conversation with these words: "Can I have a hundred and twenty seconds to tell you what a great person you are?" Then let it loose. Build him up. Drench her in words of encouragement. Don't skimp in any way.

How Happiness Happens

With Jesus by Our Side

We must all appear before the judgment seat of Christ.

2 CORINTHIANS 5:10

That "we" in Paul's letter to the Corinthians includes all humanity. Paul didn't exclude his name from this list, nor can we.

We may want to. Especially when we consider that this will be "the day when God judges people's secrets through Jesus Christ" (Romans 2:16). I don't want you to hear my secret thoughts. I don't want my congregation to know the sermons I dreaded or conversations I avoided. Why will Christ expose every deed and every desire of the Christian heart? For the sake of justice. He must declare each sin forgiven.

God filters his verdict through Jesus. Believers won't stand before the bench alone. Jesus will be at our side. As the sin is disclosed, so is the forgiveness.

"Max lied to his teacher." Jesus: "I took his punishment."
"Max stretched the truth." Jesus: "I died for that sin."
"Max complained again." Jesus: "I know. I've forgiven him."

On and on the reading will go until every sin is proclaimed and pardoned. God's justice demands a detailed accounting. Every citizen will know that every sin has been surfaced and pardoned.

Unshakable Hope

Make a Joyful Noise

*Through Jesus, therefore, let us continually
offer to God a sacrifice of praise—the fruit
of lips that openly profess his name.*

HEBREWS 13:15

In the early eighties there was a popular country song titled "Always on My Mind."[1] The singer tells his sweetheart that even though he seldom expressed his feelings through words or actions, she was always on his mind. I'm not sure where the writer of those lyrics learned the secret of romance, but he didn't consult women. No sweetheart would accept that excuse. "You never told me, never gave me flowers, kind words, or compliments, but I was always on your mind? Yeah, right."

God doesn't buy it either. He wants to hear our affection. It is out of the abundance of the heart that the mouth speaks (Matthew 12:34 NKJV), and when the mouth is silent, the heart is in question. Do you love God? Let him know. Tell him! Out loud. In public. Unashamed. Let there be jubilation, celebration, and festivity! "Shout to God with joyful praise!" (Psalm 47:1 NLT). "Make a joyful shout to God, all the earth!" (Psalm 66:1 NKJV).

Because of Bethlehem

Quiet Servanthood

*[God] will not forget the work you did and the love
you showed for him by helping his people.*

HEBREWS 6:10 NCV

In the hallway of my memory hangs a photograph of two people—a couple in the seventh decade of life.

The man lies in a hospital bed in the living room. His body, for all practical purposes, is useless, ravaged by ALS. Even though his body is ineffective, his eyes are searching the room for his partner, a woman whose age is concealed by her youthful vigor.

She willingly goes about her task of the day: taking care of her husband, as she's been doing for the past two years. It's not an easy assignment. She must shave him, bathe him, feed him, comb his hair, and brush his teeth.

She holds his hand as they sit and watch television together.

She gets up in the middle of the night and suctions his lungs.

She leans over and kisses his feverish face.

She serves him.

By the time my father took his final breath, the two had been married for more than four decades. On the day we buried him, I thanked my mom for modeling the spirit of Christ: quiet servanthood.

How Happiness Happens

Morning *Will* Come

Weeping may last through the night, but
joy comes with the morning.

PSALM 30:5 NLT

Anyone can give pep talks, but if God is who he claims to be, he sure as shootin' better have a word for the despondent. Self-help manuals might get you through a bad mood or a tough patch. But what about an abusive childhood or a debilitating accident or years of chronic pain or public ridicule? Does God have a word for the dark nights of the soul?

He does. The promise begins with this phrase: "Weeping may last through the night."

Of course, you didn't need to read the verse to know its truth. Just ask the widow in the cemetery or the mother in the emergency room. Weeping may last through the night, and the next night, and the next.

This is not new news to you.

But this may be: "Joy comes with the morning." Sorrow will not last forever. The clouds may eclipse the sun, but they cannot eliminate it. Night might delay the dawn, but it cannot defeat it. Morning comes. Not as quickly as we want. Not as dramatically as we desire. But morning comes, and with it comes joy.

Unshakable Hope

A Decision to Trust

Though you have not seen him, you love him.

1 PETER 1:8

Few people have led a more vibrant life than George H. W. Bush did. Fighter pilot. Congressman. Ambassador. CIA director. Vice president for eight years. President for four. Yet none of that mattered on November 29, 2018. His ninety-four-year-old body was frail. In what would turn out to be his next-to-final day on earth, he received his good friend James Baker. Baker called him "Jefe," Spanish for "Boss." Bush called Baker "Bake." The two often went out for lunch together. Baker would enter the house and say, "Where are we going today, Jefe?" But on this day the former president asked the question before Baker could. "Where are we going today, Bake?" His longtime friend replied, "Well, Jefe, we are going to heaven." To which Bush replied, "Good . . . because that is where I want to go."[2]

President Bush led a stellar life. But in the end it was not his accomplishments that mattered. It was his decision to trust the accomplishment of a Jewish rabbi.

You Are Never Alone

Grace Not Guilt

If we confess our sins, He is faithful and just to forgive us our sins and to cleanse us from all unrighteousness.

1 JOHN 1:9 NKJV

Humanity's first occasion of anxiety can be attributed to guilt. "That evening [Adam and Eve] heard the sound of the Lord God walking in the garden; and they hid themselves among the trees" (Genesis 3:8 TLB).

What had happened to the first family? Until this point there was no indication they felt any fear or trepidation. They had never hidden from God. Indeed, they had nothing to hide.

But then came the serpent and the forbidden fruit. The first couple said yes to the serpent's temptation and no to God. And when they did, their world collapsed. They scurried into the bushes and went into hiding, feeling shame and dread.

Note the sequence. Guilt came first. Anxiety came in tow. Guilt drove the truck, but anxiety bounced in the flatbed.

What kind of person does unresolved guilt create? An anxious one, forever hiding, running, denying, pretending. Unresolved guilt over unconfessed sin will turn you into a miserable, weary, angry, stressed-out, fretful mess.

Guilt sucks the life out of our souls. Grace restores it.

Anxious for Nothing

Jesus Intercedes

There is one God and one mediator between
God and mankind, the man Christ Jesus.

1 TIMOTHY 2:5

When Tyler Sullivan was an eleven-year-old elementary school student, he skipped a day of class. He played hooky, but not so he could hang out with friends or watch television; he missed school so he could meet the president of the United States.

Barack Obama was visiting Tyler's hometown of Golden Valley, Minnesota. His father had introduced the president at an event. After the speech when Tyler met the president, Obama realized that Tyler was missing school. He asked an aide to fetch him a card with presidential letterhead. He asked for the name of Tyler's teacher. He then wrote a note: "Please excuse Tyler. He was with me. Barack Obama, the president."[3]

I'm thinking the teacher read the note and granted the request. It's not every day the president speaks up on behalf of a kid.

But every day Jesus speaks up for you. "He always lives to intercede for [us]" (Hebrews 7:25). Jesus is praying for his people. In the midst of your storm, he is praying for you.

Unshakable Hope

The Divine Artist

God began doing a good work in you, and I am sure he will continue it until it is finished when Jesus Christ comes again.

PHILIPPIANS 1:6 NCV

Some years ago my wife and I enjoyed a dinner in the Texas hill country home of Gerald Jones. You've possibly heard his professional name: G. Harvey. He was one of the finest artists in America.

His house contained wall after wall of original paintings. Frame after frame of perfection.

Behind the house was his studio, a workroom of unfinished paintings. Partially painted canvases. People with no heads. Mountains with no peaks. Now, I'm far from an art connoisseur, but even I knew better than to say, "Hey, Gerald, this tree is half-finished." Or "You forgot to paint legs on this horse."

The artist wasn't finished yet.

The Divine Artist isn't finished either. The earth is his studio. Every person on earth is one of his projects. Every event on earth is part of his great mural. He is not finished.

This life contains many journeys between prayer offered and prayer answered. But Jesus promises a sure blessing at the end of the journey. Keep believing. God's not finished yet.

You Are Never Alone

By the Cross

No one has ever seen God; but if we love one another,
God lives in us and his love is made complete in us.

1 JOHN 4:12

Brian Reed served in a military unit in Baghdad, Iraq, in the fall of 2003. He and his unit went on regular street patrols to protect neighborhoods and build peace. It was often a thankless, fruitless assignment. Citizens seemed more interested in receiving a handout than a hand up. Brian said his unit battled low morale daily.

An exception came in the form of a church his men stumbled upon. Brian and his men, armed and armored to the teeth, entered the facility. It was filled with Arabic-speaking Coptic Christians singing and praising God. The Americans did not understand a word, but they recognized the image on the screen, a depiction of Jesus.

The Coptic Christians invited them to partake in the Lord's Supper with them. The soldiers removed their helmets and received the sacraments. Afterward they smiled, laughed, shook hands, and prayed again.

It was peace in the Middle East.

Enemies brought together by the cross of Christ.

How Happiness Happens

I AM

"I AM has sent me to you."

EXODUS 3:14

When Jesus walked out on the water and through the storm to his disciples in John 6, they were afraid. His answer was simply, "It is I; don't be afraid" (v. 20).

The literal translation of what Jesus said is "I AM; don't be afraid." I AM is God's name. If God had a calling card, it would contain this imprint: I AM. Ever since Moses saw the burning bush that refused to burn up, God has called himself "I AM." This is the title of steadiness and power. When we wonder if God is coming, he answers with his name: "I AM!" When we wonder if he is able, he declares, "I AM." When we see nothing but darkness, feel nothing but doubt, and wonder if God is near or aware, the welcome answer from Jesus is this: "I AM!"

Pause for a moment and let him tell you his name. Your greatest need is his presence. Yes, you want the storm to pass. But yes, yes, yes, you want to know, need to know, and must know that the great I AM is near.

You Are Never Alone

Play for the Father

Whatever you do, do it all for the glory of God.

1 CORINTHIANS 10:31

It was a big day in the Lucado house when we purchased a piano. Denalyn loves to play music, and we wanted our daughters to share her passion.

Jenna was five years old. Andrea was three. Sara was a newborn. They were too young to play much but not too young to put on a recital for Daddy.

It was a delight . . . most nights . . . except for the fights.

Jenna would, in Andrea's opinion, play too long. Andrea would climb up next to Jenna and start edging her off the bench. A squabble would ensue.

What they didn't understand and what I would try to explain was this: Daddy didn't need a performance or a contest. Daddy just enjoyed being with his girls. Competition and comparison turned my little darlings into tyrants.

If your desire to be noticed is making you miserable, you can bet it is doing the same for others. If you have a song to play on the piano, for heaven's sake play it. But play it to please your Father. You'll be amazed how peaceful the evening will be.

How Happiness Happens

Grace for the Humble

The high and lofty one who lives in eternity, the Holy One, says this: "I live in the high and holy place with those whose spirits are contrite and humble. I restore the crushed spirit of the humble and revive the courage of those with repentant hearts."

ISAIAH 57:15 NLT

Holy God, you are worthy of all honor and praise. You are the King of kings, the Lord of lords. All creation worships you. All good things are from you. The greatest and richest ruler is nothing compared to who you are.

God, clothe me with the humility of Jesus. Give me a gentle spirit and a kind heart—things I cannot have when my pride gets in the way. Help me put others before myself and you above all. Give me a hunger for humility and grace.

Thank you that even when my pride wells up, you will give me another chance, and in your grace, you will humble me. Thank you for your promise to give grace to the humble. Amen.

Praying the Promises

Be the Exception

*Has not God chosen those who are poor in the eyes
of the world to be rich in faith and to inherit the
kingdom he promised those who love him?*

JAMES 2:5

For many years David Robinson was a member of our congregation. He stands seven foot one and is muscular and handsome. In his NBA career he won championships and Olympic gold medals.

He did not attend church to gain attention, but the initial time he entered our sanctuary, he received just that. As he walked down the aisle looking for a place to sit, every head turned to look at him.

About the time he stepped in, so did another guest. A homeless man wandered in off the street. He was everything David was not: slight, bedraggled, and apparently poor. With only one exception, no one greeted the street dweller.

I'll always be grateful for that one exception. An elder in our church made it a point to leave his pew and take a seat next to the drifter. I've wondered if the homeless man was a messenger of sorts, even an angel in disguise, sent by God to test our willingness to receive all God's children.

Be the exception. Pass the test.

How Happiness Happens

A Storm-Free Life?

After he had dismissed them, he went up on
a mountainside by himself to pray.

MATTHEW 14:23

Lingering among the unspoken expectations of the Christian heart is this: *Now that I belong to God, I get a pass on the tribulations of life.*

To follow Jesus is to live a storm-free life, right?

That expectation crashes quickly on the rocks of reality. The truth of the matter is this: life comes with storms. Storms will come to you as they did to the disciples on the Sea of Galilee. And like them, you may be asking, *Where in the world is Jesus?*

The answer might be as surprising for you as it was for the disciples: praying.

When the disciples came upon the storm, Jesus had gone "up on a mountainside by himself to pray." There is no indication that he did anything else. He prayed all night.

Ponder this promise: Jesus, in the midst of your storm, is interceding for you. The King of the universe is speaking on your behalf. And when he speaks, all of heaven listens.

Praying the Promises

Prepare for Battle

Put on God's full armor. Then on the day of
evil you will be able to stand strong.

EPHESIANS 6:13 NCV

Soldiers know better than to saunter onto the battlefield wearing nothing but shorts and sandals. They take care to prepare. They take every weapon into the conflict.

So must we! Every conflict is a contest with Satan and his forces. For that reason "though we walk in the flesh, we do not war according to the flesh. For the weapons of our warfare are not carnal but mighty in God for pulling down strongholds" (2 Corinthians 10:3–4 NKJV). What are these weapons? Prayer, worship, and Scripture. When we pray, we engage the power of God against the devil. When we worship, we do what Satan himself did not do: we place God on the throne. When we pick up the sword of Scripture, we do what Jesus did in the wilderness. He responded to Satan by proclaiming truth. And since Satan has a severe allergy to truth, he left Jesus alone.

Satan will not linger long where God is praised and prayers are offered.

Unshakable Hope

Words of Hope

*Prayers offered in faith will restore them from
sickness and bring them to health.*

JAMES 5:15 THE VOICE

L ast evening I noticed Denalyn was texting back and forth with a
friend who was spiraling downward because of some criticism at
work. Denalyn encouraged her with this downpour of truth:

Jesus can move mountains, so he can and will act on your behalf!
He loves you, so receive his love and his power. Quit doubting the
King of kings and Teacher of all teachers. He is who he says. Believe
him! The Lord exposes our weaknesses so we'll come to him and
find our rest and hope in him. He wants you to come to him and
stop imagining terrible scenarios. Has he not brought you this far?
That's the Creator of the ends of the earth in your court, on your
side. He is for you, not against you. Trust in him! Worship him!
Take your position in praise and prayer, and he will set ambushes
for the Enemy.

Goodness gracious, would that text not stir your spirit?
Spread words of hope, and pray prayers of faith.

How Happiness Happens

Precious Promises

He has given us his very great and precious promises, so that through them you may participate in the divine nature.

2 PETER 1:4

God's promises aren't just great; they are "very great." They aren't just valuable; they are "precious." To bind them around your neck is to adorn yourself with the finest jewels of the universe. The American evangelist Dwight Moody said it this way:

> If you would only go from Genesis to Revelation and see all the promises made by God to Abraham, to Isaac, to Jacob, to the Jews and the Gentiles, and to all His people everywhere; if you would spend a month feeding on the precious promises of God, you would not go about . . . complaining about how poor you are, but you would lift up your heads with confidence and proclaim the riches of His Grace, because you could not help it.[4]

Keep this declaration handy. Say it out loud. Fill your lungs with air and your heart with hope, and let the devil himself hear you declare your belief in God's goodness.

Unshakable Hope

Focus on the Present

"Do not worry about tomorrow, for tomorrow will worry about itself. Each day has enough trouble of its own."

MATTHEW 6:34

God takes thanksgiving seriously.

Here's why: gratitude keeps us focused on the present.

The Bible's most common word for worry is the Greek term *merimnate*. The origin is *merimnaō*. This is a compound of a verb and a noun. The verb is *divide*. The noun is *mind*. To be anxious, then, is to divide the mind.[5] Worry takes a meat cleaver to our thoughts, energy, and focus. Anxiety chops up our attention. It sends our awareness in a dozen directions.

We worry about the past—what we said or did. We worry about the future—tomorrow's assignments or the next decade's developments. Anxiety takes our attention from the right now and directs it "back then" or "out there."

But when you aren't focused on your problem, you have a sudden availability of brain space. Use it for good. Focus on—and be grateful for—the present.

Anxious for Nothing

Try the Back Door

*The Lord Jesus himself said: "It is more
blessed to give than to receive."*

ACTS 20:35

The oft-used front door to happiness is the one described by the advertising companies: acquire and aspire to drive faster, dress trendier, and drink more. Happiness depends on what you hang in your closet, park in your garage, deposit in your bank account, experience in your bedroom, wear on your ring finger, or serve at your dining table. It's wide, this front door to happiness.

Yet for all its promise, it fails to deliver.

After all, we've all seen happy peasants and miserable millionaires, right?

There is another option. It requires no credit card, monthly mortgage, or stroke of lottery fortune. It demands no airline tickets or hotel reservations. Age, ethnicity, and gender are not factors. You don't have to change jobs, change cities, change looks, or change neighborhoods.

But you might need to change doors.

The motto on the front door says, "Happiness happens when you get." The sign on the lesser-used back door counters, "Happiness happens when you give."

Try the back door.

How Happiness Happens

Do You See Any Blessings?

Give thanks to the LORD, for he is good.

PSALM 118:1

My friend Jerry has taught me the value of gratitude. He is seventy-eight years old and regularly shoots his age on the golf course. His dear wife, Ginger, battles Parkinson's disease. What should have been a wonderful season of retirement has been marred by multiple hospital stays, medication, and struggles. Yet he never complains. He always has a smile and a joke. I asked Jerry his secret. He said, "Every morning Ginger and I sit together and sing a hymn. I ask her what she wants to sing. She always says, 'Count Your Blessings.' So we sing it. And we count our blessings."

Take a moment and follow Jerry's example. Look at your blessings.

Do you see any friends? Family? Do you see any grace from God? The love of God? Do you see any gifts? Abilities or talents?

As you look at your blessings, take note of what happens. Anxiety grabs his bags and slips out the back door. One heartfelt thank-you will suck the oxygen out of worry's world. So say it often. Focus more on what you do have and less on what you don't.

Anxious for Nothing

Giver of All

*"For your Father knows the things you
have need of before you ask Him."*

MATTHEW 6:8 NKJV

*Lord, you are the provider and giver of all. Nothing about me
is hidden from you. You can count every hair on my head. You
know all of my needs before I can even ask for them.*

*Sometimes it's tempting for me to believe I can rely on myself
for what I need. Instead of trusting you to provide, I think I can
look out for myself. I fear not having enough. And when I do
have enough, it never feels like it.*

*But you have promised to meet my needs out of your glorious
riches. Remind me of your kind and generous provision. Thank
you for taking care of me and meeting all of my needs.*

*Allow me to find full satisfaction in you, Father. I know you
have provided for me and you have been faithful to me in the
past. Continue to do so. Build up my trust in you. Your ultimate
provision came in the form of your Son, Jesus. May that truth
feel real to me today. Amen.*

Praying the Promises

It's More About Love

*"This is My commandment, that you love
one another as I have loved you."*

JOHN 15:12 NKJV

S ome of your greatest treasures live in your house; they share your name. You tend to think of them as the ones who forget to clean the dishes or pick up their laundry. But the truth? They are masterpieces crafted by the hand of God.

Your treasures include a host of functional folk as well. They check out your groceries, grade your quizzes, or take your blood pressure. They wear police uniforms and drive carpools and fix your computer. They compose a collage of humanity, blending in more than standing out.

All they need is someone committed to bringing the best out of them. All they need is someone who is willing to take on the greatest of the "one another" commands: "Love one another" (1 John 4:11 NKJV).

Remember, God invites us to find happiness through the back door. Most people seek joy through the front door. Buy it, wear it, marry it, or win it. The lesser-used back door embraces God's wisdom: it's less about getting, more about giving, less about being loved, and more about loving others.

How Happiness Happens

It's Not Just You

*Even though I walk through the darkest valley,
I will fear no evil, for you are with me; your
rod and your staff, they comfort me.*

PSALM 23:4

It's just me, and I ain't much."

Her seventeen-year-old son had battled opioid addiction for a year, maybe more. A car wreck had landed him in the ICU. Four days of forced detox had left him craving pills that the doctors would not provide.

It took the mom nearly an hour to tell me what I just told you in one paragraph. Her story required sob breaks and deep sighs and included flashes of anger when referring to her absent ex-husband. All in all the mom believed, "It's just me, and I ain't much."

Do you know this feeling? Convinced no one can help you, hear you, or heed your call? You aren't alone. I don't mean you aren't alone in knowing the feeling. I mean you aren't alone. Period. Belief is not some respectful salute to a divine being. Belief is a decision to lean entirely upon the strength of a living and loving Savior. And he doesn't leave us to face life alone.

You Are Never Alone

God Is Enough

Where can I go from Your Spirit? . . . If I take the
wings of the morning, and dwell in the uttermost parts
of the sea, even there Your hand shall lead me.

PSALM 139:7, 9–10 NKJV

God uses common people for uncommon works. Gideon, for example, was a simple sodbuster, yet God turned this farmer into a leader and used him to protect Israel. With only three hundred men, Gideon defeated the mighty Midianite army (Judges 7:1–25).

In this victory, Gideon learned what God wants us to learn: all we need is the presence of God. He is enough. His presence tilts the scales in our favor.

The same God who was with Gideon is right beside you. The two-dollar theological term for this is *omnipresence. Omni* is the Latin prefix for "all." God's presence is all-encompassing. Don't apply earthly physics to him. He does not have size or spatial limitation. He is present in every point of space with his whole being.

Which means he is with you as you face your armies. With you as you are wheeled into surgery. With you as you enter the cemetery. With you, always.

Praying the Promises

Be C.A.L.M.

*"Be careful, or your hearts will be weighed
down with . . . the anxieties of life."*

LUKE 21:34

Anxiety is not a sin; it is an emotion. Anxiety can, however, lead to sinful behavior. When we numb our fears with six-packs or food binges, when we spew anger like Krakatau, when we peddle our fears to anyone who will buy them, we are sinning.

Is your heart weighed down with worry?

If you answered yes to that question, I have a friend for you to meet. Actually, I have a scripture for you to read: Philippians 4:4–8. Five verses with four admonitions that lead to one wonderful promise: "the peace of God, which surpasses all understanding, will guard your hearts and minds" (v. 7 ESV).

Celebrate God's goodness. "Rejoice in the Lord always" (v. 4 ESV).

Ask God for help. "Let your requests be made known to God" (v. 6 ESV).

Leave your concerns with him. "With thanksgiving . . ." (v. 6 ESV).

Meditate on good things. "Think about the things that are good and worthy of praise" (v. 8 NCV).

Celebrate. Ask. Leave. Meditate. In other words, be *C.A.L.M.*

Anxious for Nothing

Our True Destination

*Then I, John, saw the holy city, New Jerusalem,
coming down out of heaven from God, prepared
as a bride adorned for her husband.*

REVELATION 21:2 NKJV

Life on earth meets the basic definition of an airport: a place to wait until your flight home is called.

You were never meant to stay on this form of earth. You were made for more than life in a terminal. And you can thank John for giving you a glimpse of your true destination.

John's description of the New Jerusalem stretches the imagination: fourteen hundred miles in length, width, and height. Large enough to contain the land mass from the Appalachians to the West Coast. As tall as it is wide, the New Jerusalem would have six hundred thousand floors, ample space for billions of people. Ample space for you.

This life hasn't always had space for you, has it? You learned early the finite amount of resources.

But God promises a spacious city, where he will "make all things new" (Revelation 21:5 NKJV). Because of this, we do not give up. Instead, we lift up our eyes and look. The new city is coming.

Praying the Promises

Believe His Promises

Whoever believes in him is not condemned.

JOHN 3:18

Paul had every reason to fear Agrippa's judgment. The king was the latest in the Herod dynasty, the last of the Herods who would meddle with Christ or his followers. His great-grandfather attempted to kill baby Jesus. His granduncle murdered John the Baptist, and his father, Agrippa I, executed James and imprisoned Peter.

You might say they had it out for the people in Jesus' circle.

And now Paul stood before him. He was in prison for preaching a new religion. How would Paul present his case? After a word of introduction, he said, "And now it is because of my hope in what God has promised our ancestors that I am on trial today" (Acts 26:6).

Paul's defense included no reference to his accomplishments. ("I have been known to call a person back from the dead, you know.") He demanded no preferential treatment. ("I am a Roman citizen.") He didn't attempt to justify his actions. ("I was only being open-minded.") None of that. His only justification was this: "I believed in the promises of God."

That's the only justification we need.

Unshakable Hope

It's Christ Who Matters

Though the LORD is supreme, he takes
care of those who are humble.

PSALM 138:6 NCV

Some time ago I was honored with a nice recognition. A friend learned about it and said, "Max, God gave you that honor because you were humble enough not to let it go to your head." What kind words! The more I thought about what he had said, the better it felt. The more I thought, the more I agreed. As the day went on, I felt better and better about being so humble. I was proud of my humility. That evening I was just about to tell Denalyn what he had said when I felt a conviction. I was about to brag about being humble!

Humility. The moment you think you have it, you don't.

Pursue it anyway.

A recurring message of Scripture is that God loves the humble heart.

Ponder your achievements less; ponder Christ's more. Spend less time on your throne and more at his cross. Brag on his work, not yours. You are valuable, but you aren't invaluable. It is Christ who matters, not us.

Because of Bethlehem

December

Are You Ready for Christmas?

"I bring you good news that will bring great joy to all people."

LUKE 2:10 NLT

I love Christmas. Let the sleigh bells ring. Let the carolers sing. The more Santas the merrier. The more trees the better.

I love Christmas. The ho, ho, ho; the rooty toot toot; the thumpety, thump, thump; and the pa rum pa pum pum.

Bring on Scrooge, Cousin Eddie, and the "official Red Ryder, carbine-action, two-hundred-shot range model air rifle." "You'll shoot your eye out!"

The tinsel and the clatter and waking up "to see what was the matter." Bing and his tunes. Macy's balloons. Mistletoe kisses, Santa Claus wishes, and favorite dishes. Holiday snows and Rudolph's red nose.

I love Christmas because somewhere someone will ask the questions: What's the big deal about the baby in the manger? Who was he? What does his birth have to do with me? The questioner may be a child looking at a front-yard crèche. He or she may be a soldier stationed far from home. The Christmas season prompts questions.

Let's be ready to answer.

Because of Bethlehem

The Perpetual Presence of Christ

"I am with you always, even to the end of the age."

MATTHEW 28:20 NKJV

Because of Bethlehem, I have a Savior in heaven. Christmas begins what Easter celebrates. The child in the cradle became the King on the cross. And because he did, there are no marks on my record. Just grace.

His offer has no fine print. He didn't tell me, "Clean up before you come in." He offered, "Come in and I'll clean you up." It's not my grip on him that matters but his grip on me. And his grip is sure.

So is his presence in my life. Christmas presents from Santa? That's nice. But the perpetual presence of Christ? That's life changing.

Have you let the presence of Christ change your life?

Because of Bethlehem

On Purpose with a Purpose

*I praise you because you made me in an amazing and
wonderful way. . . . All the days planned for me were
written in your book before I was one day old.*

PSALM 139:14, 16 NCV

The Christmas tree hunt is on. We lift limbs and examine needles. We measure. We ponder. We consider. We barter.

Do you purchase the first tree you see? Of course not. You search for the right one. You walk the rows. You lift several up and set them down. You examine them from all angles until you decide, This one is perfect. You have a place in mind where the tree will sit. Not just any tree will do.

God does the same. He knows just the place where you'll be placed. He has a barren living room in desperate need of warmth and joy. A corner of the world needs some color. He selected you with that place in mind.

God made you on purpose with a purpose. He interwove calendar and character, circumstance and personality to create the right person for the right corner of the world, and then he paid the price to take you home.

Because of Bethlehem

God with Us

"The virgin will conceive and give birth to a son, and they will call him Immanuel" (which means "God with us").

MATTHEW 1:23

God is always near us. Always for us. Always in us. We may forget him, but God will never forget us. We are forever on his mind and in his plans. He called himself "'Immanuel' (which means 'God with us')."

Not just "God made us."

Not just "God thinks of us."

Not just "God above us."

But God *with* us. God where we are: at the office, in the kitchen, on the plane. He breathed our air and walked this earth. God . . . with . . . us!

God is always near us. By the way, Bethlehem was just the beginning. Jesus has promised a repeat performance. Bethlehem, Act 2. No silent night this time, however. The skies will open, trumpets will blast, and a new kingdom will begin. He will empty the tombs and melt the winter of death. He will press his thumb against the collective cheek of his children and wipe away all tears. The manger invites, even dares us to believe the best is yet to be.

Because of Bethlehem

The Message of Bethlehem

The angel said to her, "Do not be afraid,
Mary; you have found favor with God."

LUKE 1:30

We can relate to the little boy who played the part of the angel in the Christmas story. He and his mother rehearsed his lines over and over: "It is I; don't be afraid." "It is I; don't be afraid."

Yet, when the Christmas pageant began, he walked onto the stage and saw the lights and audience and he froze. After an awkward silence, he finally said, "It is me and I'm scared."

Are you scared? If so, may I suggest that you need a little Christmas? I don't mean a dose of saccharine sentiment or Santa cheer or double-spiked eggnog. That's not Christmas.

Christmas is about Christ. Christ's name occupies six of the nine letters, for crying out loud. This isn't Santa-mas, or shopping-mas, or reindeer-mas. This is *Christ*-mas. And *Christ*-mas is not *Christ*-mas unless or until you receive the message of Bethlehem.

Have you? In the hurry and scurry of the season, have you taken time to receive the promise of the season?

God gets us. God saves us. That's the message of Bethlehem.

Because of Bethlehem

God Saves

[Mary] will give birth to a son, and you are to give him the name Jesus, because he will save his people from their sins.

MATTHEW 1:21

Look carefully at the words the angel spoke to Joseph.

We may not see the connection between the name *Jesus* and the phrase "save his people from their sins," but Joseph would have. He was familiar with the Hebrew language. The English name *Jesus* traces its origin to the Hebrew word *Yeshua*. *Yeshua* is a shortening of *Yehoshuah*, which means "Yahweh saves."[1]

Who was Jesus? God saves.

What did Jesus come to do? God *saves*.

God saves. Jesus was not just godly, godlike, God hungry, God focused, or God worshipping. He was God.

God *saves*, not God empathizes, cares, listens, helps, assists, or applauds. God saves. Specifically "he will save his people from their sins." Jesus came to save us, not just from politics, enemies, challenges, or difficulties. He came to save us from our own sins.

Because of Bethlehem

A Lifetime of Hope

In those days Caesar Augustus issued a decree that a census should be taken of the entire Roman world.

LUKE 2:1

No day is accidental or incidental. No acts are random or wasted. Look at the Bethlehem birth. A king ordered a census. Joseph was forced to travel. Mary, as round as a ladybug, bounced on a donkey's back. The hotel was full. The hour was late. The event was one big hassle. Yet, out of the hassle, hope was born.

It still is. I don't like hassles. But I love Christmas because it reminds us how "God causes everything to work together for the good of those who love God" (Romans 8:28 NLT).

The heart-shaping promises of Christmas. Long after the guests have left and the carolers have gone home and the lights have come down, these promises endure.

Perhaps you could use some Christmas this Christmas? Let's do what I did as a six-year-old, redheaded, flat-topped, freckle-faced boy. Let's turn on the lamp, curl up in a comfortable spot, and look into the odd, wonderful story of Bethlehem.

May you find what I have found: a lifetime of hope.

Because of Bethlehem

Missed Opportunity

Because there were no rooms left in the inn, she wrapped the baby with pieces of cloth and laid him in a feeding trough.

LUKE 2:7 NCV

Had Mary and Joseph been Queen Mary and King Joseph, the innkeeper would have responded differently. But no trumpet sounded. No herald proclaimed. No courier announced their arrival. There was only a knock.

A knock at the door . . .

by a common couple . . .

at a late hour . . .

when the inn was crowded.

So the innkeeper missed the opportunity.

Many still do. They miss the chance to open the door. They let the birth of Jesus pass them by. The miracle of Bethlehem still happens. God enters the hamlets of our lives and speaks to us. He speaks through scriptures, sunsets, or the kindness of a friend. He sings to us through Christmas carols. He calls to us through Christmas sermons. He reaches out through the Christmas story.

"Here I am!" Jesus invites. "I stand at the door and knock" (Revelation 3:20 NCV). Will you let him in?

Because of Bethlehem

What God Looks Like

The Son is the image of the invisible God,
the firstborn over all creation.

COLOSSIANS 1:15

If you want to see people on the edge of insanity, just watch the way families treat their babies at Christmastime.

The poor child has no warning. He is just starting to recover from the slide down the birth canal when the family begins decorating him with a red furry stocking cap with a white ball on the end.

We make such a fuss! This time of year, babies take center stage. And well they should. Is not Christmas the story of a baby?

This is the Christmas moment that shaped all the others to follow. On a starlit night in the company of sheep, cattle, and a bewildered Joseph, Mary's eyes fell upon the face of her just-born son. She was bone weary, surely. In pain, likely. Ready to place her head on the straw and sleep the rest of the night away, probably. But first Mary had to see this face. *His* face. To wipe the moisture from his mouth and feel the shape of his chin. To be the first to whisper, "So this is what God looks like."

Because of Bethlehem

An Invitation from God

"My Father's house has many rooms; if that
were not so, would I have told you that I am
going there to prepare a place for you?"

JOHN 14:2

It so happened that one Christmas brought with it the excitement of my daughter Jenna's pregnancy. That Christmas, Jenna asked family members to record audio messages that she could play for her yet-to-be-born daughter.

Who could refuse such an opportunity? I retreated to a quiet corner and captured this welcome.

Dear, dear child. We are so excited to welcome you into the world. We are waiting for you. Your parents have prepared a place for you. You have grandparents, aunts, and uncles ready to shower you with love. We cannot wait to spend time loving you and showing you your wonderful new home.

Only after I finished did I realize that is God's invitation to us! He has prepared a place. He has a family to love us. And he has a sparkling new world to show us. Who knows? This could be the day of our delivery.

Because of Bethlehem

Christ Came

While they were in Bethlehem, the time
came for Mary to have the baby.

LUKE 2:6 NCV

Any doubt of the Father's love for his people disappeared the night God was wrapped in barnyard towels so the hay wouldn't scratch his back.

Through a scandalous pregnancy, an imposed census, an untimely trip, and an overcrowded inn, God triumphed and Christ came.

In spite of the chaos, Christ came.

In spite of sin and scandal, Christ came.

In spite of racism and sexism, Christ came.

Though the people forgot God, Christ came.

In spite of, and out of, the pandemonium, Christ came.

The surprise pregnancy, the sudden census, the long road from Nazareth to Bethlehem. Unpleasant and difficult, yet they resulted in the world's greatest miracle. Everything before this happened so this moment would happen. God used the struggles to accomplish his will.

Don't you need that reminder? Don't we all?

Because of Bethlehem

A Gnarled and Crooked Tree

Jacob was the father of Joseph, who married a woman
named Mary. It was Mary who gave birth to Jesus,
and it is Jesus who is the Savior, the Anointed One.

MATTHEW 1:16 THE VOICE

We don't often mention the lineage of Jesus in context with his birth. Matthew did, however. He opens his gospel with a list with dozens of names. Before he presents the wise men and the star of Bethlehem, he tells us that "Abraham begot Isaac, Isaac begot Jacob, and Jacob begot Judah and his brothers. Judah begot Perez and Zerah by Tamar . . ." (Matthew 1:2–3 NKJV).

The list goes on and on (and on) for sixteen verses. Yawn. Who needs to know about Tamar, Rahab, and Ruth? Why does Matthew mention David and Solomon before he mentions Joseph and Mary?

He is making a point. The Messiah was born not because of his ancestors but in spite of them. Tamar was abandoned. Ruth was an immigrant, and Rahab was a harlot. David was an adulterer. Solomon was a philanderer. The family tree of Jesus is gnarled and crooked. Yet God had promised that Jesus would come, and Jesus came.

Because of Bethlehem

He Picked You

"I chose you out of the world."

JOHN 15:19 NKJV

One year I barely escaped the tragedy of the holiday season: a leaning tree. Denalyn and I placed the tree in the stand, stood back, and sighed at what we saw. The dreaded tilt. I crawled under the branches and began adjusting the screws until the tree stood as straight as a stalk of wheat. Denalyn placed her arm in mine, and I choked back tears of joy.

Then disaster struck. The tree started to lean again.

This time I placed the tree on its side, removed the stand, and saw the root of the problem. Our tree was crooked!

As I was retrieving a saw from the garage, it occurred to me: I'm not the first father to deal with this issue. God faces this situation on a continual basis. Don't we have our share of unattractive bents?

I know I do.

Would that I stood as straight as a sequoia, but I don't. And since I don't, I find a kindred spirit in the Christmas tree. I think you will find the same. What you do for a tree, God does for you.

He picked you.

Because of Bethlehem

The Gift of Worship

Suddenly, the angel was joined by a vast host
of others—the armies of heaven—praising God:
"Glory to God in the highest heaven."

LUKE 2:13–14 TLB

The magi gave Jesus the gifts of gold, frankincense, and myrrh. The shepherds gave Jesus the gift of their time and belief. The offerings seem practical. The wise men's treasures could be used to fund the family's escape to Egypt. The shepherds' visitation would keep the family company. But there is one gift that might appear a bit curious.

The angels' gift of worship.

The angels filled the night with light and the air with music, and, well, that's it. They worshipped. Couldn't they have done something more useful? Mary could have used a bed. Baby Jesus needed a bassinet.

These were angels. Didn't they know better?

Then again, these were angels. Who knew Jesus better than they?

God is on the hunt for those who will imitate the angels, for people who will open their hearts and mouths and declare, "Glory to God in the highest heaven." "The Father . . . is actively seeking such people to worship him" (John 4:23 NCV). Will you be one?

Because of Bethlehem

Why Such a Journey?

It was necessary for him to be made in every respect like us . . . so that he could be our merciful and faithful High Priest before God.

HEBREWS 2:17 NLT

An elementary school teacher asked her students to make a list of questions they would have liked to ask young Mary. Here are some of their responses:

"Were you scared of not doing a good job?"

"What was Jesus' first word as a baby?"

"Was he beautiful?"

"Did Jesus ever misbehave?"

"What was his favorite food?"

"Did he ever have a pet?"

These are legitimate questions. The fact that we can ask them raises a greater one.

Why such a journey? Why did God go so far?

A chief reason is this: he wants you to know that he gets you. Jesus is not "out of touch with our reality. He's been through weakness and testing, experienced it all—all but the sin. So let's walk right up to him and get what he is so ready to give. Take the mercy, accept the help" (Hebrews 4:15–16 MSG).

Because of Bethlehem

In Bethlehem

*"Does not Scripture say that the Messiah will come
from David's descendants and from Bethlehem?"*

JOHN 7:42

Maybe your life resembles a Bethlehem stable. Crude in some spots, smelly in others. Not much glamour. Not always neat. People in your circle remind you of stable animals: grazing like sheep, stubborn like donkeys, and that cow in the corner looks a lot like the fellow next door.

You, like Joseph, knocked on the innkeeper's door. But you were too late. Or too old, sick, dull, damaged, poor, or peculiar. You know the sound of a slamming door. So here you are in the grotto, always on the outskirts of activity, it seems.

You do your best to make the best of it, but try as you might, the roof still leaks, and the winter wind still sneaks through the holes you just can't seem to fix. You've shivered through your share of cold nights.

And you wonder if God has a place for a person like you.

Find your answer in the Bethlehem stable.

Because of Bethlehem

Unexpected Wrappings

You will conceive and give birth to a son,
and you are to call him Jesus.

LUKE 1:31

The large box sat unexplained in the corner of our living room for weeks. It appeared soon after Thanksgiving and sat untouched throughout most of December. Mom assumed Dad had used Christmas as an excuse to buy himself a gift.

On Christmas morning, my mom said, "Jack, aren't you going to open the big present?"

Dad looked at her with a Santa sort of twinkle. "That gift isn't for me; it's for you."

Mom pried open the top of the nondescript, unaddressed box. She reached in and pulled out nothing but tissue paper. One armful after another.

"What's in here?" she asked, still pulling out paper. Finally she struck pay dirt. A box within the box. She opened it to find another box, then another and another. At last she reached the smallest of the boxes. A ring box. She smiled. "Jack."

I didn't understand the romantic significance of a new ring. But I did learn a lesson: a remarkable gift can arrive in an unremarkable package. One did in the Lucado house. One did in Bethlehem.

Because of Bethlehem

Paul's Christmas Sermon

He made himself nothing by taking
the very nature of a servant.

PHILIPPIANS 2:7

Paul. His name seldom appears in Christmas reflections. We typically think of Joseph, Mary, the shepherds, and the magi. We
don't often refer to the reformed Pharisee. Yet we should. His words
are the Bible's most eloquent summary of the Bethlehem promise.

> In your relationships with one another, have the same mindset as
> Christ Jesus: Who, being in very nature God, did not consider equal-
> ity with God something to be used to his own advantage; rather, he
> made himself nothing by taking the very nature of a servant, being
> made in human likeness. And being found in appearance as a man,
> he humbled himself by becoming obedient to death—even death on
> a cross! (Philippians 2:5–8)

The apostle was not writing a Christmas sermon. His aim was
far more mundane. Paul was counseling a church. The Christians
in Philippi seemed to have a few issues, selfish ambition and conceit
being among them (2:3). As a result we have the heart of the gospel.
A summary of God's divine intervention.

Because of Bethlehem

Trimming the Tree

*"My Father is the gardener. . . . He trims and
cleans every branch that produces fruit so
that it will produce even more fruit."*

JOHN 15:1–2 NCV

In the manger God loves you; through the cross God saves you.
But has he taken you to his home? Not yet. He has work for you to
do. He wants the world to see what God can do with his purchased
possessions.

So . . . he prunes you.

He takes an ax to your prejudices and clippers to your self-pity,
and when there is a tilt in your character, he's been known to pull out
the old Black & Decker and even things up a bit.

Once he stabilizes us, he festoons us with love, joy, peace, patience,
kindness, goodness, faithfulness, gentleness, [and] self-control
(Galatians 5:22–23 NCV).

Then he surrounds us with his grace. We become the distribution
point of God's gifts. He wants no one to leave our presence empty-
handed. Some find the gift of salvation. Others find a kind word, a
good deed. But all the gifts are from God.

Our task is to stand tall in his love, freely giving to all who come
our way.

Because of Bethlehem

Let Him Love You

*This is what real love is: It is not our love for
God; it is God's love for us. He sent his Son to
die in our place to take away our sins.*

1 JOHN 4:10 NCV

If God was willing to wrap himself in rags and drink from a mother's breast, then all questions about his love for you are off the table.

There is no place he will not go. If he is willing to be born in a barnyard, then expect him to be at work anywhere—bars, bedrooms, boardrooms, and brothels. No place is too common. No person is too hardened. No distance is too far. There is no person he cannot reach. There is no limit to his love.

When Christ was born, so was our hope.

This is why I love Christmas. The event invites us to believe the wildest of promises: God became one of us so we could become one with him. He did away with every barrier, fence, sin, bent, debt, and grave. Anything that might keep us from him was demolished. He only awaits our word to walk through the door.

Invite him in. Let him love you.

Because of Bethlehem

A Friend in Heaven

*The Word became flesh and blood, and
moved into the neighborhood.*

JOHN 1:14 MSG

As kids, my brother and I had a chest at the foot of our bed that contained children's books. The three bears lived in the chest. So did the big, bad wolf and seven dwarfs and a monkey with a lunch pail. Beneath the fairy tales was a book about baby Jesus.

On the cover, a star glowed above the stable. Joseph and a donkey, equally big eyed, stood nearby. Mary held a baby in her arms. She looked down at him, and he looked up at her, and I remember looking at them both.

My dad, a man of few words, had told my brother and me, "Boys, Christmas is about Christ."

In one of those bedtime, book-time moments, I began asking the Christmas questions. In one way or another, I've been asking them ever since.

I love the answers I have found.

Like this one: God knows what it is like to be a human. When I talk to him about deadlines or long lines or tough times, he understands. He's been there. He's been here.

Because of Bethlehem, I have a friend in heaven.

Because of Bethlehem

Finding Your Way Home

They came to the house where the child was and saw him with his mother, Mary, and they bowed down and worshiped him.

MATTHEW 2:11 NCV

Behold the first Christian worshippers. The simple dwelling became a cathedral. Seekers of Christ found him and knelt in his presence. They gave him gifts: gold for a king, frankincense for a priest, and myrrh for his burial.

They found the Christ because they heeded the sign and believed the scripture. Noticeably absent at the manger were the scholars of the Torah. You'd think they would have accompanied the magi to Bethlehem. The village was near enough. The risk was small enough. But the priests showed no interest.

The wise men earned their moniker because they did. Their hearts were open to God's gift. The men were never the same again.

Called by the sign of a star. Instructed by Scripture. And directed home by God.

God uses every possible means to communicate with you. The wonders of nature call to you. The promises and prophecies of Scripture speak to you. God himself reaches out to you. He wants to help you find your way home.

Because of Bethlehem

The Wise Men and the Star

"Where is the Messiah supposed to be born?"
"In Bethlehem in Judea," [the priests and teachers]
said, "for this is what the prophet wrote."

MATTHEW 2:4–5 NLT

M atthew loved the magi. He gave their story more text than he gave the narrative of the birth of Jesus. He never mentions the shepherds or the manger, but he didn't want us to miss the star and the seekers. It's easy to see why. Their story is our story. We're all travelers. In order to find Jesus, every one of us needs direction. God gives it. The story of the wise men shows us how.

God uses the natural world to get our attention. "The heavens declare the glory of God" (Psalm 19:1 NKJV). God led the wise men to Jerusalem with a star. But to lead them to Jesus, he used something else: "And you, O Bethlehem in the land of Judah, are not least among the ruling cities of Judah, for a ruler will come from you who will be the shepherd for my people Israel" (Matthew 2:6 NLT).

The star sign was enough to lead the magi to Jerusalem. But it took Scripture to lead them to Jesus.

Because of Bethlehem

It All Began with Worship

Because your love is better than life, my lips will glorify you.

PSALM 63:3

It was Christmas Eve 1915 near the village of Laventie in northern France. World War I was raging. Bombs shook the soil of Europe. Frigid temperatures shook the bones of the fighters. Germans were entrenched on one side and the Royal Welsh Fusiliers on the other. Christmas seemed far away from this blood-soaked land.

At one point from the German side of the field came a chorus of voices singing a Welsh holiday hymn in German.

Soldiers on both sides set down their weapons. In that moment, there were no enemies; there was just the song. What happened next could only be described as a miracle. The night was spent in carol singing. Around dawn the feelings of goodwill emboldened the soldiers to step out of their trenches and greet their foes. They shook hands in no-man's-land and exchanged gifts. German beer, sausages, and spiked helmets from one side. Canned corned beef, biscuits, and tunic buttons from the other. They even enjoyed a soccer game against one another.

And it all began with worship.

Because of Bethlehem

A Christmas Prayer

The LORD your God in your midst, the Mighty One, will save.

ZEPHANIAH 3:17 NKJV

May this prayer be yours:

My Heart, Your Manger

Like the stable in which you lay,
my heart is simple, frail as hay.
But if you would within me stay,
Make my heart your manger, I pray.
Make my world your Bethlehem,
centerpieced with heaven's Son.
Make this night a shepherd's sky,
quickened bright with holy dawn.
Rush the air with cherub wings.
Brush this earth. Let angels sing.
A glimpse of your face. A taste of your grace.
Be born in this place.
I pray.
Amen

Because of Bethlehem

Always Near

The LORD is my shepherd; I shall not want. . . . Yea,
though I walk through the valley of the shadow
of death, I will fear no evil; for You are with me;
Your rod and Your staff, they comfort me.

PSALM 23:1, 4 NKJV

God, you are Immanuel, God with us. You did not leave your creation to fend for itself. You have been near to us and present with us all along. Through your Son, you have saved us, and with your Spirit, you have guided us.

When I am fearful and anxious, I can forget you are here. Give me a sense of your presence. May I feel you in the quiet moments and know that you are near. When a worry arises, remind me of your presence so that I will turn to you and not fear. Help me know that it is going to be okay and that you are on my side, fighting for me.

Thank you for always being near. How grateful I am to serve a God whose tender presence I can always trust. Amen.

Praying the Promises

What's So Special?

[God] sent his one and only Son into the world that we might live through him.

1 JOHN 4:9

Imagine two angels on a tour of the universe, as J. B. Phillips did. The senior angel calls attention to planet Earth. "I want you to watch that one particularly," said the senior angel, pointing.

"Well, it looks very small and rather dirty to me," said the little angel. "What's special about that one?"

His superior explained that the unimpressive ball was the renowned Visited Planet. The lesser angel was surprised.

"Do you mean that our great and glorious Prince . . . stooped so low as to become one of those creeping, crawling creatures . . . ?"

"I do, and I don't think He would like you to call them 'creeping, crawling creatures' in that tone of voice. For, strange as it may seem to us, He loves them. He went down to visit them to lift them up to become like Him."[2]

It really comes down to that: the story of Christmas is the story of God's relentless love for us.

Because of Bethlehem

378

The Most Beautiful Tree

Christ . . . died for sins once for all, the righteous for the unrighteous, that he might bring us to God.

1 PETER 3:18 RSV

We don't know why the cross of Christ is often called a tree. Perhaps the earliest crosses were actually trees. Or since crosses were formed from trees, maybe the name stuck. But whatever the reason, the first-century writers often called the cross a tree. Peter did when he declared, "[Jesus] Himself bore our sins in His own body on the tree" (1 Peter 2:24 NKJV).

Somewhere on the timeline between the Tree of Knowledge in the garden and the Tree of Life in heaven is the Tree of Sacrifice near Jerusalem. And if Christmas trees are known for beauty and gifts, then who would deny that the most wonderful Christmas tree was a rugged one on a bald knob? "God . . . loved us and sent His *unique* Son *on a special mission* to become an atoning sacrifice for our sins" (1 John 4:10 THE VOICE). Jesus took on our sin. He was covered by the rebellion that separated us from God. He endured what we should have endured. He paid the price to save us.

Because of Bethlehem

Between the Advents

*Christ . . . will appear a second time, not to deal with
sin but to save those who are eagerly waiting for him.*

HEBREWS 9:28 RSV

We live between the Advents.

The Second Advent will include the sudden, personal, visible, bodily return of Christ. Jesus promised, "I will come again" (John 14:3 RSV). But he won't come the same way.

He came quietly in Bethlehem. He will return in glory with a shout (1 Thessalonians 4:16–17 NKJV).

At his first coming few noticed. At his second "all the nations of the world will be gathered before him" (Matthew 25:32 NCV).

In Bethlehem, Joseph placed Jesus in a manger. At his return Jesus will be seated on a throne (v. 31 NCV).

"*What will happen next,* and what we hope for, is what God promised: a new heaven and a new earth where justice reigns" (2 Peter 3:13 THE VOICE). History is a directed movement toward a great event.

We enjoy the fruit of the first coming but anticipate the glory of the second. We refuse to believe that this present world is the sum total of human existence. We long for the next coming.

Because of Bethlehem

Our Ever-Present Help

God is our refuge and strength, an ever-present help in trouble.

PSALM 46:1

God is our "ever-present help in trouble." Don't you love that phrase?

Ever present. Not occasional or sporadic help. You'll never be put on hold or told to check back later. He's never too busy or preoccupied. God is . . .

Ever *present*. As near as your next breath. Closer than your own skin. "Where can I go from your Spirit? Where can I flee from your presence? If I go up to the heavens, you are there; if I make my bed in the depths, you are there" (Psalm 139:7–8). Rehab clinic? He is there. Prison cell? He is present. No palace is too royal. No hovel is too common. He is present. And he is present to . . .

Help. Not hurt or hinder. He is here to help.

Hang on! Hold on! Don't give up. Help is here. It may not come in the manner you requested or as quickly as you desire, but it will come. Assume that something good is going to happen. The door to tomorrow is unlocked from the inside. Turn the knob and step out.

You Are Never Alone

His Presence

*In peace I will lie down and sleep, for you
alone, LORD, make me dwell in safety.*

PSALM 4:8

When my daughters were small, I made a practice of returning from travel with a gift for each one. I would walk through the door and yell, "Daddy's home!" and they would scurry to give me a hug. I wasn't insulted when they would take the new toy and scamper off to play. I knew they would come back. At some point before bedtime, we'd read a book, and soon they'd fall asleep.

I knew it wasn't my presents that brought them comfort. It was my presence.

May God bless your life with more miracles than you can count. May your water become cabernet. May your dark storms turn into springtime sun. May he feed thousands upon thousands through your picnic basket of faith. May you walk like the just-healed cripple, see like the was-blind man, live like the was-dead Lazarus. May you dwell in the grace of the cross, the hope of the empty tomb, and the assurance of restoration power. But most of all may you believe that God is your ever-present help. And in his presence may you find rest.

You Are Never Alone

Notes

January 1-31

1. Sonja Lyubomirsky, *The How of Happiness: A Practical Approach to Getting the Life You Want* (London: Piatkus, 2007), 150–51.
2. Kasley Killam, "A Hug a Day Keeps the Doctor Away," *Scientific American*, March 17, 2015, https://www.scientificamerican.com/article/a-hug-a-day-keeps-the-doctor-away/.
3. "The United Healthcare/Volunteer Match Do Good Live Well Study," March 2010, pp. 19, 33, 43, https://cdn.volunteermatch.org/www/about/UnitedHealthcare_VolunteerMatch_Do_Good_Live_Well_Study.pdf.

February 1-29

1. Ian Fisher, "Fingers That Keep the Most Treasured Violins Fit," *New York Times*, June 3, 2007, https://www.nytimes.com/2007/06/03/world/europe/03cremona.html. See also Martin Gani, "The Violin-Makers of Cremona," *Italy Magazine*, January 20, 2012, http://www.italymagazine.com/featured-story/violin-makers-cremona.
2. L. B. Cowman, *Streams in the Desert: 366 Daily Devotional Readings*, ed. Jim Reimann, updated ed. (Grand Rapids, MI: Zondervan, 1997), 462–63.
3. John Henry Jowett, *The Best of John Henry Jowett*, ed. Gerald Kennedy (New York: Harper and Brothers, 1948), 89, https://archive.org/stream/bestofjohnhenryj012480mbp/bestofjohnhenryj012480mbp_djvu.txt.
4. Teresa Woodard, "80 People Went to Dallas Emergency Rooms 5,139 Times in a Year—Usually Because They Were Lonely," WFAA, May 28, 2019, https://www.wfaa.com/article/features/originals/80-people-went-to-dallas-emergency-rooms-5139-timesin-a-year-usually-because-they-were-lonely/287-f5351d53–6e60–4d64–8d17–6ebba48a01e4.
5. "Chambers, Gertrude (Biddy) (1884–1966); Archival Collections at Wheaton College," Wheaton College, https://archon.wheaton.edu/index.php?p=creators/creator&id=198.
6. Louis J. Cameli, *The Devil You Don't Know: Recognizing and Resisting Evil in Everyday Life* (Notre Dame, IN: Ave Maria Press, 2011), 79.
7. Story contributed by Alice H. Cook, *Reader's Digest*, December 1996, 140.

8. John Stott, *Romans: God's Good News for the World* (Downers Grove, IL: InterVarsity, 1994), 395.

9. "Aristobulus," Bible Hub, http://biblehub.com/topical/a/aristobulus.htm.

10. E. Badian, "Narcissus: Roman Official," *Encyclopaedia Britannica*, http://www .britannica.com/biography/narcissus-roman-official.

March 1-31

1. "Water Scene," *The Miracle Worker*, directed by Paul Aaron (1979; Atlanta, GA: Half-Pint Productions).

2. W. E. Vine, *Vine's Expository Dictionary of New Testament Words: A Comprehensive Dictionary of the Original Greek Words with Their Precise Meanings for English Readers* (McLean, VA: MacDonald Publishing, n.d.), "Admonition, Admonish," 32.

3. "Telegram from Anna Spafford to Horatio Gates Spafford re Being 'Saved Alone' Among Her Traveling Party in the Shipwreck of the Ville du Havre," Library of Congress, https://www.loc.gov/item/mamcol000006.

4. Horatio Spafford, "It Is Well with My Soul," https://hymnary.org/hymn/CYBER/3106.

5. Bill Bryson, *A Walk in the Woods: Rediscovering America on the Appalachian Trail* (New York: Random House, 1998), 161.

6. Zach C. Cohen, "Bill Irwin Dies at 73; First Blind Hiker of Appalachian Trail," *Washington Post*, March 15, 2014, https://www.washingtonpost.com/national/bill -irwin-diesat-73-first-blind-hiker-of-appalachian-trail/2014/03/15/a12cfa1a-ab9b -11e3-af5f-4c56b834c4bf_story.html?utm_term=.23d11af6b3c2.

7. Henry Blackaby and Richard Blackaby, *Being Still with God: A 366 Daily Devotional* (Nashville, TN: Thomas Nelson, 2007), 309.

8. Some Bible versions say about one hundred pounds. Other versions say about seventy or seventy-five pounds.

9. William Barclay, *The Gospel of John*, rev. ed. (Philadelphia: Westminster Press, 1975), 2:263.

April 1-30

1. "The grave-clothes were not dishevelled and disarranged. They were lying there *still in their folds*." Barclay, *The Gospel of John*, 2:267.

2. Gary M. Burge, *John, The NIV Application Commentary* (Grand Rapids, MI: Zondervan, 2000), 554.

3. Used by permission.

4. Kennon M. Sheldon, Todd B. Kashdan, and Michael F. Steger, eds., *Designing Positive Psychology: Taking Stock and Moving Forward* (New York: Oxford University Press, 2011), 249–54. See also Amit Amin, "The 31 Benefits of Gratitude You Didn't Know About: How Gratitude Can Change Your Life," Happier Human, http://happierhuman.com/benefits-of-gratitude/.

5. "Chris Tomlin Most Sung Songwriter in the World," *The Christian Messenger News Desk*, July 3, 2013, www.christianmessenger.in/chris-tomlin-most-sung -songwriter-in-the-world/.

6. Gerhard Kittel, ed., *Theological Dictionary of the New Testament*, trans. and ed. Geoffrey W. Bromiley (Grand Rapids, MI: Eerdmans, 1964), 2:588–89.

7. W. E. Vine, *Vine's Expository Dictionary of New Testament Words: A Comprehensive Dictionary of the Original Greek Words with Their Precise Meanings for English Readers* (McLean, VA: MacDonald Publishing, n.d.), "Gentle, Gentleness, Gently," 484–85.

8. Andrew Shain, "As He Heads to the U.S. Senate, Tim Scott Praises Early Mentor," *Beaufort Gazette*, July 2, 2013, http://www.islandpacket.com/news/local/community /beaufort-news/article33492450.html.

9. Carter Conlon with Leslie Quon, *Fear Not: Living Courageously in Uncertain Times* (Ventura, CA: Regal Books, 2012), 52–53.

May 1-31

1. W. E. Vine, *Vine's Expository Dictionary of New Testament Words: A Comprehensive Dictionary of the Original Greek Words with Their Precise Meanings for English Readers* (McLean, VA: MacDonald Publishing, n.d.), "Comfort, Comforter, Comfortless," 209–10.

2. Spiros Zodhiates, ed., *Hebrew-Greek Key Word Study Bible: Key Insights into God's Word, New International Version* (Chattanooga, TN: AMG Publishers, 1996), #5770, 2122.

3. Quoted in Alan Loy McGinnis, *The Friendship Factor: How to Get Closer to the People You Care For* (Minneapolis: Augsburg, 1979), 70.

4. Thomas Lake, "The Way It Should Be: The Story of an Athlete's Singular Gesture Continues to Inspire. Careful, Though, It Will Make You Cry," *Sports Illustrated*, June 29, 2009, www.si.com/vault/2009/06/29/105832485/the-way-it-should-be.

5. Translation by Frederick Dale Bruner, *The Gospel of John: A Commentary* (Grand Rapids, MI: Eerdmans, 2012), 359.

6. Extract by C. S. Lewis © copyright C. S. Lewis Pte. Ltd. Used by permission.

June 1-30

1. Henri J. M. Nouwen, *The Essential Henri Nouwen*, ed. Robert A. Jonas (Boston: Shambhala, 2009), 131–32.
2. W. E. Vine, *Vine's Expository Dictionary of New Testament Words: A Comprehensive Dictionary of the Original Greek Words with Their Precise Meanings for English Readers* (McLean, VA: MacDonald Publishing, n.d.), "Longsuffering," 694.
3. David Hocking, "The Patience of God," *Blue Letter Bible*, https://www.blueletterbible.org/comm/hocking_david/attributes/attributes14.cfm.
4. "Mr. Happy Man—Johnny Barnes," YouTube, May 6, 2012, https://www.youtube.com/watch?v=v_EX5NzqNXc. See also Jarrod Stackelroth, "Mr. Happy Man," *Adventist Record*, July 21, 2016, https://record.adventistchurch.com/2016/07/21/mr-happy-man/.
5. Told to me in person and used by permission.
6. Deborah Norville, *The Power of Respect: Benefit from the Most Forgotten Element of Success* (Nashville: Thomas Nelson, 2009), 6–8.

July 1-31

1. Os Guinness, *Unspeakable: Facing Up to the Challenge of Evil* (San Francisco: Harper San Francisco, 2005), 136–37.
2. Lee Strobel, *The Case for Miracles: A Journalist Investigates Evidence for the Supernatural* (Grand Rapids, MI: Zondervan, 2018), 141.
3. Tom Doyle, *Dreams and Visions: Is Jesus Awakening the Muslim World?* (Nashville: Thomas Nelson, 2012), 127.
4. W. E. Vine, *Vine's Expository Dictionary of New Testament Words: A Comprehensive Dictionary of the Original Greek Words with Their Precise Meanings for English Readers* (McLean, VA: MacDonald Publishing, n.d.), "Made," 709–10.

August 1-31

1. John MacArthur Jr., *Philippians, The MacArthur New Testament Commentary* (Chicago: Moody Press, 2001), 273.
2. William C. Frey, *The Dance of Hope: Finding Ourselves in the Rhythm of God's Great Story* (Colorado Springs, CO: WaterBrook Press, 2003), 175.
3. John Newton, "Amazing Grace," *Timeless Truths*, https://library.timelesstruths.org/music/Amazing_Grace/.
4. Rick Warren, *The Purpose of Christmas* (New York: Howard Books, 2008), 41.

5. Lee Strobel, *The Case for Miracles: A Journalist Investigates Evidence for the Supernatural* (Grand Rapids, MI: Zondervan, 2018), 101–4. Billy Hallowell, "The Real-Life Miracle That Absolutely Shocked Lee Strobel," Pure Flix, April 24, 2018, https://insider.pureflix.com/movies/the-real-life-miracle-that-absolutely-shocked-lee-strobel.

September 1-30

1. Randy Alcorn, *Happiness* (Carol Stream, IL: Tyndale, 2015), 19.
2. Lynne Malcolm, "Scientific Evidence Points to Importance of Positive Thinking," ABC RN, June 17, 2015, http://www.abc.net.au/radionational/programs/allinthemind/the-scientific-evidence-for-positive-thinking/6553614.
3. Quoted in Alan Loy McGinnis, *The Friendship Factor: How to Get Closer to the People You Care For* (Minneapolis: Augsburg, 1979), 69.
4. Jayson Casper in Cairo, "Forgiving ISIS: Christian 'Resistance' Videos Go Viral in Arab World," ChristianityToday.com, March 17, 2015, http://www.christianity today.com/gleanings/2015/march/forgiving-isis-christian-resistance-viral-video-sat7-myriam.html.
5. Jeane MacIntosh, "Homeless Heir to Huguette Clark's $19M Fortune Found Dead in Wyoming," *New York Post*, December 31, 2012, http://nypost.com/2012/12/31/homeless-heir-to-huguette-clarks-19m-fortune-found-dead-in-wyoming/.
6. Terry Wardle, *Exalt Him! Designing Dynamic Worship Services* (Camp Hill, PA: Christian Publications, 1992), 23.
7. Story related to me in person. Used with permission.

October 1-31

1. Joel J. Miller, "The Secret Behind the Bible's Most Highlighted Verse," *Theology That Sticks* (blog), AncientFaith.com, https://www.patheos.com/blogs/joeljmiller/2013/06/the-secret-behind-the-bibles-most-highlighted-verse/.
2. W. E. Vine, *Vine's Expository Dictionary of New Testament Words: A Comprehensive Dictionary of the Original Greek Words with Their Precise Meanings for English Readers* (McLean, VA: MacDonald Publishing, n.d.), "Love," 702.
3. "Religion: Promises," *Time*, December 24, 1956, http://content.time.com/time/magazine/article/0,9171,808851,00.html.
4. Brennan Manning, *Lion and Lamb: The Relentless Tenderness of Jesus* (Grand Rapids, MI: Chosen Books, 1986), 21–22.

5. Gary Smalley and John Trent, *Leaving the Light On: Build the Memories That Will Draw Your Kids Home* (Sisters, OR: Multnomah, 1994), 27–28.

6. Nika Maples, *Twelve Clean Pages: A Memoir* (Fort Worth, TX: Bel Esprit Books, 2011), 129–30.

November 1-30

1. "Always on My Mind," by Wayne Carson, Johnny Christopher, and Mark James, published 1972.

2. Used with permission of Russ Levenson.

3. Nick Schifrin, "President Obama Writes Fifth Grader's Excuse Note," ABC News, June 3, 2012, https://abcnews.go.com/blogs/politics/2012/06/president-obama-writes-fifth-graders-excuse-note.

4. Dwight L. Moody, *How to Study the Bible*, updated ed. (Abbotsford, WI: Aneko Press, 2017), 114–15.

5. Spiros Zodhiates, ed., *Hebrew-Greek Key Word Study Bible: Key Insights into God's Word, New International Version* (Chattanooga, TN: AMG Publishers, 1996), #3534, p. 2093.

December 1-31

1. Frederick Dale Bruner, *Matthew: A Commentary*, vol. 1, *The Christbook: Matthew 1–12*, rev. and exp. ed. (Grand Rapids, MI: Eerdmans, 2004), 29–30.

2. J. B. Phillips, *New Testament Christianity* (Eugene, OR: Wipf and Stock, 2012), 15–16.

About the Author

Since entering the ministry in 1978, Max Lucado has served churches in Miami, Florida; Rio de Janeiro, Brazil; and San Antonio, Texas. He currently serves as the teaching minister of Oak Hills Church in San Antonio. He is the recipient of the 2021 ECPA Pinnacle Award for his outstanding contribution to the publishing industry and society at large. He is America's bestselling inspirational author with more than 150 million products in print.

Visit his website at MaxLucado.com
Facebook.com/MaxLucado
Instagram.com/MaxLucado
Twitter.com/MaxLucado
Youtube.com/MaxLucadoOfficial
The Max Lucado Encouraging Word Podcast

Everyone Needs Grace for the Moment They Are In

Grace for the Moment by *New York Times* bestselling author Max Lucado continues to touch lives as it emphasizes the help and hope of God in everyday moments. This 365-day devotional speaks to the heart and mind of each person in a special way. Available in hardcover, note-taking, and leathersoft editions.

ISBN 978-0-8499-5624-9 (Hardcover)

ISBN 978-1-4002-3633-6 (Note-taking)

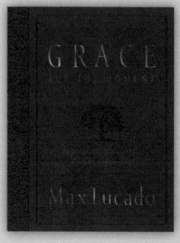

ISBN 978-0-7180-8977-1 (Leathersoft)

Timeless Messages of Comfort, Grace, and Encouragement

Do you sometimes wonder where God is in the midst of your daily battles with loneliness, grief, change, and doubts? In *God Is with You Every Day, New York Times* bestselling author Max Lucado uses his signature reassuring and encouraging voice, paired with practical, relevant, and personal messaging, to remind you that God is with you every day. Available in hardcover and leathersoft editions.

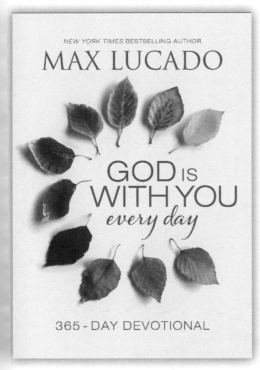

ISBN 978-0-7180-3463-4 (Hardcover)

ISBN 978-1-4002-0996-5 (Leathersoft)

Release Your Anxieties into the Safe Hands of God

In an uncertain world, it's not always easy to put our worries into God's hands. In *Calm Moments for Anxious Days*, beloved author and pastor Max Lucado weaves together biblical promises, gentle illustrations, and thoughtful practices to help you exchange your anxieties for God's peace.

ISBN 978-1-4002-4349-5 (Hardcover)